8th April 2015
To Rosemary & I
Hoping you will
interesting —
from Justine – Anthea's mum

IN THOSE DAYS

The Author—aged 17

IN THOSE DAYS

A SCRAPBOOK OF GROWING UP IN INDIA IN THE DAYS OF THE RAJ

Justine Dowley-Wise

iUniverse, Inc.

New York Lincoln Shanghai

IN THOSE DAYS
A SCRAPBOOK OF GROWING UP IN INDIA IN THE DAYS OF THE RAJ

Copyright © 2005 by Justine Dowley-Wise

All rights reserved. No part of this book may be used or reproduced by any means, graphic, electronic, or mechanical, including photocopying, recording, taping or by any information storage retrieval system without the written permission of the publisher except in the case of brief quotations embodied in critical articles and reviews.

iUniverse books may be ordered through booksellers or by contacting:

iUniverse
2021 Pine Lake Road, Suite 100
Lincoln, NE 68512
www.iuniverse.com
1-800-Authors (1-800-288-4677)

ISBN-13: 978-0-595-36350-6 (pbk)
ISBN-13: 978-0-595-80787-1 (ebk)
ISBN-10: 0-595-36350-4 (pbk)
ISBN-10: 0-595-80787-9 (ebk)

Printed in the United States of America

This book is dedicated to Bill, without whose assistance and encouragement I could not have completed it, especially as computers were completely new to me when I started writing it. Having completed it at long last, I still do not understand their complexities and have discovered that they seem to have a mind of their own. Bill has been patient, longsuffering and helpful throughout, whenever I have called upon him for advice and help, or to sort out some technical problem, be it day or night, and I will be for ever grateful to him for this.

CONTENTS

PREFACE

People who have become famous or have lived interesting lives usually write memoirs. So some may wonder why I should have decided to record my life in India. As I was born in 1926, I was fortunate to have lived during the remarkable period that has come to be known as **The Days of the Raj**, which ended when India obtained her Independence in 1947.

Once, when we were on holiday at Victoria Falls in Zimbabwe, we joined a small group for a spectacular sunset cruise on the Zambezi River to view the wildlife. On our return, we were greeted by a candle-lit banquet that had been prepared for us by the riverbank. That night there was a full moon and the deep blue sky was studded with a myriad of bright twinkling stars, with the whole of the Milky Way visible across the heavens. All around us were sounds of wildlife, and a herd of elephants could be heard trumpeting close by. After enjoying a fabulous feast, there was a buzz of animated conversation around the table about the wildlife we had encountered that day. This reminded me of an exciting elephant safari that we had enjoyed in Nepal a couple of years previously, when we had encountered tiger and the white one-horned rhino. As I was recounting this to the couple seated opposite to me, I became aware that everyone at the table had ceased talking and were listening to my story. The conversation then turned to India, and I told them about some of my experiences out there. Afterwards there were several people in the group who came to me and asked if I had ever written about them, and when I told them that I hadn't, they suggested that I should. It was then that I decided to make the effort, especially as a similar request had been made on many previous occasions. So this is a record of my life from the 1920s to 1948. Although almost sixty years have passed since I left India for good, my memories are as vivid as though they took place only yesterday.

No one else will ever again have the chance to experience the kind of life I led, or see any of the amazing sights that I saw, because those days are history now. My wish is that this record will succeed in giving the reader a glimpse into that past.

Our Elephant Safari in Nepal with the author on the nearest tusker, 'Shamsher Bhadur'.

I wanted to continue living in that wonderful country, and was devastated when I had to leave, but due to the strife everywhere in 1946, my parents decided that it was no longer safe for us to remain there, so very reluctantly we returned to England to start a new life.

CHAPTER 1

BEGINNINGS and SMALLPOX

Can you imagine India in the 1920s? An era often referred to as **The Days of the Raj.** Rich and powerful Maharajahs ruled over their individual states with their own military forces to protect them and keep order. They lived in vast, richly decorated palaces set in gardens full of exotic tropical trees and flowers and sparkling fountains which cascaded into pools covered with lotus flowers. Harems of beautiful wives were adorned in brightly coloured gold brocaded saris with heavy gold necklaces studded with diamonds and precious stones. Golden earrings dangled from their ears, and jewelled rings shone on their fingers and toes. Lavish banquets were held in these grand palaces, attended by hundreds of guests who ate off solid gold plates, waited on by a multitude of servants attired in red and gold brocaded livery. Afterwards they were entertained by groups of beautiful dancing girls dressed in exotic colourful clothing, with golden bells around their ankles, which jingled as they swirled to the music of the sitars and the beat of the drums.

A Maharajah's Ceremonial Procession. A sketch created by artist Sian Rosamund.

In their stables were many magnificent horses and exquisite carriages. All the maharajahs and rulers also owned many elephants for ceremonial events, which carried them in procession, seated in golden-canopied howdahs strapped upon their backs. For these special occasions the elephants were painted with brightly coloured intricate patterns and covered in richly embroidered colourful drapes. Golden bells around their necks and feet jingled as they passed through the crowds. These elephants were also used when hunting parties were organized for their friends to hunt tiger and big game in the jungles of their hunting reserves. Their palaces and hunting lodges were filled with many trophies from these hunts. Every maharajah and nawab also owned a fleet of Rolls Royce cars that were custom built in various colours especially for them and shipped out from England. In those early days it is recorded that one in every five of the Rolls Royce cars built, were sent out to India. This is the era into which I was born in the great city of Calcutta, in Bengal.

My paternal great grandparents settled in India in the 1800s, and I believe their parents were connected with the East India Company, formerly The Honourable East India Company that had been established towards the latter part of the 16th century to protect Britain's trade interests in India. I think they were involved in the production of jute and owned mills on the banks of the Hooghly River, not far from Calcutta. My father was born there on the 24th March 1896 and christened Arthur Arnold Wise. He had two brothers, Sidney and Freddie, and four sisters, Myra, Irene, Marjorie and Cherry who were also born in India. I remember Irene and Marjorie as being strikingly beautiful girls. Cherry married a Merchant's Assistant in Calcutta called Harold Fox when she was 19years old, but died when her first child was born. Harold later became a missionary. Marjorie emigrated to America and married a millionaire there. She had a daughter called Una who became a film star in Hollywood. When Marjorie's marriage failed, she returned to live in Calcutta. Irene also married a British Merchant in Calcutta, and after living there for many years with her four daughters, Zena, Christina (Tena), Geraldine and Justine, she returned to settle in England, where she lived to be 96 years old.

Arthur grew up with his family in India, and when he was 16 years old he was confirmed in the Old Church in Calcutta shortly before his father died, leaving his business in difficulties and his wife with seven children to care for. Not surprisingly Arthur had no desire to take over his father's business, so planned to make a career in the Indian Army.

Father loved to go on safari to hunt the black buck deer. This was the favourite pastime of the Europeans, especially amongst military personnel and the maharajahs. Records show that next to the tiger, this was the favourite animal to hunt, and in the 18th, 19th and early 20th century this was the most hunted wild beast all over India. Being one of the fastest animals on earth that could run at a sustained speed of 50mph, it could out-run any other animal across the open plains, and some maharajahs kept specially trained cheetahs to hunt it down.

The black buck is a strikingly beautiful and graceful creature with the upper part of its body black and the lower part white, with its spiralling horns growing in the shape of a V to a length of about 28 inches in the adult male. They are regarded as sacred in Hinduism and venerated and vigorously protected by the nature loving Hindu Bishnois tribal people who inhabit the western region of the Thar Desert in Rajasthan. Their faith teaches that man lives by conserving the flora and fauna to the extent of sacrificing their lives to protect the environment, and they have been known to beat up hunters. The Kathis people in the North East Province as well as the Haryanas in Northern India also venerate the black buck.

A Black Buck antelope.
Photo by the author.

Rock paintings of this animal can be seen on the walls of caves in central India dating back to 5000 BC, and on seals of the Indus valley civilization two millennia later. They also appear in many ancient miniature Mogul paintings. One of them shows the Emperor Akbar the Great, circa 1590, hunting black buck with his pet cheetahs. In 1555 he was given one, which he referred to as 'this strange animal' and grew very fond of it. Within a month it had been trained to obey its keepers who would release it to stalk and kill black bucks and then return with them after the kill, much like a hawk. These magnificent animals were draped in coats studded with jewels and were transported to the hunt sitting blindfold on beautiful carpets, as is depicted in an ancient miniature Mogul painting. In 1572, when one of the emperor's cheetahs leapt a wide ravine as it was chasing a black buck, he was so astounded that he elevated it to the rank of Chief Cheetah and had a drum beaten before it in procession!

In 1500 BC the black buck also featured in Hindu mythology and religious myths and fables following the Aryan invasion. About 500 years ago a man named Jhambhezi, a member of the Kshatriyas, the second highest caste of the ruling Brahmin class, was venerated as a mystic with many followers. One of his teachings was that no one should kill black buck that he held to be sacred, and in certain parts of India this belief is still held, but obviously not amongst the European community.

Whilst out on a hunting safari searching for this animal, my father recalls in his own words, the appalling disaster that befell him.

'One day my friend Harry and I decided to go on safari to shoot black buck at a place called Sarwar, where we stayed in the Dak bungalow. After enjoying some exciting days searching for wildlife, I returned to the bungalow one evening feeling very ill. During the night I developed a high temperature with severe pains in my head and back. My Indian servant was so concerned that he hurried to the nearest village in search of the hakeem (the local Muslim healer.) When he found him and brought him back to the bungalow, they were greeted by Harry in a state of panic, because we were miles from any hospital and he didn't know what to do. The hakeem examined me thoroughly and upon finding a telltale pockmark announced that I was suffering from the deadly smallpox, and must be isolated immediately and not moved from the Dak bungalow. You can imagine my distress at the predicament I now faced, especially as my two younger brothers had died from the same disease within a short time of each other when they were little children. Harry was distraught, but had no option but to leave me there, though my dear faithful Indian bearer decided to stay by me and continue to do what he could to help me, thus putting himself at the grave risk of catching this dangerous disease himself. I never ceased to marvel at the care and dedication he showed towards me during that terrible time. The bond of loyalty was so great that he remained in service with me for many years afterwards.

'The hakeem instructed him to remove all the furniture from the room, leaving me lying on an Indian charpoy, (a wooden framed bed with a base of loosely woven string,) upon which was to be placed a thick layer of banana and neem leaves, which possibly had some healing properties. At that time there was no known treatment for smallpox, which was a scourge all over India, and once contracted, often caused death. He instructed my servant to paste red tissue paper over all the glass windowpanes of the room to filter the light shining through, thus giving the whole room a red glow. As the disease developed, my whole body from head to foot was covered with large sores of the most distressing nature. As I lay there feeling so desperately ill day after day, I was deeply depressed as I contemplated the prospect of the awful disfigurement that invariably occurred should I survive this dreadful disease.

'As the days passed I was lonely and saddened at not having a single visitor except for the hakeem and my faithful servant. I knew when epidemics of smallpox occurred in India thousands die because of its highly infectious nature, so I did not see myself recovering. In my distress I cried out to God to heal me, but in my heart of hearts wasn't really hopeful of recovery because this disease had killed both my brothers. So I lay there resigned to my fate with only the faintest glimmer of hope, because I knew the hakeem was experienced in treating this disease and would be doing his very best for me. No medicine of any kind had passed my lips throughout this ordeal and I couldn't eat any solid food at all. I was given only liquids such as milk whey, fruit juice and water.

'When the hakeem came to visit me one day and told me that he felt the worst was over, I found it difficult to believe him. I had now reached the stage where the scabs had dried and was itching all over. To alleviate this he coated my body with some herbal potion, and bound my hands in cloth, warning me that I must never touch the sores or I would be pockmarked for life. I remember this period as one of complete torture. Gradually I recovered, and when I was well enough to return home, I embraced the hakeem in grateful thanks for all he had done. When I offered to pay him, he refused, saying it was reward enough that I had survived and regarded it an as honour to have been able to save the Sahib. I also expressed my gratitude to my faithful Indian servant who had remained with me throughout this dreadful period and amazingly did not contract smallpox. As I look back on this period of my life, I feel sure that although I was not a Christian at that time, God's hand of healing was upon me, and that the hakeem had been guided rightly in his treatment, as I have no pockmarks left on my face or body.

'When I returned to my home in Calcutta, my mother was so overjoyed to see me that she wept with relief and emotion. Being a devout Christian, she had been praying for me throughout this terrible time, and thanked God that He had heard and answered her prayers.'

CHAPTER 2

A SOLDIER OF WW 1 AND BHOPAL

War had been declared with Germany in 1914, and my father decided to join up in the Indian army. In January 1915, he was commissioned into the 92nd Prince of Wales Punjab Regiment. As a commissioned officer, then with the rank of Captain, he was later sent with his regiment from India to Mesopotamia to fight against the Turks. After a successful campaign in 1917, his regiment was moved to Palestine, where they fought under General Allenby against the Turks to bring relief to the Jews and return their Holy City of Jerusalem to them. He recalled how he entered Jerusalem on 9th of December 1917 with General Allenby and his fellow officers on foot in a triumphal procession, and afterwards when they remounted their horses outside the Jaffa Gate to ride away, they were mobbed by hundreds of cheering Jews waving palm leaves and shouting, 'Praise God that you have come at last and delivered us from Turkish rule.'

Many, many years after this event, when my father was in his eighties, I was on a visit to the Holy Land and

My father in regimental uniform in 1915

wandered into a small museum in the old part of Jerusalem and was amazed to see an enormous and very old photograph of this very scene that he had described to me all those years ago. There was General Allenby outside the Jaffa Gate, on a magnificent charger at the head of his troops, and riding in that procession somewhere behind him, was my father!

When I returned to England and told him about the photograph, he remembered the occasion and proceeded to tell me how, amidst the deafening noise, he was pulled off his horse and embraced by some of the excited Jewish people in the crowd. He recalled what an alarming experience it had been for him as he tried to remount his frightened horse to rejoin his men.

His regiment remained in Palestine for several months to maintain the peace before returning to Calcutta. Shortly after, he was offered a permanent commission in the regular Indian army in the same regiment, and remained with them for a further five years. After completing this period, he retired from the army under a Royal Warrant for officers surplus to government requirements.

Having left, he then sought new employment. After making enquiries about a post he had heard of in Bhopal, for a military officer required to command the state troops, he travelled there for an interview with the Begum, a woman, who was ruling at that time, and was accepted.

World War 1 Palestine Campaign. Capt Wise (centre) with fellow officers. 1917

Bhopal is the Indian capital of Madhya Pradesh and the city is situated on seven gently rolling hills at an altitude of 532m. It has an interesting history, having been founded in the 11th century by Raja Bhoja, a ruler who had murdered his mother. To atone for this crime, his courtiers ordered him to construct a pal (dam) across one of the seven rivers that flowed through his Kingdom, thus forming two lakes around which he built a new capital and this was called Bhojapal. Over the centuries it fell into ruin until the 17th century, when it was restored by Dost Mohammed, a chief in the army of the Mogul Emperor Aurangzeb who built a walled city and a grand palace above the lake with sheer walls down to the lakeside. The Muslim dynasty, which he established, eventually became one of central India's leading royal families, remaining Muslim to this day. In the 19th century Bhopal was presided over by women rulers who held court behind a wicker screen of *purdah*. Because no man other than her husband may view a Muslim woman's face, they wear the long *burkhas* covering the body from their heads to the ground. These powerful women rulers were also responsible for the building of the magnificent mosques and palaces and these buildings remain there to this day. The old city with its teeming markets and fine buildings still bear the aristocratic imprint of its former rulers who ruled Bhopal from 1819 to 1926.

The city of Bhopal was brought to the attention of the world on 3rd December 1984 when 40 tonnes of a lethal cloud of toxic chemical gas (methyl isocyanate—MIC) escaped at night from the Union Carbide plant. In an attempt to cut costs, vital safety measures had been drastically reduced and, during routine maintenance, an error by workmen led to a sudden and catastrophic flow of water into a storage tank that held the MIC, an unstable and extremely dangerous compound. This caused an explosion that led to the world's worst industrial disaster, killing thousands of poor unsuspecting people as they slept in their shanty settlements. By the third day of the disaster, it was estimated that 8,000 had died from direct exposure to the gasses, and the toxic cloud of gas that covered an area of 40 square kilometres injured a further 500,000. Many times that number continued to suffer, and still do, from chronic and incurable health problems, leading to an early death. The sensitivity and care needed to handle these traumatized victims has been missing all along. To add to the tragedy, due to bureaucratic wrangling, it was years before paltry sums in compensation reached any of the victims, and by the time it did, most of them were dead. Sadly, hundreds living there today still show the scars of that horrendous night and are still left hoping for some compensation, because those responsible for the tragedy will not accept liability.

It was to this city that my father went in 1923, and was offered the military post that he sought, which was to take charge of the state troops for the Nawab Sultan Jehan Begum, who was ruling in her own right at that time. She was a powerful ruler who had good relations with Britain throughout her rule. Her son, His Highness Zadar Hamadullah Khan, was an accomplished sportsman and an international polo player. When she abdicated in his favour, the Prince proved to be a wise administrator and, anxious to improve the welfare and productivity of his subjects, formed the Bhopal Productivity Trust. Finding that my father also had expert managerial administrative abilities, he appointed him as manager.

My father was invited to live in the Noor-Us-Sabah palace built in the 1920s as the residence of the eldest daughter of H.H. Nawab Hamid Ullah Khan. Reputed to be one of the best palaces, it overlooked the famous Bhopal Lake. It is still a magnificent place set in beautiful gardens, and is now a Heritage Hotel. At the back of the palace adjoining it, there is a very large courtyard enclosed by impressive colonnades. The many rooms still have magnificent furnishings, depicting the rich and lavish lifestyles of the Royal Rulers. My father lived there in grand style and accompanied the Royal Family wherever they went. As he was a crack shot with a rifle, he went out hunting tiger and other big game on the great hunting parties that the Prince organized for his friends, on elephants he kept for this purpose.

In those days tiger hunting was a great social occasion when maharajahs, nawabs, important dignitaries, district commissioners and other guests would gather for a week's hunting, while staying at a hunting lodge or palace. Anything from twenty to fifty trained elephants would be assembled to carry them out into their private hunting reserves. Two guests rode on each elephant seated comfortably in a howdah, with the mahout astride the elephant's neck, while another man balanced precariously on its back, in order to attend to their needs and help them on or off to join the elaborate picnics that were prepared for them on such occasions.

In the early 1920s, tigers abounded in spite of such large numbers being shot on these safaris. It was recorded that on one such hunt at that time, no less than one hundred and eighteen tigers were shot. It is little wonder that the marble floors in so many palaces were adorned with the skins of these magnificent beasts. In the present day, with many people against hunting, the methods adopted then would now be considered barbaric. My father described such a hunt, explaining how the elephants would gather near an area where a tiger had been seen. One or two buffalo calves were then tethered to a stake, where their cries would soon attract the tiger. Once it had moved into the area, the elephants formed a large circle around it, whilst the native 'beaters' on foot unrolled a very large continuous roll of cloth attached to stakes within that circle, which prevented the tiger's escape. Two elephants then moved inside to flush it out, and once it broke cover they shot it, so the poor beast never had a sporting chance to get away. But that was how things were done during the days of the Raj.

As manager of the Princes Trust, my father found the work very rewarding as he travelled all over the State visiting people in the surrounding villages, to find out how the various projects that the Trust had set up were progressing, and whether the people were benefiting from them.

Unfortunately after father had been working for the Prince and the Begum for about two years, he contracted typhoid, and with no modern medicine in those days to treat such a serious disease, his condition very rapidly deteriorated. The Prince was so concerned that he sent for his personal physician, Colonel Crawford, who lived in Indore, 250 miles away from Bhopal; in the hope he could save him. He came at once, but after examining him, said nothing more could be done for him and confirmed he was not likely to survive. Father must have sensed this, because he asked for a priest to be summoned to pray over him. As there was no Anglican Church there, the Roman Catholic priest, Father De Souza was summoned to perform the last rites. My father recalled a strange sensation as the priest prayed while anointing his feet, hands and forehead, with oil. As he made the sign of the Cross over his body, he recalled just before losing consciousness, that he felt a strong blast of cold air pass over him. The Prince, not expecting him to survive, had ordered a coffin to be made following the custom in the East that, when someone died, they had to be buried or cremated the same day. Fortunately this was not required because he came out of his coma and gradually recovered.

When Father De Souza returned to visit him, and father told him about his strange experience, he said that he believed it to be 'an act of God'. Father agreed with him, and as a result of this, after many discussions with this priest, decided to adopt the Roman Catholic faith. To help with his recovery, the Prince sent him to convalesce in the military cantonment at Rawalpindi. It was during his stay there that he met my mother, who had just come out from England with the Havelock family as the children's governess.

CHAPTER 3

A NEW ADVENTURE. India and Cupid's arrow

My mother's parents were devout Roman Catholics when she was born on the 2nd July 1904, and christened Violet Gertrude Duffield. But she was always known as Ivy. The family lived near Chelsea, London, by the River Thames, where they remained until about 1918. She had five brothers whose names were Frederick, William, Percy, Stanley, and Reggie, and two sisters, Rosina and Lillian. Rosina was a nurse in Queen Alexandra's Imperial Military Nursing Service, nursing the wounded soldiers in field hospitals on the Western Front during the First World War. Percy joined the East Surrey Regiment and was sadly killed in action on the 20th April 1915. His name appears on the Menin Gate Memorial in Ypres. Another of her brothers joined the Royal Defence Corps and was also killed in the war. Stanley was only two years old in 1917.

My mother was educated at the Sacred Heart Convent in Putney, London, where she was so impressed by the devoutness and dedication of the nuns, that she felt she would like to take up Holy Orders and train to become a nun herself. After she had completed her studies there, she expressed this wish to the Mother Superior, who suggested that before making such a momentous decision, she should first 'taste of the world' for at least two years, to discover what it had to offer. If after that time she still felt a strong desire to become a nun, she could return for an interview to determine whether she was a suitable candidate. Should she prove to be, she would then be accepted for training. This was wise advice, because had she not taken this suggestion to heart, she might have become a nun and later lived to regret that decision. The course of her life was to be changed by the death of her mother who suffered ill health from consumption, and succumbed to the deadly influenza virus when it swept across Britain as the First World War with Germany was ending.

The influenza epidemic started in the spring of 1918 and killed 25 million people in one year. It first appeared in Glasgow in May of that year and spread across Britain killing 228,000 people and little could be done to prevent this in spite of efforts to spray the streets with chemicals and the wearing of gas masks. In one sector of the Western Front 70,000 American troops were hospitalised and a third of these died. It then spread to the German population and caused the death of 400,000 civilians. In June it spread to India, and between that month and July 1919, 16,000,000 died from the virus. Most of the Indian doctors were away serving in the British forces, so no one was left to tend the sick. In that country alone, it was estimated that more people died of this virus than were killed all over the world during the First World War. This influenza virus was so deadly that it is believed a total of 70 million people died from it throughout the world.

My mother was only thirteen years old when her mother died, but she did her best to help in the home and look after her younger brother Stanley, and seek to comfort her distraught and grieving father. She told me of a strange incident that occurred prior to her mother's death. One evening when the family were sitting around the table together enjoying a meal, they were startled by a loud crash. The large framed picture of Percy, taken in his military uniform just before he left for the battlefront, suddenly fell off the wall, scattering smashed glass all over the floor. Her mother's face turned deathly white as she jumped up from her chair shouting, 'It's Percy! Percy has been killed!' Naturally they were all shocked and fearful by what had just happened. Not long afterwards there was a knock at the door, and when her mother opened it, she was handed the telegram that the family had been dreading, stating Percy had been killed on the battlefield on the same day that his picture had fallen off the wall!

Percy was her favourite son, and his death and also the death of another son, so affected her, that my mother was quite convinced that the shock and grief which she suffered after this, contributed to the break down of her health, causing her speedy death.

The Menin Gate, in Ypres, has the name of thousands of other brave soldiers who gave their lives during the Great War for the freedom of Great Britain, and who have no known grave, inscribed on its great arches. This Memorial Gate that took some years to build after the war ended, was completed in 1929, and every evening since the 11th November of that year to the present time, the moving ceremony of the 'Last Post' takes place there at sundown. I have had the privilege of attending this on two occasions and each time found it a deeply moving experience. Mother gave me a very old photograph which I treasure, of a hand pointing to the name J.H.P DUFFIELD inscribed on the walls of the arch, and on the back of it are the words 'Menin Gate. November 11th 1929', which signifies that she must have been present at the very first opening ceremony held there to honour her brother who so tragically lost his life during the fierce battles that raged in that region.

Mother told me how her father was devastated by the loss of his beloved wife as well as their two sons, and became so deeply depressed that he was unable to cope with his home or all his family commitments. Sadly it was due to these circumstances that led to the break up of the family, and the decision to send my mother and young Reggie away for adoption. Rosina her sister, took Stanley and brought him up in her home.

Their family doctor Dr. Cator and his wife had retired and moved away to live by the sea in Boscombe near Bournemouth, Dorset. It was they who offered my mother and Reggie a home. They were a wealthy couple with a lovely home, and having no children of their own, were delighted to welcome them and treated them as if they were their own son and daughter. Mrs Cator, an eccentric lady, lived in fear of having the valuable antiques in her home stolen, so used to bury some of them around the garden, then forget where they were. It upset mother one day to see her burying a beautiful musical box in a rosewood case. She had often enjoyed listening to it as it played many lovely tunes. As the brass drum revolved, moving sprockets activated brightly coloured enamel butterflies, which flapped their wings as the tunes were played.

Whilst living with Dr and Mrs Cator, she saw an advertisement in a Bournemouth newspaper offering a post as governess to two girls aged six and eight years old and decided to apply for it. When she went for the interview she was delighted when she was accepted. At the time, she didn't know that this family were descendants of a very famous man, Major General Sir Henry Havelock, a hero of the Indian Mutiny. There is an impressive bronze statue of him in Trafalgar Square, where it stands in the shadow of Nelson's Column. Because he was famous, almost every town in Britain has a Havelock Street or road named after him. He was a true British hero as well as being a sincere Christian, and introduced the distribution of

Mother as she prepares to travel to India.

Bibles to soldiers of all ranks. It is recorded that when he died the national mourning was greater than that for Nelson, which showed the sense of loss ordinary people felt at his death. Little did mother know then how the course of her life was about to be changed when she joined this family, or that it would lead her out to live in India. She enjoyed her work with them, and soon felt accepted as part of the family, as the little girls grew to love her. Colonel and Mrs. Havelock were on furlough in England at this time, but were shortly due to return to the military base where they were stationed at Rawalpindi in India.

Mrs Havelock came to her one day, and asked if she would like to go to India with them and continue as the children's governess for a period of two years. She was delighted at the idea, and willingly accepted. She knew nothing about the kind of life that she might lead in that far off country, but felt it was an opportunity not to be missed.

In 1924 the family and my mother set sail as first class passengers from Liverpool, on the Anchor Lines' new ship **California**, bound for Bombay. She kept an account of the voyage in her diary where she says that she enjoyed the experience tremendously; especially dancing at night with some of the interesting young men she met on board. Their voyage took three weeks via the Suez Canal, and as the ship approached land, her first sight of India was Bombay's most famous landmark, the great archway of the Gateway to India, built in 1911 to commemorate the visit of King George V and Queen Mary. Ironically it is only remembered now, as the place where the British staged their final departure from India. The last detachments of troops remaining on Indian soil set sail from there, on 28th February 1948, after India gained her independence from Britain.

She records that as the ship finally docked alongside the quay, they were welcomed by a military brass band wearing scarlet and gold uniforms and white helmets, playing rousing tunes. After disembarking, they made their way accompanied by a long line of coolies carrying a vast amount of luggage, to board the special boat train that would take them on the three-day journey to Rawalpindi. This semi-hill station was founded in 977A.D with an impressive fort overlooking the city and is situated on the famous Grand Trunk Road that runs right across India. In 1849 it became a major British military outpost and to the present day is still an important military centre, now being the army headquarters of Pakistan.

Colonel Havelock and his family were quartered there in a splendid bungalow with many servants to wait on them. They were soon engaged in a busy social life, and my mother was invited to attend many events with them. She was a very beautiful and elegant young woman, but shy by nature, so found this new lifestyle completely overwhelming. During the day she carried out her duties as a governess with the girls, and in the evenings was often invited to dances, where she met many young officers.

On the advice of Mrs Havelock, mother had taken dancing instruction before leaving England and purchased several ball gowns in preparation for the life that she would lead in India. The contrast in lifestyle was quite extraordinary for someone who had previously led such a sheltered life, and been educated in the strict confines of a convent.

One evening when she was invited to a dinner dance in the officers Mess, she dressed up in her favourite black lace gown embroidered with hundreds of tiny black glass beads, which she called her 'Charleston' dress. She clipped back her dark brown wavy hair with a sparkling diamante slide in the shape of an arrow, but was unaware when she placed it there, that it would play a part in changing the course of her life.

As she danced, whirling around the room with her partner, this sparkling arrow in her hair, caught the attention of a young officer who couldn't take his eyes off her. When the dance ended, he went over to ask if he might have the pleasure of the next dance with her, which she coyly accepted. With him, it was love at first sight As they danced and talked together during the evening, he told her how the sparkling slide had, like Cupids arrow, 'pierced his heart', and he had fallen for her and wanted them to meet again. Taken completely by surprise, she wondered at his sincerity, so asked him to wait for a few days before contacting her again. As she thought about what had happened, she felt that she would like to get to know him better. Another meeting was arranged, and after that they met together several times over the next few weeks, during which time she realized that she had also grown to love him.

When he told her how he had come to Rawalpindi to convalesce after almost dying from a deadly disease, and of the miraculous cure which he had experienced which led him to adopt the Catholic faith, she realized that they had much in common. As his leave was coming to an end and he was to return to Bhopal, she was sad and wondered if she would ever see him again. She tells how she went to her room and prayed before her statue of the Virgin Mary, and pleaded that such love would be put in his heart for her, that he would ask her to marry him. Shortly afterwards, he proposed to her and she joyfully accepted.

Before his departure, they went to see Colonel and Mrs Havelock to tell them that they wished to marry, but though they wished them well, they were upset at the prospect of losing a much loved governess. She'd signed a two-year contract and they had paid all the expenses of bringing her out to India, but an amicable solution was reached when my father offered to reimburse them for these expenses, and friends of the Havelocks agreed to share their children's governess with them.

CHAPTER 4

BHOPAL. A wedding in a palace

My father returned to Bhopal to find that the Prince's Productivity Trust had been thrown into chaos when this important work had been interrupted by his illness. When he told the Begum and the Prince about the beautiful girl that he had met whilst he had been away recovering, whom he wished to marry, they said that she would be most welcome, and insisted that the wedding should take place in the Royal Palace. As it would be a grand affair, invitations would have to be sent out to all the Maharajahs and Nawabs and heads of departments in the neighbouring states, as well as important people within Bhopal. After this was done father returned to Rawalpindi to bring his bride back to the palace to finalize the arrangements for the wedding, which had been fixed for 9th February 1925.

On her arrival in Bhopal, she was warmly greeted by the Begum and the Prince, who provided her with a suite of rooms within the palace, and a retinue of servants to take care of her every need. As she was the only white woman in the whole of the State of Bhopal, this caused a great deal of interest and curiosity, especially as she was able to show her face in public, which was forbidden to the Muslim women who wore the long *burkhas* that covered the whole of their bodies.

Mother's arrival at the palace had caused great excitement amongst all the Prince's many beautiful wives and concubines in his harem. When they expressed a wish to see this English lady, a visit was arranged. As she was the first white woman they had ever seen, she told me how fascinated they were as they examined her western dress, and her tiny size two high-heeled shoes intrigued them. As was their custom, they offered her exotic sweetmeats and fruits, and afterwards invited her to partake of 'pan', which she reluctantly accepted, not wishing to offend them.

The chewing of *pan* is something of a national obsession in India, from royalty in palaces to natives in the lowliest hovels of the bazaars. Wherever you go in India there are *pan-wallahs* with their laden baskets on top of their heads. Often they wander up and down the railway platforms whenever a train stops, be it day or night, shouting loudly '*pan, birree,* (a rolled dry leaf cigarette) cigarette'. Elsewhere these men will be seen sitting cross-legged in the niche of a wall by the wayside with a basket full of *pan* leaves, as well as numerous little tins full of various concoctions including ground betel nut, ash lime paste, tobacco, flower essences, *catachu* and a variety of spices. A selection of these ingredients can be mixed and folded into the edible leaf, which is then chewed, and eventually the residue is spat out as a blood red liquid. You can see this spattered over the walls and pavements everywhere you go. The betel nut in pan can cause addiction to it and if chewed over a long period the teeth eventually become an unsightly red-black colour. Included in the more expensive types of pan, is a mixture of silver or gold leaf, cocaine, opium, powdered rhino horn and other traditional aphrodisiacs with exotic names such as *palang tor*. ('bedbreaker') It is said that sometimes this is given to the groom on his wedding night!

My poor mother put this *pan* into her mouth and started to chew it, watched closely by the women. She soon realized that she couldn't continue because it tasted so awful, so made signs that she wanted to spit it out. A silver spittoon was brought to her; and much to their amusement and her great embarrassment; she spat out the red *pan* liquid.

Since my parents were the only Europeans in Bhopal at this time, apart from a German scientist who was doing some research for the Prince, an English wedding would be difficult to arrange. In the local bazaar there were no shops where a wedding dress or morning suit could be purchased, so an order was sent to the Army and Navy Stores in Calcutta to send all the items that had been chosen for the occasion from their catalogue. This included a wedding gown and veil, a going-away outfit and a bouquet of white silk arum lilies.

When the wedding morning dawned and all the arrangements were in place, mother looked radiant in her beautiful white silk wedding gown as she left the palace in the Prince's magnificent Rolls Royce to be driven to the Roman Catholic Church for the wedding service. The church had no organ, only a small portable harmonium. When mother recalled the scene she laughed. As she solemnly walked up the isle to the strains of the Wedding March, she caught sight of the large lady playing it, who was frantically working the foot pedals to obtain the maximum volume from it. So much so, that it was rocking precariously to and fro and appeared to be in danger of tipping over at any moment.

Father De Souza conducted the wedding service, which was the first English wedding that had ever taken place in the State. As a result of this, vast crowds gathered outside the church to witness this momentous occasion.

A guard of honour from the Prince's State troops formed a triumphal arch over them with their lances as they came out from the church after the service to be greeted by cheers and clapping from the many onlookers. As they were driven to the Durbar Hall, where the reception was to take place, they were followed by a long procession of guests in their grand horse-drawn carriages and limousines. The route to the palace was lined with curious Indians, who had also come to watch this *burra tamasha*, (a special occasion).

THE WEDDING—9th February 1925

This vivid account of the first meeting of my parents, their wedding, and the many other stories of their early life were related to our family when we made a three-hour video recording whilst they spent Christmas with us in 1984. Both being splendid raconteurs, they vividly brought those early days to life. It was an enthralling experience to be able to listen to them. As I look back over my life, I am grateful and feel privileged to have been blessed with two such remarkable parents.

The wedding reception was held in the magnificent Durbar Hall. Seated over the ornate entrance on a decorated platform, was the band with a group of musicians playing their various Indian musical instruments, and in mother's own words, 'making a most dreadful noise.' Hundreds of guests all dressed in the most fabulous clothes, filed in and were greeted by my parents. The master of ceremonies announced each one by name preceded by their full title, so instead of Mr and Mrs So-and-So, it was His Royal Highness the Maharajah Abdullah Zadum Akbar of this State and that State, and there were numerous States in those days, each ruled by Nawabs, Princes, Begums and so on, each with a string of unpronounceable names. Mother recalled how she had to greet each one with a smile and a nod as she said, 'Pleased to meet you…Pleased to meet you.' She remembers feeling quite confused and rather dizzy by the time she had greeted the last guest.

The richly decorated tables were laden with a variety of Indian delicacies and a wonderful four-tier wedding cake took pride of place. On the topmost layer were two little porcelain figurines of a bride and groom, and a tiny silver shoe for luck. I know mother was relieved when all the various speeches had been made and they could return to their rooms to get ready for the departure on their honeymoon. My father said she looked absolutely fabulous in her beautiful going-away outfit of blue silk with a pink and blue Dolly Varden hat tied under her chin with a silver ribbon and dainty little blue satin shoes. He wore a smart suit with a flower in his buttonhole, and from the photograph they look a most handsome couple. Father's two sisters Irene and Marjorie came to the train to see them off.

Going away—9th February 1925

The Prince owned a magnificent hunting lodge near the town of Jhansi, which he used for the great hunting parties he organized for his guests to hunt tiger and other big game in the jungle on his private reserve. He kindly let my parents have this wonderful place for their honeymoon. By train, it was about a day's journey from Bhopal. The Prince had reserved a first-class compartment for them on the Delhi to Bombay Express steam train, and plans had been made to coincide with their being able to catch this particular train after the wedding. Unfortunately their schedule was running late, and when His Highness the Prince realized this, he sent a message to the station master informing him of the delay, so they arrived at the railway station to discover that, upon his instructions, the Bombay Express had been held up for over an hour awaiting their arrival. As they stepped from their Rolls Royce and made their way to the train along the red carpet laid down for them, a brass band struck up a rousing tune, 'It's a long way to Tipperary,' played Indian style, off key, and to an Indian rhythm, which was quite inappropriate for such an occasion. Even though the band's choice of music was less than melodious, they looked splendid in their red and gold uniforms.

There was a crowd of British soldiers on this train who must have been wondering why the train had been held up for so long. When they saw my parents arrive they cheered and lustily sang along as the band played. My mother had found the whole scene most embarrassing, as she recounted it to me many years later.

The following morning the train arrived at Jhansi Halt, which was the special stop for access to the Prince's hunting lodge. As there was no station platform, my father clambered down on to the trackside and bodily lifted my mother down, still dressed in her going-away clothes. As he did this, the British troops who had been gleefully watching, shouted out some typically bawdy remarks, once more causing mother acute embarrassment One of the Prince's elephants and a horde of coolies were waiting there to carry them and their vast complement of luggage away to the Prince's lodge. The noisy troops were obviously enjoying this unexpected and what must certainly have been a rare spectacle and clapped and cheered as the elephant knelt down to allow my parents to clamber up into the splendid howdah upon its back. These raucous men last viewed them as they disappeared deep into the jungle followed by a long line of coolies carrying their luggage on their heads.

A tiger shoot had been arranged for them the next day. Late in the afternoon they clambered aboard an elephant and were conveyed to a clearing in the jungle where a poor little goat had been tied up as bait. It was getting dark as they waited, and it was not long before the bleating of the goat attracted a tiger, which came into the clearing. As it did so, a man stationed in a tree above it lit a flare, and as the tiger looked up, my father shot it straight between the eyes. Mother was greatly distressed at this savage introduction to tiger hunting in India, especially when the body of the magnificent beast was brought back slung from a pole on the shoulders of two coolies, to be skinned. She was quite relieved though, that the life of the goat had been spared.

After spending only four days of their honeymoon in the jungle, an urgent message arrived from the Prince requesting them to return to Bhopal at once as an administrative crisis had developed within the Bhopal Productivity Trust, which only he would be able to resolve. So the following day they reluctantly had to return so the matter could be dealt with.

Back at the Palace, a very apologetic Prince greeted them. He informed them that a bungalow had been prepared for them in the grounds of the palace in a lovely position on the shores of the lake. It was a beautiful building called *Kala Burra Koti*, (The Big Black House) so named because of the black-grained marble facade. It had been exquisitely furnished and appointed, and he had arranged for them to have their own retinue of servants. This was a completely new and strange experience for mother who had never run a home. To make matters worse, she hadn't learnt a word of their native language.

Soon after they moved into their new home, whilst father was away at work and she was alone in the house, a troupe of large black-faced grey langur monkeys invaded the house, chattering noisily as they scampered through the rooms scattering everything in the their path. Terrified, she screamed for the servants who had heard the commotion and came running to chase them out. Shortly after this incident they were both sitting on the verandah enjoying a 'sundowner' drink in the cool of the evening, when two large black panthers appeared on the lawn immediately in front of them. When one of them proceeded to rub his back against a tree in the garden, they were so amazed at this sight that they just sat there transfixed watching them. Evidently they were often seen after this in the same location, wandering about in the cool of the evening.

Mother told me that she was not happy about living in that bungalow, because 'it gave her the creeps', and she was becoming increasingly convinced that it could be haunted. She had observed various objects around the house moving about of their own accord, and lights in various rooms switched on and off as if by an unseen hand, when she was certain that no one else was in the room. Her fears were heightened one night, when the cook's wife who lived in the staff godowns close by, ran into the garden screaming that she had seen an apparition rise out of the ground in front of her and it had tried to strangle her Because they were both so worried about these strange occurrences, father related them to the Prince. He was amazed when he showed no surprise, but casually remarked that the house had been built on an ancient burial site.

There was another frightening experience that she had in that house. Just before going to bed one night, she went into the bathroom to wash and noticed something shiny under the washstand. Thinking it was a broken vase that one of the servants had swept under there, she bent down to pick it up. As she did so, a cobra shot out raising itself to strike at her. Thankfully she managed to avoid being bitten and shrieked for father who came and shot it with the revolver he always carried. This incident made her feel even more nervous about living in this house in the jungle. The fact that it was built on a burial site, however ancient, did nothing to allay her fears.

One evening father came home from work feeling very unwell. During the night he developed violent pains in his abdomen, which worsened throughout the night, and in the early hours was groaning in agony with violent diarrhoea. The doctor was called at once and after examining him was puzzled by father's unusual symptoms, so took a sample of stool away for analysing. When he returned later, they were horrified when he informed them that finely ground tiger's whiskers that could perforate his bowel had been found in the sample. Fortunately the doctor was able to treat this with various herbal potions to relieve the symptoms and his condition gradually began to improve, but it was some weeks before he felt strong enough to resume his duties.

Naturally, they were distressed by the doctor's discovery and wondered who could possibly have wanted to harm him. The doctor told them that this was a well-known method used to kill people, because when mixed with food, the whiskers were impossible to detect, but could cause internal haemorrhaging which often led to death.

The Prince was quite mystified and angry when he was told about what had happened and ordered an immediate full-scale police investigation. Suspicion fell upon the servants who were interrogated, but later ruled out because of the high regard they all held for my parents. It was felt that this attempt to murder father was more likely to have been carried out by a jealous rival, because the Prince and the Begum thought so highly of him. Apart from that, he had a beautiful white woman as his wife.

Even though the police carried out extensive investigations, the person who attempted to kill him was never caught. Thankfully father had survived but was now fearful of his position within the Princes Trust. This attempt on his life was the last straw and prompted them to make immediate plans to move to Calcutta. There my mother could enjoy a more social environment amongst other Europeans, as she had been the only white woman in Bhopal all the time that they had been there. Father also felt that there would be better opportunities for him to find suitable employment for advancement in the city. Reservations were made on the express train and they prepared to leave to start a new chapter in their lives.

The Begum and the Prince were upset by their departure, especially under such unpleasant circumstances, but respected their wishes and gave them a memorable send off. They accompanied them as they were driven by the Prince's chauffeur to Bhopal station, where a group of dignitaries and members of father's staff were waiting to bid them goodbye. When the train arrived and all the farewells were said, they were garlanded with marigolds and sweet smelling flowers as they boarded the train. I'm sure they were glad to be leaving Bhopal as the train steamed away and relieved that they had both survived their sojourn in that place. The journey took about three days, and when they reached Howrah Station in Calcutta, they found father's sister, Cherrie, and her husband, Harold Fox, waiting there to meet them.

CHAPTER 5

CALCUTTA. NEW OPPORTUNITIES

Howrah Station is the main line terminus for trains that come from all over India for passengers bound for Calcutta. It was built on the west bank of the Hooghly River opposite the major part of the great city of Calcutta and covers a vast area with fifteen or more platforms. Because it offers shelter from the burning sun and monsoon rains, it has a resident population of several hundred poor homeless people, as well as many orphaned street children who camp there permanently on the platforms amongst numerous wandering sacred cows, bulls, goats and monkeys, stray pariah dogs and cats. On all the platforms there are always crowds of people squatting, waiting patiently for trains. Some are asleep, covered from head to foot wrapped in their dhotis, looking like dead bodies swathed in white shrouds. Amongst them, little groups of families with their babies and children all wait patiently. Many of the women are Muslims in *purdah*, wearing *burkhas*, a thick voluminous cloth enveloping the whole of their bodies with just a small net window through which to view their surroundings. Rising above this mass of humanity is the endless noise and piercing calls of the vendors weaving their way amongst the crowds and animals.

This scene of total chaos greeted my parents as they alighted from the train just before the Christmas of 1925. To my father who had been there before, it was nothing new, but my poor mother was quite horrified and overwhelmed as she surveyed the scene. A horde of coolies swarmed around them jostling each other as they grabbed their entire luggage, piling it high on their heads to carry it to the car that awaited them. Because they had so much luggage, it had to be stacked into two open cars, which followed them as they were driven with Harold and Cherrie across Howrah Bridge over the Hooghly River which took them half an hour just to cross because it was so tightly congested with bullock carts, horse gharries, buses tooting their horns with the passengers sitting on the roof or hanging out of the doors, rickshaws, taxis, and pedestrians. As they neared the city, they passed areas of squalor, noise and smells, and the cars had to wind their way around the many sacred cows that were lying around in the road, as they drove to their new home.

On the other side of the river from Howrah station, in complete contrast, was British Calcutta founded in 1690 by the remarkable English merchant trader Job Charnock. He was in charge of the East India warehouses by the Hoogly River, which was then the centre of British trade from eastern India. He was an interesting character who became the first Governor of Calcutta, where he lived with his Indian wife whom he had rescued from committing *suttee*.

Suttee is a very ancient Hindu practice in which the widow demonstrated her utter devotion to her late husband by immolating herself on his funeral pyre. It was supposed to be voluntary on her part and an act of peerless piety, guaranteed to purge the couple of all sin and to ensure their reunion in the afterlife and the veneration of the widow. This horrifying way of dying is believed to have often been forced on the widow by social pressures and even by the use of drugs. It did not pervade the whole of India, but was restricted to certain castes such as the Rajputs and to certain locations, such as Rajahstan, Bengal and parts of the Gangetic plain. The savage custom was abolished by law in British India in 1829, but was still followed illegally in certain remote districts, even to recent times. There was a quite remarkable case in 1988, when a childless 19-year old widow named Roop Kanwar was immolated, purportedly voluntarily, on her husband's funeral pyre in the village of Deorala, Rajasthan. A large-scale investigation led to the arrest and trial of eleven people who were charged with the crime. But on 31st January 2004 a special court in Jaipur acquitted all the accused on the grounds that the prosecution had failed to prove charges that they had glorified *suttee*.

Calcutta was almost a world apart with its vast open area of the Maidan, which only two hundred years ago was covered with jungle, but which was transformed into what is believed to be the largest urban park in the world, known to Calcuttians as The Lungs of the City. Palatial colonial and government buildings flanked this area along its main thoroughfare, Chowringhee, which also houses several interesting museums. On this street facing the Maidan were the great British department stores of Army and Navy and Hall and Anderson, as well as several hotels, the grandest of which were the Princes Grand Hotel and the Great Eastern Hotel, which was the first place in Calcutta to have air conditioning.

Across the Maidan lies the massive Fort William, built in 1707 and named after King William III. It was surrounded by a deep defensive moat that could in times of trouble be flooded from the river Hooghly close by. In spite of these defences, the twenty-year old Nawab of Bengal had captured the city in 1756. The one hundred and forty six British residents who were sheltering there failed to escape by the fort's river gate. Many of them were captured and imprisoned in a tiny room only six metres by five metres with one tiny window, causing most of them to suffer a terrible slow death from suffocation in the sweltering heat. This place came to be known as the Black Hole of Calcutta. After this disaster, Robert Clive retook the city the following year and a massive new Fort William was erected that was strong and large enough to house all the Europeans of the city in case of any future attacks.

In the southeast corner of the Maidan was the one mile five furlong racecourse, and near it, the great St Paul's Cathedral with its two hundred foot high spire. This was the original metropolitan church of British India, completed in 1847 and where there are many interesting plaques commemorating famous people. In the northeast corner of the Maidan was the magnificent white marble monument of the Victoria Memorial to Queen Victoria and the Raj.

In spite of all these wonderful places and the fact that Calcutta was the proud Imperial capital of India until 1912 when the capital was transferred to Delhi, it had a reputation for poverty, squalor and deprivation. Because of this, outsiders have been known to refer to it by many names such as 'the dustbin of the world' or 'the a—-hole of the Far East'. Winston Churchill once visited it when he served as a soldier, and when asked if he was glad to have been there, he replied that he was very glad that he had, because it meant that he would never have to go there again! I believe that it acquired this bad reputation because of the terribly primitive conditions in which the local population were forced to live, in the many areas that surround the heart of the city, and where many Hindus and Muslims lived in such squalor and close proximity to each other.

Harold had been fortunate in being able to obtain an apartment for my parents to rent from friends of his, at 10 Middleton Street, in a pleasant road just off Chowringhee. The couple that owned it had returned to England on furlough, so they were happy for them to rent it, especially as all their servants could be retained.

They soon settled in there, and it was not long after their arrival that my father joined Andrew Yule & Co, a company of managing agents. It was the practice for such companies to manage the affairs in India of other companies world wide, and he became the managing director for an American firm called Tide Water Oil, for the marketing of Veedol Oil in Bengal, and later extended to the whole of India. As a result of this new post they were invited to many social functions and exclusive clubs where they dined and danced until the small hours of the morning. There were also many invitations to private dinner parties, and they would reciprocate by holding dinner parties and social functions in their home for the new friends that they had made.

When mother first arrived in Calcutta, she was afraid to go out anywhere alone, because she was unaccustomed to being jostled by the crowds of Indians that surrounded her and the way in which they stared at her whenever she went shopping to the New Market or the local bazaars. Because of this fear my father always accompanied her. She told me of an unpleasant incident that greatly concerned her, when on one occasion as she was walking through the crowds in the market keeping close to him, an Indian crept up behind her and pinched her bottom! As she shouted out in distress, he was so angry that his instinctive reaction was to grab the nearest man believing him to be the culprit, and start hitting him. As he was doing this, she was shouting, 'Stop Arthur! It's **not** that man, it's **that** man!' pointing to the fleeing Indian. But as it was too late to go after him, his excuse was—'Well he's probably done that to some other woman before, anyway!' She was quite horrified that the poor innocent man had suffered unnecessarily by being in the wrong place at the wrong time.

Father could speak fluent Urdu having lived in India for so many years, so mother didn't see the need to learn the local dialect, but as he was at office during the day and she was left alone at home to manage the servants and run the home, she soon realized that it was an absolute necessity, because they couldn't speak or understand a word of English. So it was arranged for a *munshi* (language teacher) to come to the house to give her instruction in Urdu. After several weeks of trying to master the language, she decided to show off her knowledge of it, in front of her guests at a dinner party one evening, As they were sitting around the table waiting for the meal to be served, she called to the bearer, '*Juldi kurro! Hum bahut baugh kurta*'. Her guests started laughing as the servant hurried away to the kitchen, greatly amused. Feeling embarrassed, she asked them what she had said that so amused them. One of them explained to her that what she had said was, 'Hurry up, because I have a strong smell', and pointed out that what she must have intended to say was, '*Jeldi kurro. Hum ko bahut bukah hai*', that is to say, 'Hurry up! I am very hungry'. Needless to say it was a long time before she ventured to speak Urdu again when any of her friends were present.

Both my parents enjoyed the new lifestyle that was so different from the life they had led in Bhopal, and made many friends. Father excelled in all sporting activities. He joined the Calcutta Soccer Club and was made Captain of the European team and played in many matches against the Indians. He was also an excellent tennis player, so they were often invited to tennis parties and other sporting functions.

It was partly due to all the help and advice that Harold and Cherrie gave my parents that they were enabled to settle down so quickly in their new home in Calcutta. Harold's friendship with them especially, had a powerful effect on their future lives in quite a remarkable way. He was a devout Christian, and as such, lived a simple godly life in complete contrast to my parent's attitude to life. 'Eat drink and be merry for tomorrow we die'. He looked upon this as ungodly and sinful. It shocked him that they were Catholics in name only, and that my mother who had once been so devout and had even wanted to become a nun, was now living such a worldly lifestyle. As my mother recalls, 'He set out to convert us both'.

As a missionary, Harold was in charge of the Birkmire Hostel in Calcutta for homeless Eurasian teenage boys, who were sent to him from Dr. Graham's Missionary Homes situated up in the hill-station of Kalimpong where homeless and orphaned children were cared for and lovingly brought up by a dedicated team of missionaries. Once they had reached their teens they were sent to the Birkmire Hostel and placed in Harold's care and taught Christian principles and prepared for a career. When they were ready to leave and start a job, he helped to find them suitable employment. Sadly in those days this was a difficult task, because of the stigma on Eurasians, as Indians wouldn't accept them because they weren't pure Indians and the British likewise, but thankfully this attitude has changed. My parents were impressed by the dedication which Harold showed in helping these boys, so gave his work their financial support.

On Sunday evenings a service was held in the hostel, attended by all the boys, and they often went there to hear Harold preaching. His sermons were always powerful and thought provoking but he used to get worked up during them, often warning the boys of 'hellfire and damnation' if they didn't accept the Christian way of life!

It was due to his influence and example and their association with him, that my parents gradually came to the realization that there was a deeper meaning to life than the shallow frivolous one they were leading. They said that they were sure it was due to his earnest prayers on their behalf that they both became Christians in the truest sense of the word, and remained so for the rest of their lives. Throughout the many years they lived in Calcutta, their home was a 'home from home' for many missionaries, and later to members of the forces during the war.

Wherever Europeans settle in foreign parts of the world, they manage to create a little bit of their homeland around them, banding together to form clubs where they can socialise, building beautiful churches where they can meet to worship, get married and be buried in consecrated ground. Hospitals and clinics are built where their own doctors from their homeland can treat them, but where the locals can also get medical help. So whenever someone new arrived on the scene, people opened their homes to them and they were at once made to feel welcome. This was not done in a random way, especially if you lived in a big Indian city. In those early days, etiquette—'Conventional rules of personal behaviour in polite society'—was an important factor of the social scene. In fact it was as if they still lived in the Victorian age.

In the early 1930s, for the newcomer to India, one of the first social functions was the dropping of visiting cards on the various British residents in your area. Beside every front door there was a small black box where anyone who was a newcomer, or wished to make contact with you, could drop in their visiting card giving details of who they were and their reason for calling. In those days before the war, no newcomer would just 'drop in' without an official invitation. The head bearer, ever alert to what went on around the house, would present this card to my parents, who could then decide whether or not to contact them. Invitations to dinner parties and various functions abounded, so they soon became part of this social scene. For these grand occasions all the ladies dressed in extravagant evening gowns and the men in full evening dress, even though there was no air conditioning in any of their homes or the clubs, and in the Hot Season the intense heat was unbearable. In spite of this they would sit down to a six-course meal, followed by dancing that would continue throughout the night. This was the usual lifestyle for the British in the days of the Raj..

Another most important necessity for newcomers was to join the various clubs, but this could only be achieved through being introduced by friends who were already members. The famous Tolleygunge Golf Club on the outskirts of Calcutta had a waiting list of six years before one could become a member. This was a very select club solely for Europeans, set in acres of beautiful well kept grounds with a large swimming pool, a racecourse, riding stables with a gymkhana club, and one of the worlds finest golf courses. When my parents settled in Calcutta in the 1920s they were introduced to the club by a member and in those early days you were accepted only after you had been vetted to ascertain your social standing within the European community.

At that time most of the European clubs had excellent residential quarters that were the hub of the social scene where you could meet for a game of bridge, a meal, or spend some time in their library. The gentlemen would meet for a game of billiards, play bridge and drink at the bar where ladies were not permitted. They had special areas set aside for them, which they called the *moorghi-khana*, meaning, in Urdu, the 'hen house'. In the evenings these clubs held dinner-dances for their members who would dance to the lovely old melodious tunes of the 1920s and 1930s played by their resident bands.

In Calcutta nearly everyone belonged to one club or another of which there were many. They were purely for the Europeans and some of them were confined to categories within that community. If you held a senior post in commerce, then you were eligible to join the Bengal Club, which was especially famous for its cuisine, but if it was only a junior post, you might only be able to join the Saturday Club for social activities such as dancing, swimming, squash, tennis, etc Because of the intense heat, one of the most popular clubs was the Calcutta Swimming Club, where in those early days during the war, we also spent many happy hours in and around the pool.

Generally, except for the war years, the senior British businessmen (*burra sahibs*) that settled in India, were entitled to return to England with their families every two years for a 6 month paid furlough with first class passages also paid, which enabled them to continue to enjoy the same lavish lifestyle during their sojourn there.

CHAPTER 6

MY ARRIVAL!

My parents were still living at number 10 Middleton Street, Calcutta, when I was born there on 26th September 1926 and christened Pamela Justine Gloria Dowley-Wise. Being my parent's first child, great preparation was made for this momentous event. I understand that they had a complete baby layette shipped out to Calcutta by an exclusive London firm, The Treasure Cot Company of Bond Street that specialised in everything required for the new baby. As this layette was also used for my sister Patricia who was born eighteen months later, as well as my youngest sister Claire born six years after that, I can clearly recall some of the details. The oval pale pink woven wicker cot stood on a stand with wheels. Around the rim, draped to the ground, were white organza pleats dotted with pink satin rosebuds. The inside was lined with pale pink satin, and attached to the frame overhead was a brass rail with white organza frilled drapes on either side. The shiny black coach built pram with chrome

The new arrival in christening robes

My first outing

fittings, was of an unusual design, having a deep body with a central panel inside which could be removed to enable two small children to be seated facing each other. The baby clothing was quite exquisite, especially the long delicately embroidered lace christening robe. The layette also contained a silver-backed baby's brush, a silver rattle with an ivory handle, an ivory 'teething' ring and an engraved silver christening mug with a baby's 'feeding spoon', and every other conceivable item that a baby might need.

Not long after I was born, my father was due to take 6 months furlough in England. Families from India that took this leave there would usually employ a nanny to look after the children whilst they were there, and on arrival, purchase prams and any other items that were necessary. When my parents arrived they soon found a pleasant young girl to care for me, and bought the latest model pram for me, to take back to India. After their stay in England, which seldom lasted for much more than six months, they would return and have to set up home once more. So my early life was one of comings and goings.

During the days of the Raj, it was also customary for all British parents living in India to employ nannies and ayahs to look after their children. These nannies could usually to be found amongst the Eurasion community, and proved to be reliable and very capable in the care of their charges. Seeing that they had to spend more time in looking after and training them than did their parents, it was of great importance that the right nanny was chosen for their children.

Often these special nannies, which were held in high esteem, were passed on amongst families when they left India and returned to England for good.

My father had the latest model Studebaker car shipped out from America for him and this photo shows mother with the ayah waiting to take me out for a drive.

Father's Studebaker 1926

On their return from furlough they also employed a nanny who was never expected to perform any menial tasks in the care of her children, so an ayah had to be found to help her. Her duties consisted of bathing the children, nappy changing, dressing them, keeping the nursery tidy, wheeling the pram out whilst nanny walked beside it, and so on. For the older children in the family, often a governess would be brought out from England with the sole task of teaching the children various subjects, because there were often no suitable schools nearby that they could attend.

Mother was fortunate to find an experienced Eurasian nanny called Bessie Smith, who remained with our family for several years, as well as an ayah to perform all the chores connected with caring for us. I can still picture Bessie's diminutive figure, dressed in crisp white uniform, with white stockings and shoes, and on her head a very large three-cornered starched white cap that almost concealed her face. She was gentle-natured, and even though she was always strict with my sister and me, we grew fond of her.

Mary ayah came from Madras in South India, and like all the other Tamil people who inhabited that part of India, had a very dark skin. She was always dressed in a spotless white sari with brightly coloured borders and a short matching blouse that exposed her bulging midriff. She too was kind and tolerant and laughed a lot. Sometimes, sitting crossed-legged on the floor she sang a Hindi nursery rhyme whilst rocking me to and fro in her arms. It was a strange rhyme that didn't make sense when translated into English, but anyway it seemed to rhyme in Hindi!

'*Neeni baba neeni, roti, mucken, cheni, goosli goosli unda, baba ke unda tunda*', (Sleep baby sleep, bread, butter, sugar, bath, bath, egg. Baby's egg is cold.)

After I'd been bathed and put to bed at night, she would sit by my cot humming softly and gently patting my back until I went off to sleep.

On March 22nd 1928 my sister was born. Like me, she was given several names—Patricia Dolores Govina. I think our parents wanted to choose names that had some meaning. Patricia—'of noble birth', Dolores-'grief, sorrow', Govina—'joy'. They told me that as she was born a few weeks after my father's mother died of cancer when she was only 54 years of age, their new baby was

Patricia, the new baby

their joy in their sorrow. All the beautiful baby clothes that I had worn were passed on to her, and as she now lay in my cot, mother told me that at first I so resented the new arrival that was receiving all the admiration and attention from them and their friends, that I used to hide under the drapes of the cot and refuse to come out. Once she was able to walk and play with me, I grew fond of her and sometimes wheeled her around in my dolls pram under the watchful eye of Bessie and Mary ayah.

Every afternoon when it was too hot to go out, we used to rest in our nursery, look at picture books,

Friends at my 3rd birthday party with their nannies.
Centre. Bessie with baby Patricia

or nanny would read us a story. Because we believed in fairies, our favourite stories were about them. At night when we should have been asleep, we stayed awake to wait for them to visit us. Because of the stifling heat in the days before air conditioning, we slept under our mosquito nets with the windows open. Soon tiny flickering lights would fly into our room and flit around us. We were so sure that they were fairies that we gave them names like Tinkerbell and Twinklebell, and believed they were the same fairies that came to visit us every night. Especially when one of my baby teeth fell out I wrapped it in silver paper and put it under my pillow, because my mother told me a fairy would exchange it for a beautiful silver charm of a fairy, while I was asleep. Sure enough, I found one when I awoke in the morning. I was so excited about this, and showed nanny what the fairies had brought me, but she didn't have the heart to tell me that my fairies were only little fireflies!

From an early age I was fond of animals, especially the friendly and very lovely black Cocker Spaniel that my parents bought for me on my third birthday. Because she was so beautiful we called her Bella. Whenever we were wheeled out in our pram, she always accompanied us. She also loved going out for drives with us in our open-topped car and as we drove along her long ears flapped about like two sails in the wind.

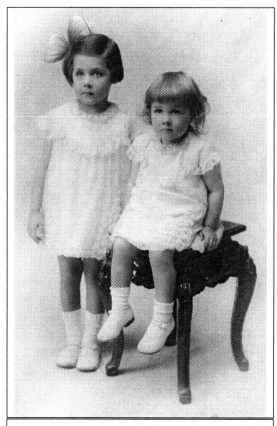

Calcutta 1930

In the early mornings and late afternoons when it was cooler, we were dressed alike in pretty dresses with large taffeta bows in our hair, and taken out by Bessie and Mary ayah to play with our friends in the beautiful gardens of St Paul's Cathedral or the Victoria Memorial close by. While we enjoyed ourselves, all the nannies used to congregate to discuss the gossip of the day. Because we were always in the care of Bessie and Mary ayah throughout those early years, we didn't see much of our parents, though mother always made a point of coming to kiss us good night before going out to the club or some social function with father.

In the great cities of the plains, the hot season usually began in April when the temperatures could soar to 130 degrees Fahrenheit in the shade, especially in Calcutta. Because of this, generations of Britons would make for the Hills to find some relief from the searing heat. This hot season would last for as long as five months. Should you remain in the heat too long, you would find yourself covered all over in 'prickly heat', a sweat rash, from which there was no relief from the constant itching, as there were no antihistamines then to ease the irritation. The other danger was from sun-stroke, so we always had to wear our topees, a pith helmet with a long brim at the back which gave the back of your neck protection from the sun's rays.

Very few houses had the luxury of air-conditioning, so we were lucky to have an electric *punkah* (fan) suspended from the ceiling in all the rooms of our home. Those who did not have this had to employ a *punkah-wallah* whose sole job it was to pull on the rope attached to a heavy length of cloth suspended on a beam across the ceiling, which swung to and fro as it fanned the sweltering occupants beneath it. These poor *punkah wallahs* would have to keep at this job day and night and often got shouted at if they went to sleep and the *punkah* stopped swaying. Because it was a lowly job they would have got very little reward for their efforts.

CHAPTER 7

KALIMPONG

To escape the heat mother took us up to the hills to remain there until the cooler weather returned. Sometimes it was to the beautiful hill-station of Darjeeling or to another equally beautiful place, Kalimpong, as both were not too far from Calcutta.

Kalimpong is a hill-station situated at an altitude of 1,250 metres, and therefore enjoys a pleasant climate. As it is not far from Tibet, it has always been a crossroads for Tibetans, Sikkimese and Gurkhas, who bring their goods there to trade with the locals.

Because of the lovely climate, orchids and many other beautiful flowering plants grow there in profusion. There were no passenger planes then, so travel was restricted and being rather difficult to reach, it was a quiet town with pretty chalet type houses nestling amongst the pine-clad hills.

In the hot season of 1933, when Patricia was only three and a half years old and I was five, mother took us up to the hills to stay at 'Ahava', a missionary guest house in Kalimpong run by Gwen Hastings, a retired missionary friend of theirs.

Ahava. On the edge of the cliff

The journey from Calcutta took us about 12 hours by overnight train to the foothills at the little town of Siliguri. From there we took a three and a half hour taxi ride up a steep winding road through thick pine forests to Kalimpong. When we stopped now and then for a break, we had wonderful views of the magnificent snowy mountain ranges in the distance.

The guesthouse was in an isolated position situated at the end of a long drive through a dense forest. It was surrounded by lawns and a garden full of flowers, and as we walked around the corner of the house, we were amazed to see that it was perched right on the edge of a sheer precipice which dropped away for thousands of feet to the plains below, then

'Bacha'. My birthday present

rolled away for hundreds of miles to the foothills of the snowy Himalayan mountain range. Clearly visible in the distance was mighty Kinchenjunga, the third highest mountain in the world at 8,500 metres above sea level, dominating the whole range. The sight was so amazing, that even though I was so young at the time, I still remember that wonderful view.

After spending a few days to see us settled in, mother left us in the care of Gwen to rejoin father, who was rarely, if ever, able to get away from his business commitments. Poor mother. She was often torn between the decision as to whether she should remain with us or stay with her husband. On this occasion it must have been hard for her to leave this lovely place and us and return to Calcutta, knowing that there would be no relief from the heat for five months until the Monsoon rains broke. These were the difficult decisions that had to be faced on many occasions throughout the time that we lived in India.

When mother left, I cannot remember feeling unduly upset by her departure. Even though we were very fond of her, I think we had grown used to being without her because we had always been in the care of our nanny and ayah.

Although Gwen was kind to us, there were no other children to play with, so there was little to amuse us. Sometimes we went for walks along the mountain tracks with Gwen to pick blackberries and then help her make blackberry jelly and cookies for tea.

We both loved to go out riding, so before mother left, she bought us a small dun pony named 'Bacha', (Little One) who was looked after by a Nepali *syce*, and a donkey for Patricia that was cared for by a Tibetan woman. As this was our only mode of transport, we rode everywhere. Sometimes Gwen allowed us to go off without her and ride through the forests and along the mountain tracks knowing that we would be safe in the care of the two trusted *syces*.

Riding from an early age

Because of the hilly terrain and the lack of proper roads, transport was nearly always by horseback. Even tiny babies rode on the donkeys and ponies secured within a ring saddle, as this photograph shows when we stayed in Kalimpong on a previous occasion.

One evening as Patricia and I were returning from a ride, we were terrified when we saw many eyes glaring at us from the bushes. I think they were hyenas. We often heard them howling at night as they prowled around the house, and we called them 'laughing hyenas' because of the strange sound that they made, which is difficult to describe. One of them would start with a spine-chilling howl, and then the whole pack would gradually join in with the pitch rising ever higher, until their cries sounded like the hysterical laughter of a crowd of crazy women. We were so terrified when we heard them that we used to dive under the bedclothes and put the pillow over our heads to shut out the noise.

Gwen had a large friendly Tibetan-Mastiff-Mountain dog called '*Bhuta*', who was kept chained by the entrance to guard the house. One night we were awakened by his barks, so guessed some animal must be prowling around. The barking changed to terrible howls and shrieks, but suddenly stopped. We realized then that something must have attacked him. This so upset us that we couldn't sleep again. When I asked Gwen what had happened to him the following morning, she told us he was missing and had probably been killed and dragged away by a leopard because it had left its pug marks in the soil, and there was a trail of blood along the path into the woods.

After this terrible event, we were worried about going outside in the garden by ourselves, because the house was in such an isolated position in the forest, which we knew was also the home of those terrible laughing hyenas.

A Tibetan mastiff—like Bhuta

The balcony of our bedroom overlooked the beautiful view I described when we first arrived. Everyday we watched the magnificent sight of the sun rising and setting on the range of these wonderful mountains, when the snows glowed with amazing hues of red, orange and gold, then changed to glisten silvery white by the light of the full moon. Patricia and I were sitting out there one evening before going to bed, when we heard a loud rasping, purring sound right below us. As we leant over the balustrade to see what it was, we were amazed to see a large leopard rubbing his back against a tree. We watched it in silence not daring to call anyone for fear of alarming it. It must have been the same leopard that killed poor *Bhuta*. The next morning we showed Gwen where we'd seen it, and sure enough, it had left its pugmarks in the flowerbeds under our balcony. It was very unnerving to know that there were such dangerous wild animals prowling around so close to us, and were glad that our bedroom was upstairs.

One night I had a frightening experience of a different kind. I was suffering from a tiresome chesty cough that must have disturbed Gwen, because she came to me in the night to give me what she mistakenly thought to be Owbridge's Cough Mixture. She poured out a large spoonful of the brown liquid, and as I swallowed it I let out a yell because it burnt my throat. Startled by my violent reaction, she looked closely at the label only to discover she had given me **Tincture of Iodine**. Realizing her mistake and that this was poisonous, she panicked and thrust her finger down the back of my throat hoping that this might help to make me vomit, but apart from causing me further distress, this didn't have the desired effect. So she prepared a strong mixture of hot salty water, which she made me drink in the hope that it might act as an emetic. Eventually I was sick, probably more out of fear and stress than her efforts. The only advantage of this unpleasant experience was that the coughing stopped but my throat remained sore from the iodine for some time afterwards.

While we were there I suffered a further disaster. A missionary lady had occupied the bedroom next to ours with her black Scottie dog. Several weeks after she left, I went into her bedroom to fetch something, and within minutes was covered from head to foot with fleas. I rushed out calling for Gwen who hustled me into the garden and told me to lie on the grass whilst she got something to get rid of them. Hurrying back to me, I was horrified to see that it was **kerosene,** because I knew this was used for lighting lamps, but had to lie there as she poured this stinking fluid all over me. As expected, this drastic treatment made my skin smart but it killed the fleas. After bathing I turned red and was sore for days. There were no aerosol sprays or insecticides then, so she was forgiven for the unusual treatment.

At the end of the Hot Season mother returned to Kalimpong to take us back home to Calcutta. We had enjoyed our stay with Gwen but it had been several months since we had last seen mother so we were delighted to be with her again. Our young lives seemed to be made up of so many partings and reunions. But then that was what we had come to expect when we lived in India. Although we had been looking forward to returning to Calcutta with her, we knew it would not be possible to take my pony *Bacha* and the dear little donkey back home with us. So we were very sad to have to say goodbye to them after they had given us so much pleasure.

CHAPTER 8

DARJEELING and St. Michael's Convent

While were away in Kalimpong we received a letter from mother telling us the exciting news that we had a new baby sister called Claire. This came as a surprise to us because mother hadn't said anything about it before.

When we arrived back home it was the midst of the monsoon rains and difficult to go out anywhere as many of the roads in the city were flooded. In some ways this was an advantage because it gave Patricia and me time to be with mother and enjoy our new baby. After we had left for Kalimpong we were sorry that mother had dispensed with the services of Bessie and Mary ayah, but pleased that she was now going to take care of us herself, and to enable her to do this she employed another nanny, Connie Gilson to especially look after baby Claire.

It was wonderful to experience the love and affection she showed towards us having been separated from her so often, and sometimes for long periods. Having always had a nanny and ayah caring for us, these were happy days, except that we didn't see father very much because he spent long hours working at the office or was often away on business in New York. I never felt able to get very

Goodbye to dear Mary Ayah

close to him because at times he could be short tempered, so I was afraid of upsetting him. But he was always generous and kind-hearted towards us and brought lovely gifts for us on his return from America. On one occasion he brought Patricia and me two large exquisitely dressed porcelain dolls and two beautiful doll's prams so we could wheel them out when we went to play with our friends in the grounds of the Cathedral or the Victoria Memorial. On a previous visit he brought me an enormous teddy bear that was larger than I was, and a life-like white dog that I loved. Unfortunately all these lovely gifts would often disappear because they would be packed away when my parents went on furlough to England every two years, and when they returned they

Father's lovely gift to us

would find that they had been damaged or destroyed by the white ants or cockroaches, no matter how carefully they had tried to preserve them.

One of father's office staff had an unusual pet. It was a fully-grown leopard called Rajah that lived in his home as if it were a dog! One day Father saw this man leading it through the crowds that thronged the main Chowringhee Street. Even though it appeared to be docile, its presence was causing the Indians to flee in panic. Because of father's love of animals, he asked if it would be safe for him to bring Patricia and me to see it, and was told we would be welcome. When we entered his house and this great creature came forward to greet us, I was scared because he looked so ferocious, but thankfully he wasn't, and let us stroke him. When we were invited to have our photo taken with him in the garden, I still felt I couldn't trust him, but surprisingly Patricia appeared to be quite unconcerned.

Father loved animals and had a way with them. He sometimes took us to visit the Calcutta Zoo to watch him feed an enormous black Himalayan bear, which used to lick Lyles Golden Syrup off the palm of his hand. We then went to see his favourite wild timber wolf that would always leave the pack whenever he saw him, and come over to greet him. Surprisingly it would allow him to put his hand into the cage to stroke its back! I remember seeing an Indian who had been watching, attempt to do the same thing, but as he touched the wolf it bit his hand.

I remember my father telling me about his uncle that lived on the outskirts of Calcutta, who had two Bengal tiger cubs as pets, which used to wander freely around his house and the grounds. Even after they were fully grown, they still had their freedom in

Is he really friendly?

the confines of the large compound. One day one of his tigers was lying by him licking the back of his hand, which was becoming increasingly sore by his rough tongue, and when he tried to pull it away, the tiger became aggressive and refused to let it go. Fortunately in those days most men usually carried a revolver strapped to their belt, so sadly he had no alternative but to shoot it between the eyes, killing it instantly.

Since returning to Calcutta, our parents had been searching for a suitable kindergarten for us to attend, but were unsuccessful. Two sisters living locally became aware of this need and opened one close by. They were Jo and Rumer Godden. (Rumer later became an author and wrote several novels including The Peacock Spring and The Black Tulip. All these novels were set in India, and some were made into films.) We attended there daily and enjoyed our time with them, especially the tap dancing lessons that were great fun.

We continued there until the New Year when our parents found a convent in the hill-station of Darjeeling where they planned to send us before taking us 'home' to England to be left at a school there. This was sadly inevitable for every child born to British parents who settled in India. I often heard them discussing the problem of schooling, and was puzzled why they referred to England as 'home' when India was my home. I asked them about this but they never really had an explanation that I could understand or accept.

For most British families, life in India would always be full of the heartaches of separation. For a wife it would be goodbye to the husband for several months when she took their children away to a hill-station to get away from the heat of the plains, whilst the husband would have to stay behind at his job and sweat it out throughout the hot season. Then there were the unending long separations and painful partings for the children when the time came for them to be taken to England and left there to be educated. We remained there alone for years without seeing father, and mother only came home to England twice for short periods. In those early days it took as much as three weeks to receive a letter, so how could anyone keep in close touch and still feel part of a family?

Ready for St Michael's Convent

Even though my sister and I were so young, our parents went ahead with the plan to send us to this boarding school up in the hills of Darjeeling because they felt it would help to prepare us for boarding school life in England. I didn't understand the significance of this, neither could I see how it would make the parting from them any easier when the time came.

The school they chose for us was St. Michael's Convent because since it was up in the hills we wouldn't have to suffer the heat of the plains during the hot season. We were both upset when we discovered that the term would be for nine months. This seemed to be a very long time to be away from home, especially as we discovered that we wouldn't be seeing our parents at all during that term, so I decided that I didn't want to go there, but knew I had no choice in the matter.

In April 1935, preparations were made for our departure so we went to the Army and Navy Stores to be kitted out in the school uniform. Dark navy gymslips, navy blazers, black stockings, and brown lace up shoes. I was quite upset at the thought of wearing these dull clothes instead of my pretty dresses, for such a long time.

As the trunks were packed, I became increasingly worried about what lay in store for us and resentful at our parents' decision to send us away. Although we'd stayed in Kalimpong without them for some time, that was different because of the friendly home environment. I wondered now what life would be like in this convent. I was soon to find out.

When it was time for us to leave, our parents accompanied us to Sealdah station. After a tearful goodbye, we were handed over to the care of Blossom, a young Eurasian woman who was to escort the school party on the train journey to Darjeeling. The express steam train only went as far as Siliguri, a small town situated at the foothills, where we would change to the Toy Train which climbed up the winding railway track to Darjeeling. I can remember a macabre spectacle in the station there of a goat with two heads preserved in a glass container.

Because it is such a unique and ingenious feat of engineering, this amazing Toy Train is known worldwide. In 1870 an agent by the name of Franklyn Prestage of the Eastern Bengal Railway first thought of building a little railway up to Darjeeling, because the only way then was by a difficult and circuitous route. Eight years later he submitted his scheme to Lt Governor Sir Ashley Eden who sanctioned it and appointed a Committee to examine the feasibility of the project, and it was decided to start building it in 1879. By 1880 the first 20 miles to Tindharia were completed and a miniature steam engine built by the Atlas Works in Manchester, England, was shipped out to India, and three carriages completed in time for the viceroy to travel on it as far as the first station at Tindharia. The little train was known then as The Viceroy's Train. When the railway line was completed on the 4th July 1881 as far as Darjeeling, it was named 'The Darjeeling Himalayan Railway Co'. The same engine is still operating today, albeit with the help of many spare part replacements manufactured in the workshops at Tindharia. The railway track is only 2ft wide and the line includes four complete loops and five switchbacks, some of which had to be added after the initial construction had been completed, because the gradients at certain points were found to be too steep. There are also numerous zig-zags along the 87 km route and no less than one hundred and seventy seven (no! I didn't count them) unsupervised level crossings, five major bridges and four hundred and ninety eight minor bridges. Before the train reaches Darjeeling it stops for water at Ghoom, the highest railway station in the world to be reached by a steam engine.

In the early days when the narrow track ran through thick jungle, there was a report of the train being held up because a tigress was lying across the line whilst her cubs played around her.

When we alighted at Siliguri and I saw the brightly painted little train standing at the station with clouds of smoke belching forth from the engine, I felt happier as we boarded it in anticipation of what might, after all, turn out to be an exciting adventure. Suddenly there was a shrill whistle and we set off at what seemed to be a walking pace. As the train increased its speed to about 10 mph, I heard amusing sounds coming from the engine which seemed to have a language of its own, because throughout the journey as it met varying gradients the rhythm changed. As it approached a steep part of the track, the puffing sounded like: 'Can I get up-can I get up-can I get up,' then after a while it would change to, 'I think I can-I think I can-I think I can,' and when it had finally reached the top of a hill, it would let out a triumphant burst of steam followed by, 'I thought I could-I thought I could-I thought I could.'

When we travelled on this train, there were about three little carriages with hard wooden benches and there was no glass in the windows. Because the train travelled at such a slow pace, I saw people getting off and walking or running along by the train for a while, then clambering back whilst the train was still moving. When the guard came on at one of the stations to check the tickets, I saw people hurriedly getting off when they saw him coming, and getting on again after he'd gone. It was obvious that they were travelling without tickets.

It was a fascinating journey as there was so much to see en route. Because there were no tunnels, the views were magnificent and changed as we rounded each bend. In some places, where the train went so near to the edge, you looked over a sheer precipice. We passed through forests of great trees, cascading waterfalls, and areas that were covered with colourful bougainvillea, poinsettia, purple orchids and yellow flowers. As I lent out of the window, I saw two men perched precariously on the front of the buffers pouring sand onto the rails on either side to enable the wheels to grip the track as the engine pulled the train up the steep gradients. When the train passed through the villages at the foothills, the track ran so close to the little wooden houses that you could put your hand out of the window and pull the washing off the clothesline. As the train ascended into the mountains and we reached the tea gardens, we saw many women in brightly coloured clothing, with baskets on their backs, picking the tips of the leaves from the bushes.

Another wonderful view en route

As the train rounded a bend I noticed a dark cloud approaching us at great speed and wondered what it was. Suddenly we were hit by a swarm of large insects and I was horrified when I found them crawling all over me and didn't know what they were. They may have been locusts, but whatever they were I was glad they didn't sting us as we tried to get them off us and remove them from our carriage.

It took about five hours to reach the halfway halt before we were able to alight from the train to refresh ourselves. When the whistle sounded again and we clambered back into our carriage, the train set off even though some of the passengers were still not aboard. I saw several of them running alongside and clambering into their carriages whilst it was still moving.

As we climbed higher into the mountains, the scenery changed again, this time to thick dense pine forest, and every now and then through a break in the trees, we caught glimpses of the magnificent snowy mountains of the Himalayan range. When we reached Darjeeling, this wonderful view was ever present.

We were met by a group of nuns in their black habits and driven to the convent. As we turned into the drive and I saw this formidable looking building, my heart sank. Was this the place where we would be living for nine long months without a break? As we entered the vestibule, I was horrified to see a large wooden cross with a life-size statue of a Man with a great red gash in His side hanging there by great metal spikes driven through his feet and outstretched hands.

Sister Georgina, who was the principal of the convent, came forward to greet us,

Darjeeling with Kinchenjunga

then handed us over to a nun who led us along dark gloomy corridors until we reached our dormitory, which was a large long narrow room with bare wooden floorboards and windows along one wall. On each side were ten beds facing each other, with a small bedside locker between them. Down the centre of the dormitory were five large chests of drawers. Each child had been allocated a single drawer to contain all her belongings. It was obvious there would be no home comforts here. I felt most uncomfortable as I lay on the wooden-slatted bed with a lumpy kapok mattress, and found it hard to get to sleep, especially when I heard Patricia crying in the next bed. This upset me so much that I cried as well until I fell asleep.

Certain incidents that took place at that time stand out vividly in my memory, but I don't remember much about other things such as the girls that shared our dormitory, or the subjects we were taught, but I can never forget the wonderful sight of the sun rising and setting on the magnificent mountains of Himalayan range that was always in view.

Every night before we went to bed we were bathed in small tin tubs laid out in a long line on the stone floor of a cold draughty room which had no heating in it, not even in winter, neither had it any running water. The task of bathing us was allotted to Tibetan ayahs from mountain villages. They carried heated water in large kerosene cans slung from poles across their shoulders, which they emptied into the tubs. We waited in line for our turn, and when one child had been bathed, the ayah just tipped the water out of the tub onto the stone floor, and refilled it for the next one. I remember the rough texture of their horny hands as they scrubbed my tender body and the strange smell they exuded. Because they lived at high altitudes, these women wore layers of brightly coloured thickly woven clothing that they seldom removed. Their long black hair was plaited and smeared with the grease obtained from their yaks. These simple peasant women probably performed these tasks for just a few annas a day but even though they were poor, they all wore heavy gold earrings, large beaten gold studs in their noses and turquoise beads and silver disks strung around their necks.

A Tibetan Ayah

After our bath, dressed in our nightclothes with no dressing gowns to keep us warm, we lined up along the length of the dormitory in front of the chests for prayers before bedtime. We had to chant in unison, 'Hail Mary' and 'The Lords Prayer,' several times under the watchful eye of Miss Swanson, who wasn't a nun but the junior dormitory assistant to the senior nun. I can see her now, standing in front of us holding a ruler, which she used like a conductor's baton to beat out the rhythm at which we were to chant these prayers. I think she must have been in her thirties, tall and thin, with short black hair and a fringe that met her horn-rimmed spectacles. Her cold steely dark eyes glared at us as we stood in line in front of her. I hated these boring prayer sessions during which time I froze as I stood there in the cold. When we were eventually allowed to get into bed, it was difficult to warm up again.

One evening as I was reciting these prayers, I discovered that as I lent back against the chest, it made a creaking noise, so started rocking back and forth in rhythm with the chanting. As there were twenty children in line, she had no idea who was doing this. In the midst of a 'Hail Mary' prayer she stopped abruptly and shouted,

'Which one of you is making that noise?'

I had been brought up to tell the truth, so raised my hand and said,

'I was, Miss Swanson.'

'Come here at once.' she yelled.

I stood meekly in front of her expecting a scolding.

'Hold your hands out in front of you.'

Obeying immediately, I held up my outstretched hands, palms facing upwards.

'No, turn your hands over.' As I did so, she raised the ruler high about her head and with a lightning stroke, brought the sharp edge down with full force across my knuckles. Although my hands were smarting with pain under this savage blow, she ordered me back into line to continue the prayers as though nothing had happened.

My hands were hurting as I was trying to get to sleep. It was pitch black in the dormitory, so I was startled when I sensed that someone was leaning over me. It was Miss Swanson. I hoped that she might have come to say she was sorry, but no such thing. All she said was, 'Don't you dare tell anyone who made those marks on your hands, or you'll be sorry!' So far from feeling any regret at having savaged a young defenceless child, this sadistic woman was interested only in saving her own skin.

Next day during class, my teacher noticed the welts across the back of my hands and asked me how it happened, but I was too scared to tell her, so just had to grin and bear it. There was no one to turn to or that seemed to care about us. Patricia often cried because she was so homesick. The only highlight of each day was when we lined up after lunch for the single sweet that we were allowed from the tuck boxes we brought with us. This special privilege was only allowed if you had been good. Needless to say that there were many days when I went with out my sweet. Such were the simplest of pleasures that meant so much to me then.

All we could look forward to was the end of term, and when it finally came in November, we were thrilled when both mother and father came to take us back home for Christmas. I'm sure they never realised what a terrible experience it had been for us in that awful place or how we had suffered for so long. If this was what boarding school in England would be like, then I certainly didn't like the idea of going there.

We returned home again and were enjoying home life once more, but I was upset when I heard our parents discussing which boarding school they should choose for us in England. They heard about one in Malvern, Worcestershire, from a missionary couple whose daughter was attending there. It was a school with Christian principles, so they were considering placing us there, but first there were many arrangements that would have to be made. A guardian must be found who could be responsible for us while our parents were in India. There was also the question of where we could spend our school holidays, as we had no friends or relatives in England. Returning to visit them was not an option, as there were no aircraft then. Many letters passed to and fro during this time in an effort to resolve these problems. A friend of my parents put them in touch with a Swedish lady in England, Dagmar Andre, who kindly agreed to be our guardian. As she had no children of her own, she told them she would be pleased to take care of us. We discovered that she was a very wealthy widow whose husband had been connected with the invention and marketing of the famous Andre Shock Absorber, and that he owned racing cars, which he raced on the Brands Hatch circuit. So with most of these problems resolved, final arrangements were made and passages booked for us to leave for England in the spring of 1936.

CHAPTER 9

THE EARTHQUAKE

While we had been away at school in Darjeeling our parents had moved house once again. This time it was to a third floor apartment in Bishop Lefroy road near the Maidan. Houses and apartments were rarely owned by the British who were domiciled in India, probably because it was the custom for anyone in business to be granted furlough every few years to return to England for several months. Consequently, one was never able to acquire any permanent possessions. Even if your things were packed away in lead lined trunks, when you returned you would often find they had been destroyed by white ants or cockroaches that had entered through the keyhole. It was found to be more practical for houses or apartments to be exchanged amongst friends, so you were able to retain your servants that went with them whilst you were away.

This apartment had no lift so we had many stairs to climb. It was whilst Patricia and I were there having our afternoon siesta one day, that we heard a loud rumbling sound and the whole house started shaking violently. Mother was unwell at the time so was confined to bed.

'It's an earthquake!' she called, 'I can't come with you, but hurry downstairs into the garden and stay away from the building.'

It was my first experience of an earthquake and I was petrified as the house shook and strange rumblings could be heard sounding like a train rushing through a tunnel. As we hurried through the lounge, the furniture was sliding about and things were falling from shelves and smashing onto the floor. As we tried to hurry down the stairs it was like being on a ship in a rough sea. When we reached the garden the sound changed to a strange rhythmic 'brrum-brrum-brrum-brrum'. Out in the streets we could hear people screaming as they rushed about in panic. Father was so worried about us that somehow he managed to drive from his office through all the chaos, to see if we were alright. Fortunately the house had been well built and so withstood the violent shaking. When we returned to the apartment, it was a scene of devastation with smashed china and everything strewn all over the place and even the heavy furniture had moved across the room. Father discovered that the earthquake had been so severe that it registered 7.6 on the Richter scale and had lasted for about eight minutes, but it seemed much longer.

It had caused devastation in an area of several hundreds of miles, and the Indians that lived in poorly built buildings and shacks had suffered the most damage. I believe it was known as the Bihar earthquake, after the place where its epicentre was. Nearly every earthquake in India was violent and caused devastation and death to millions because of the *kutcha* (shoddy) workmanship in the construction of most of their buildings. If they weren't killed or injured by the collapse of their homes, then they died from some disease, which invariably followed its aftermath.

When earthquakes were felt in Calcutta, a strange and terrifying phenomenon also occurred on the Hoogly River. A tidal bore, which was a great wall of water many feet high, would sweep at a great speed all the way up the river from its mouth at Diamond Harbour, past the city and continue far beyond into its upper reaches. When this happened, because it was completely unexpected, all the boats moored along its banks, especially the little sampans that were home to many poor families, were swamped or totally submerged, causing death to thousands.

These poor people who already had so little and only existed on any fish they might have been able to catch and a daily handful of rice with which to feed their families, suffered untold hardships. There were no welfare agencies to turn to as there are today, so those that survived this tragedy had no alternative but to join the thousands of beggars who already thronged the streets of Calcutta. But these people were resilient and accepted whatever happened to them as their *kismet* (fate).

Whilst we were living in this apartment, my parents became friendly with a German couple living in the flat below us, by the name of Mr and Mrs Wecksler. He was a talented artist whose paintings were sometimes displayed at the Royal Academy in London. He told my parents that he was keen to paint my portrait and have it displayed there. I didn't like the idea of having to sit still for long periods whilst he painted me, but mother persuaded me to do this, and these two photos are the result. He was pleased with his efforts, but told mother that I was one of the most difficult models he had ever had to paint, because I kept fidgeting and getting up to have a look to see how the painting was progressing. He wanted to take it to England but my parents were so keen to have it that they offered to buy it from him, so he let them have it.

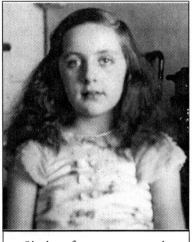

Sitting for my portrait

The result!

CHAPTER 10

HOMEWARD BOUND

In the early part of the 1930s there was a vast army of 'Soldiers of the British Empire' stationed in cantonments right across India. The British Garrison in 1935 numbered as many as 60,000, and were placed there to maintain order and keep India safe from invaders. Soldiers who were drafted out there were expected to serve for a term as long as six years, and they travelled by train the length and breadth of the vast sub-continent, packed tightly in terrible conditions in the intense heat, without even a fan to relieve their sufferings. It was one such train that my parents boarded in Bhopal on their way to Jhansi where they were to spend their honeymoon, when those troops whistled and shouted out bawdy remarks to them. It was a strange fact that the Indians held the British soldier in high esteem, but there was no contact at all between them and the European civilians in those early days.

Every New Years Day on every parade ground in India, the Army of India showed its military splendour in the King-Emperor's Parade, and at that time Calcutta was no exception. My parents took my sister and me to witness this grand event. I remember the magnificent spectacle of Imperial pomp held on the Maidan with the Viceroy of India seated on the saluting base. The parade went on for hours like a continuous conveyor belt of colours. The Indian cavalry in their red and gold uniforms with pennants flying from their lances, mounted on their magnificent shining horses with harnesses jingling as they tossed their heads in a cloud of dust. Following them rank upon rank were British soldiers dressed in smart khaki uniforms all wearing topees, marching past to the beat of the military bands. Regiment after regiment passed by, some Indian, some British, all to the sound of the rousing marches played by their various military bands. For me, the most exciting part of the parade was the sight of the elephant gun-batteries with the elephants in their leather harnesses, their regimental banners draped on their foreheads and their toenails painted white. They came by in a phalanx of six in line to the slow loud beat of the heavy drums, which kept in time to their lumbering step, dum-da-da-dum, dum-da-da-dum. At a signal from their mahouts, they raised their trunks in unison to salute the Viceroy as they passed the dais. Such were the magnificent spectacles to be seen in those glorious days of the Empire.

It was dark when we drove away in our open Pontiac tourer that night, and because there were no lights to guide us to the exit, our driver failed to see a slanting steel hawser that was holding taut a tall pole, and drove right under it. It struck mother just above her left eye, causing a deep gash. We heard her cry out but didn't notice her face covered in blood until we reached a light. We had no means of calling for help, so father told the driver to hurry to the hospital. By the time we arrived she was feeling faint from pain and shock. After the wound had been stitched and dressed we were called to her room to see her. We were concerned that the accident might have damaged her eye or left her face badly scarred. Thankfully when the bandages were removed we were relieved that her sight had not been affected and as the scar healed it was scarcely visible under her eyebrow.

It was a miracle that it healed quickly as antibiotics were not yet available. Sulfonamide powder produced by a firm called May & Baker was widely used to treat infections, but there wasn't much else. Our cuts and scratches were painted with a bright red liquid called Mercurochrome, which helped to heal them quickly. (It has recently been banned in the UK.) Father treated us for any illness with Homeopathy. He had a black leather box that opened up to reveal several shelves with an array of identical small bottles containing tiny round white sugary pills. With it went a reference guide produced by Nelsons of London, to all the labels, which father would study, and depending on what the symptoms were, he would dispense the relevant pills to us. The fact that we survived speaks well for his skill and knowledge in treating us, and the efficacy of those little pills.

Smallpox was still one of the worst scourges in India with no known cure. The only way to avoid it was by vaccination. This was done each year regardless of age. Four small scratches were smeared with the serum on either the arm or the leg, which was then covered by a circular mesh cage strapped over it to protect it. I always had a violent reaction to it which caused unbelievable itching lasting for days, and wasn't relieved until it healed. This left me with scars that lasted for many years.

We were never allowed in the sun without our white pith topees, for fear of getting sunstroke. Even though we had to cope with the strong glare of the sun, I can't recall any of our friends or us, ever wearing sunglasses. I never got used to the heat, or the months of incessant heavy rain during the monsoon. India's climate followed an annual cycle of three distinct seasons. Cold weather, when it was never really cold, at least not in the plains. Hot weather lasted for five months of intolerable heat with temperatures soaring to 130 degrees Fahrenheit in the shade without a breath of wind. That's why we always escaped to the hills during this period. This was followed by the Monsoon when it rained so much that everywhere was flooded. In spite of this, I was happy there because India was my home. England, on the other hand, meant nothing at all to me at that time.

The time arrived all too soon for us to leave for England. Father was granted six months furlough from his firm so he would be able to spend time with us and see us settled in our new school there before returning to India. During that time he planned to buy a car and take the family on holiday to Cornwall. But it was with heavy hearts that we helped mother pack our trunks in readiness for our departure. Because this was all we were permitted to take with us to school it meant leaving behind all our precious belongings knowing that we would probably never see them again. Our parents had found friends to rent the house while we were away, and all the servants were pleased that they would be retained. They lined the drive to bid us farewell and were sorry to see us children leave knowing that it would be many years before our return.

When we arrived at Howrah station we were greeted by a group of father's Indian office staff that had come to see us off and, as is the Indian custom, place garlands of marigolds and sweet smelling jasmine around our necks. Although we travelled first class, the carriage was still rather basic. A *maund* (80 lbs) block of ice had been placed in a tin tub in the centre of the floor and an electric fan played on it, which was the only method of keeping cool on trains at that time. As bedding was not supplied, we took our own canvas bedding rolls with the bed already made up inside it, which we simply unrolled on our bunks at night. After a journey of thirty-six hours we were relieved to reach Bombay and embark on the ship.

Happy days afloat

Although the S.S Britianna was smaller than some of the other great liners, it was a lovely ship. As we boarded, a friendly ship's officer greeted us and took us to our luxuriously appointed Stateroom cabins. Then we were taken on a tour around the ship and shown all its amenities and told about the various daily activities that would be organized for the children during the voyage.

There was a flurry of activity as the ship slowly eased her way from the quayside as the band played. People shouted and waived and all the passengers threw their coloured paper streamers down to those that had come to see them off, as a last parting gesture.

I had made this voyage twice before, but this was the first time that I was old enough to enter into all the excitement of the moment. Soon we were out of the port and passing the great Archway of India that was built to represent the might of the British Empire. This was the first and last view of India that Britons had from their ship. For me this was the first time that I had seen it, and as it faded away into the distance I wondered how long it would be before I would see it again.

With father on our way to school in England

When we reached Aden at the entrance to the Suez Canal, many small canoes surrounded the ship. They were full of colourful wares that the locals hoped to sell to the passengers. It was amusing to watch them as they hauled their goods up onto the decks in little baskets amidst much shouting and bargaining. Father bought us each a small stuffed leather camel with colourful drapes. Unfortunately they had such a dreadful smell that we had to throw them overboard. We were fascinated as we watched a group of young Egyptian children diving off a bank close by and wondered how they could stay underwater for so long. We discovered they were diving for the coins that passengers were throwing overboard for them to retrieve.

As the ship moved slowly through the canal, we saw long lines of camels laden with goods walking along its banks. When we reached Port Said, the passengers were able to disembark for a short while, but we decided to stay on deck to watch a conjuror's show being given by a large man wearing a fez and colourful robes, who shouted 'Gully-Gully-Gully', as he produced live fluffy baby chicks out of nowhere—by magic.

One night we were awakened by our parents and taken on deck to see an amazing sight. We were passing close by the Stromboli volcano as it was erupting. It was an awesome sight in the pitch black of the night, as rivers of molten lava rushed down the steep slopes, hissing as it reached the sea. The sound of the great explosions was deafening, as molten rocks, which lit up the sky, were hurled hundreds of feet into the air. It was an unforgettable sight.

After we left the calm waters of the Mediterranean Sea and sailed into the Bay of Biscay, we met with a terrible storm. The ship pitched and tossed as the sea crashed over the bows each time it dipped into the trough of the waves. It was impossible to walk around without being thrown off your feet. Everything that was moveable was battened down or chained. It was then

Our last day on board, so we throw our topees overboard!

that I realised I wasn't such a good sailor after all, as I had to remain on my bunk until the storm abated. What a relief it was when land was sighted and we sailed towards the shores of England and finally berthed at Southampton. In spite of this unpleasant experience, I had enjoyed the voyage.

CHAPTER 11

HAPPY DAYS

After disembarking at Southampton, we travelled by train to London where we were met by our agents and transferred to Denmark Hill, Dulwich, not far from London. A suite of rooms had been reserved for our family at The Ruskin Manor Hotel that had once been the home of writer John Ruskin, who died in 1900. He was a champion of the working classes, and wrote many books and articles on the social issues of his day. In 1899 he founded Ruskin College in Oxford for the underprivileged. Over the years it expanded, and is still offering a high level of education today. It was also interesting to discover that Mahatma Gandhi had read and studied all his works and, as a result, had sought to follow these principles when he fought to help the underprivileged and outcastes in India.

It was an imposing building standing in acres of parkland, which swept downhill to a lake with a small island in the middle. There were caves on it that were believed to be prehistoric. The house was filled with fine antique furniture and a vast collection of paintings. Everything had been preserved as he had left it. Although he was a champion of the underprivileged, it was obvious that he had lived in grand style. From our lounge upstairs we could see for miles across the parkland and woods over to Sydenham Hill where the sun was glinting on the glass of the beautiful exhibition building, the Crystal Palace.

We visited this vast exhibition on several occasions. There was so much to see that it is difficult to describe all the wonderful things that were on display there. The India Pavilion was particularly interesting with its full sized model of a richly decorated ceremonial elephant complete with a golden howdah on his back, also there was a magnificent display of the grand robes and jewels worn by some of the maharajas. There were also exhibits from other countries around the world, but it would take many visits to see everything.

After having spent the day there, we returned to the Manor for our evening meal. As we entered the dining room we could see a bright red glow in the distance and were horrified when we realized that it was the Crystal Palace on fire. As we rushed out on to the terrace to watch this tragic sight, we could hear the awful sound of the great explosions as the glass shattered in the inferno and shot high into the sky, like some bizarre firework display. It was devastating to know that all those wonderful exhibits that we had so recently marvelled at, were now being destroyed. I don't know the cause of that fire, but felt privileged to have been able to see such wonderful things there before it was burnt to the ground.

We remained at Ruskin Manor for some time, and often made trips into London to see the sights and also paid a visit to the London store of Daniel Neale to be kitted out with school uniform for our boarding school.

The school that our parents had chosen for us had been founded in 1898, and had a good reputation for its Christian principles. Its motto demonstrated its lofty ideals 'Non ministrari sed ministrare', (Not to be ministered unto to, but to minister.) with the aim of helping all the girls that attended there to put these important values into practice. Many of the pupils were children of missionaries serving in various parts of the world, and we were told that some went out to the mission field as doctors, nurses, and specialists in different fields of medicine after they had finished their studies there. Others married clergymen and did valuable work amongst local communities. Many went on to take degrees in various subjects at universities.

Looking back, I'm thankful my parents chose that school for us, even though the years I spent there turned out to be the most difficult of my life. The education that I received which covered such a wide diversity of subjects and the lessons that taught me self-discipline and self-control, two of the most difficult things to learn, and which I so strongly resented during those years at school, have stood me in good stead throughout my life, and I am grateful for them.

On one of our visits to London we were taken to meet our guardian who lived in a large house in Rosslyn Road, Twickenham. As we entered, a pleasant lady greeted us who mother introduced as Auntie Andre. She led us into a beautiful room full of amazing objects. An enormous lifelike polar bear rug lay spread-eagled across the floor with its gaping mouth showing a ferocious set of teeth. Around the room was a collection of antiques and fascinating ornaments including a colourful bird in a golden cage, which when wound up, flapped its wings and sang like a canary. The intriguing collection of musical boxes included an enormous carved wooden bear standing on its hind legs, which poured water into a silver cup then raised it to its mouth to drink. The room was like an Aladdin's cave.

Auntie Andre in 1948

We discovered that Auntie Andre had a great sense of humour and we grew to love her and looked forward to our short visits to her, and although we weren't able to spend our holidays with her, she spoilt us by her kindness whenever we were in London. Sometimes she took us for a drive in her chauffeur-driven Rolls Royce to see the deer in Richmond Park, or down to the river to feed the swans. We were grateful for these happy times, and remained firm friends with her throughout her life.

Before starting school in the September term, we were to spend a holiday on a farm in the grounds of Treasowe Manor, near the village of Marazion on the Cornish coast. There were five of us, which included our baby sister Claire, as we set off in father's new green Hillman Minx car. During our time at Ruskin Manor we had acquired a kitten and a bowl of goldfish. As we couldn't leave them behind, they came too, which turned out to be a very unwise decision.

During our journey, as we were driving across Dartmoor, the goldfish bowl tipped over spilling the fish onto the floor. We were in a state of panic as the kitten, which had been lying on the parcel

A picnic on Dartmoor.

shelf, jumped down to play with them. Fortunately father spotted a cottage a short distance ahead and sped towards it. As we reached it, I rushed to the front door shouting' Water! Water!' A very surprised lady opened the door and led me to her kitchen sink where I filled the bowl and hurried back to rescue them. Luckily they were none the worse for their ordeal.

In 1936 a motorway system across Britain had yet to be developed so the journey to Cornwall took us two days. We were relieved when we reached the farm and the friendly farmer and his wife showed us to our chalets. I was delighted when I discovered that animals surrounded us, even though I was awakened on the first morning by the floor heaving up and down, which made me wonder if they had earthquakes in England. When I looked underneath the chalet, I saw a large sow rubbing her back on the beam under the floorboards. A few days later we were awakened again in the early hours by the crowing of a cockerel perched on our bedroom windowsill.

Patricia and I enjoyed helping the farmer and his wife with various jobs around the farm, but

Caught by the tide

sometimes we were more of a hindrance than help as when we were given a basket and asked to look for hen's eggs in the hedgerows. In our ignorance we took the eggs about to hatch from underneath a hen that was incubating them and mixed them up with newly laid ones. Consequently all of them had to be thrown away.

One morning we set out to visit St Michael's Mount, a mediaeval castle set high on a small island about half a mile off shore at Marazion. An ancient cobbled stone causeway to the mainland connects it. As the tide was out we decided to walk across to explore the castle. When we started the tide was still out, but on the way back, when we were about a quarter of the way across, we were horrified to find it flowing in fast from around the island. It was too late to turn back, so we hurried hoping to reach the mainland before the water rose too high, but it was coming in so fast that we risked being drowned. We were the only people on the causeway at the time and still about a quarter of a mile from the shore, so no one could have heard our shouts. We waved our arms frantically to try and attract attention and were relieved when a local fisherman spotted us and rowed out to rescue us in his boat.

After spending the rest of a wonderful holiday visiting other places of interest and helping on the farm, it was time to return to Ruskin Manor and prepare for the departure to our new school. Before we left the farmer's wife offered to give our kitten and the goldfish a home, which pleased us all, especially father.

Back at the Manor, our school trunks were packed and sent in advance, so we would be able to travel in our car together with our parents to Paddington Station to join the school party for the journey to Malvern. Sadly we now had to dress in our drab winter school uniform. A thick woollen vest that made me itch, navy bloomers, serge pleated gymslip and beige Lisle stockings held up by a suspender belt. I wondered how I was going to be able to cope with wearing such awful and uncomfortable clothing for so many years. For such a little girl with a sister eighteen months younger to care for, the days ahead were surely going to be difficult.

When we arrived at the station and located the reserved school compartment, we went in search of the teacher who was to be in charge of us. After finding her, I heard her trying to reassure my parents by telling them that we were the youngest pupils that had ever attended the school and they need not worry because the staff would take good care of us. Though reassured by what I heard, this did nothing to ease the pangs of parting. When the whistle blew, we were hugged and kissed, and as the train steamed away, I remember feeling forlorn, worried and abandoned as I saw them waving and blowing kisses to us. That was the last image I had to remind me of them, and especially of my father, until I saw him again as a stranger almost five years later. Sadly during this period the memory of both of them soon faded, and I almost forgot what they looked like, and don't remember even having a photo to remind me of them.

CHAPTER 12

ABANDONED AT BOARDING SCHOOL

L ater that afternoon we arrived at the school and were met by a lady dressed in a dark blue uniform and a starched white frilled bonnet. She said that she would be in charge of us, and we were to call her Sister. We followed her along various corridors until we reached a room she referred to as the 'Baby Dorm', which we were to share with other young girls. There were six black iron framed beds in the dormitory, each with a small bedside locker, and apart from the curtains, the room was bare. Memories of the dormitory at St Michaels came flooding back and, when I got into bed on that first night, I discovered that the bed was just as uncomfortable. The lumpy horsehair mattress sagged so deeply that it was difficult to turn over.

Patricia and I were very homesick in those early days because everything was so unfamiliar, and with no one to comfort or reassurance us, it was difficult to adjust to the baffling school routine with all its rules and regulations. Our lives were now regulated by the ringing of bells, rigid time-keeping, homework, strict discipline, silence at meals, no talking after 'lights out', making your bed with hospital corners, tidiness, food that we found difficult to eat, order-marks, detention, punishments, strange and uncomfortable clothing and so on. Right from the start we were required to wear liberty bodices with suspenders on them—nothing to do with freedom, but because they were exclusive to Libertys of London—to hold up our thick lisle stockings which we were required to wear at all times, even in the heat of summer. I could never fathom the reason for this.

It wasn't long before I found myself breaking the rules, which landed me in trouble with the inevitable punishments that followed. I admit that the more punishments I was subjected to, the more resentful and rebellious I became. For what I considered a minor offence such as talking after 'lights out', the staff considered a major one worthy of severe punishment. Every night we had to be in bed by 7pm after which time we were expected to lie there in those uncomfortable beds in silence until the wake-up bell rang at 7am. I found it particularly difficult to get to sleep in the summertime when the sun was still shining and the birds singing. I had learnt a poem by Robert Louis Stevenson called 'Bed in Summer', which expressed the same feelings that I had then.

> In winter I get up at night,
> And dress by yellow candlelight.
> In summer it's quite the other way.
> I have to go to bed by day.

I have to go to bed and see
The birds still hopping on the tree,
Or hear the grown-up people's feet,
Still going past me in the street.

And does it not seem hard to you,
When all the sky is clear and blue,
And I should so much like to play,
To have to go to bed by day?

On several occasions Sister had warned me not to talk after 'lights out', but being a talkative child, I found this particular rule difficult to observe, and was surprised that the other girls managed to obey it so meekly.

We had been put to bed at the usual early hour. It was a cold dark winter night, and feeling cold I was finding difficulty in getting to sleep, so was talking quietly to the girl next to me. Sister must have been listening outside the door determined to catch me in the act, because quite suddenly, she burst into the room demanding that those who were talking should own up. I put up my hand and was surprised that I was the only one to do so. Surely she didn't think that I was talking to myself! It was obvious that she was determined to make an example of me in front of the other children.

'You were caught talking after 'lights out', so you will be punished. Get out of bed, put on your dressing gown and slippers, collect your quilt and pillow and follow me'.

Wondering what punishment she had in store for me, I followed her fearfully as she led me along dark corridors, up two flights of winding stairs to a small attic room with only a bed in it.

'You will sleep here alone for a week, and possibly longer if I think it necessary, until you learn to be obedient and keep silent when you are told to. Get into bed and I'll call you in the morning.'

It was very cold and draughty up there and I couldn't get to sleep, so just lay there for hours feeling angry, frightened and upset, and to make matters worse, I was sure there were rats in the room, because I could hear scratching sounds. Every night she escorted me to this room, and every night I heard these strange sounds, so I opened the door in the hope of hearing human voices, but there was no lights or anyone on that floor. I had been alone there for two days when I was awakened during the night by a strange sensation on my legs. The ginger school cat 'Marmalade' had found me and was lying on my bed purring. He had probably come up there to hunt for rats or mice, so every night I kept the door ajar in the hopes that he would come back to keep me company. He came without fail and I found his presence a great comfort, which helped me to sleep more easily.

I had been sleeping there alone for a week when the headmistress came to see me. She sat on my bed, and as she held my hand she said:

'My little black lamb, I have come up here especially to see you and try to discover why it is that you find it so difficult to be obedient. While you are at this school it is the duty of my staff to teach you to be cooperative and obey its rules, and until you learn this lesson, you will always find yourself in trouble. Now it is up to you to mend your ways, so we will say a little prayer together and ask God to help you.'

So she prayed that 'God would bless His little lamb and help me to see the error of my ways, so that I might grow up to be a blessing to others.' In my heart of hearts I knew that I should agree with these sentiments, but at that time I found it extremely difficult to put them into practice, partly because I felt rebellious at the way in which I was being treated, and I resented the fact that our parents had left us amongst strangers who didn't understand our background that was so different to the other children. It was not that my actions were premeditated or that I deliberately went out of my way to do something wrong. It just seemed to me that I couldn't do anything that **was** right. As I look back to those difficult days I would like to think that her prayer made so long ago, was eventually answered.

Having admitted that I found it difficult to keep quiet, this caused me further problems at mealtimes. We ate at long tables under the eye of a strict mistress, whose task it was to teach us good table manners. We were not allowed to talk during meals or help ourselves to anything on the table but had to be aware of the needs of the girl on either side of us and pass to her whatever was required, neither were we allowed to ask for second helpings, but wait until we were asked by the mistress.

On one occasion I was overheard talking during a meal and severely reprimanded in front of everyone and ordered to leave the table and go to my dormitory to wait there. So I sat on my bed for ages wondering if my supper would be brought to me. Eventually this mistress appeared carrying a plate with a slice of white bread on it and a small glass containing a yellowish liquid. As she approached I could tell by the dreadful smell that it contained castor oil. This was to be my supper, and she insisted that I have it whilst she waited. Naturally I felt upset at what I considered to be an unjust punishment for such a minor offence. Having had a dose of this vile medicine before and remembering the painful results, I told her that I didn't think my stomach should have to suffer for my brief moment of forgetfulness. She scolded me for being insolent and daring to answer her back, and promptly gave me a 'broken rule' which carried with it a detention period as further punishment. Such incidents as these have remained clearly imprinted in my mind even after the passing of so many years. Sometimes I wonder why I always seemed to be in some sort of trouble during all the years we were at school together, but Patricia never.

The pupils in the school were divided into three groups chosen at random from each form and divided equally between three sections, Red, White and Blue. I was placed in the Red House. The girls would compete against each other for the award of the highest number of Stars gained by this arrangement at the end of each term. Stars were awarded for all manner of things such as good behaviour, top marks in any subject, an award gained in music examinations and so on. Stripes were given for various misdemeanours, and broken rules for the worst offences. A certain number of stars could cancel out stripes and broken rules, and vice-versa. If a girl received either she had to go to the head prefect of her particular house and hand it to her personally when she would either receive praise or the appropriate lecture. A tally was kept so that the house with the greatest number of Stars by the end of term could be awarded the House Shield. I must admit I sometimes wondered why the Red House was never the recipient of this coveted award during all the years that I belonged to it and it would have been interesting to discover whether it ever won the shield after I left school.

During the terms that we slept in the Baby Dorm, we shared it with three little girls who were Ethiopian princesses and the granddaughters of the Emperor Haile Selassie. He ascended the throne of Ethiopia in 1930 but was deposed and sent into exile in 1936–1940, when he came to England to live in the city of Bath. It was during this period that he sent Ruth, Seble, and Sophie Desta to be educated at my school. Their mother Princess Tenagne Worq, was the eldest daughter of the Emperor, and died in April 2003, aged 91 years. With her death ended a dynasty that was said to descend from the union of King Solomon and the Queen of Sheba many centuries before the birth of Christ. This reign was largely unbroken from the early Christian centuries, making it one of the oldest dynasties in the world. Their father Ras Desta was assassinated soon after Ruth, Seble and Sophie started their schooling. We became good friends as we shared the same dormitory and were in the same class till 1940.

Many years later, I heard that these three girls who had been my friends for so many years when I was at school, were thrown into prison when they returned to Addis Ababa because the brutal dictator Mengistu had deposed the Emperor again. Not only they, but their mother, brothers and sisters and other close relatives were also imprisoned, where they suffered brutal and inhuman treatment for fifteen long years. During which time some of them contracted leprosy and others died as a result of starvation and the harsh conditions they were forced to endure until 1989, two years before the downfall of Mengistu. Members of the family that had survived were welcomed back to live in England and I know for a fact, that there had been negotiations going on throughout this time by Britons here who were pleading for their release.

In 1974 another young Ethiopian girl, Maza, connected to Sophie, Ruth and Seble's mother through her father's side, was also being educated at my old school and unexpectedly came into my life. In front of the family, the rebels had shot her father who was a minister in the Emperor's Government, and had also imprisoned her mother. Somehow she was able to flee to England, but when she arrived at the school, she had no friends or anywhere to go during the holidays, neither could she ever return to her own country again. When I heard of her plight, I offered to become her guardian and helped her to obtain a British passport as a genuine refugee, and she still remains a loving member of our family.

In fairness to the reputation of the school, I must say that in spite of its rigid regime and total lack of creature comforts, we were taught an extensive range of subjects. Besides the usual ones, we were introduced to nature study, when we were taken out into the woods and fields to observe and learn about wildlife and the names of wild flowers and plants. We were taught painting, sketching, and needlework, and how to do fine and intricate embroidery, dressmaking so that we could make clothes for poor orphan children in the slums of the East End of London that were cared for by the Mildmay Mission. One subject that I enjoyed was domestic science (which sadly didn't include cookery), homecare, and hygiene, which stood me in good stead later on in life, when I set up my own home. Two other subjects I enjoyed were elocution and poetry appreciation, when we were given long poems to commit to memory, including whole Psalms and chapters from the Bible, some of which I can still recite. One subject, for which I often achieved good marks, was composition, when we were given a specific subject to write about and I was able to freely express my thoughts.

Our dear Maza

The school also had an extensive programme of various sports in which every pupil was expected to take part. I soon discovered unfortunately that I was not a 'sporty' person, so found hockey, lacrosse, tennis, swimming and rounders were not for me. Nevertheless I had to take part and hated them. The only game that I enjoyed was netball, and surprisingly rarely missed scoring for the team, and in gymnastics I learnt to do vaults and somersaults off the springboard over a wooden horse. One of my favourite subjects was singing under the tuition of Miss Whitaker who was patient and good-natured as she conducted our singing with her hands high above her head. She found interesting songs for us and I still remember some of them. 'Argos the Puppy', was one that never failed to bring tears to my eyes.

Argos was a puppy, frisky full of joy.
Ullyses was his master who sailed away to Troy.
Argos on the seashore, watched the ship's white track
And barked a little puppy bark, to bring his master back.

Argos was an old dog, too grey and tired for tears.
He lay outside the house door and watched for twenty years.
When twenty years were ended, Ullyses came from Troy,
Argos wagged an old dog's wag, and then he died for joy!

The school had a very good reputation in the realm of music under the direction of Miss Peggy Spencer-Palmer, a brilliant musician and composer. It was under her tuition that the musical talents of the pupils flourished. She formed a large school orchestra, a choir, a percussion band, of which I was a member, as well a pipe band where we learnt how to make our own pipes out of short lengths of bamboo and play lovely tunes on them. Another interesting subject was musical appreciation when we learnt about the lives of various classical composers, which led to my love of classical music, which continues to give me pleasure.

Miss Spencer-Palmer composed a rousing tune for our school hymn.

> Fight the good fight, with all thy might.
> Christ is thy strength, and Christ thy right
> Lay hold on life and it shall be
> Thy joy and crown eternally.
>
> Run the straight race through God's good grace,
> Lift up thine eyes and seek His face.
> Life with its path before us lies;
> Christ is the way, and Christ the prize.'

I can see her now seated at a large grand piano, thundering out her version of the rolling drums as the prelude to the singing of the hymn, after which the whole school joined in singing lustily. Sometimes she gave us a musical recital, which would include comical songs such as 'The monkey up a stick', and 'You don't get bread with one meat ball!' A poignant song about a poor tramp that had only a penny left to buy a meal, and dared to ask for a slice of bread to go with it. This song could have been a reflection of conditions in many of the slums in the big cities across Britain at a time when there was no system of benefits for the poor.

She also composed other beautiful arias and anthems that the school choir and orchestra performed. One I loved, which they sang at its Centenary Service, was taken from the Bible. Psalm 103, and verse 13 onwards. 'Like as a father pitieth His children, so the Lord pitieth them that fear Him…He knoweth our frame and remembereth that we as dust. As for man his days are as grass: as the flower of the field, so he flourisheth. For the wind passeth over it and it is gone; but the steadfast love of the Lord is from everlasting to everlasting…' The lovely melody and poignant words brought back many memories.

Miss Spencer-Palmer was a personal friend of the famous pianist Dame Myra Hess, who during the Second World War organized morale-boosting lunchtime concerts, in which she also performed. These were held in the National Gallery situated in the heart of London, which had been emptied of all its treasures for safekeeping during the London Blitz. Even during the height of the air raids with the nightly bombing, she continued her concerts and became known as a musical heroine. It was there that those weary war-torn audiences could for a short time escape the horrors and devastation that surrounded them, as they listened to the soaring beauty of the music, and hopefully gain fresh hope and courage as they came out to face the scenes of devastation all around them. For her splendid services, throughout the War, she was made a Dame in 1941. She had arranged over 1,300 such concerts.

Soon after arriving at school in 1936, my sister and I had piano lessons with Miss Spencer-Palmer, which involved daily practice sessions and preparation for music examinations up through the various grades.

During our first year at school we played a piano duet at the annual End of Term Concert and Prize Giving, which was held in the Great Hall of the Winter Gardens in Malvern. We were so young and very nervous as we sat at the large grand piano in the centre of this vast hall and played a jolly little tune entitled 'Here come the farmer's men.' What made it all the more daunting was that we were playing before the Emperor of Ethiopia, his family and a large retinue of bodyguards and other personnel that always accompanied him. He had come there especially to see his three little granddaughters taking part in the Prize Giving concert. I recall that when he had to unexpectedly exit the hall for a short time, it brought the concert to an abrupt end whilst everyone respectfully rose to their feet as he and his retinue filed out of the hall and returned a short while later. When it resumed, it was the turn of my little sister Patricia to take her place alone in the centre of hall, and in her high-pitched voice, recite A.A.Milne's poem, 'The Brownie', from Christopher Robin's lovely book of poems. As she concluded, I remember her embarrassment as she ran back to her seat amidst loud applause. I was surprised and delighted when the time came for the Prize Giving and my name was called, and as I went up to receive a prize for Nature study, was also applauded.

Sundays were spent in a special way. The motto for that day was taken from the Bible, 'Thou shalt remember the Sabbath, to keep it holy', and I soon discovered what that meant. No chores to be performed, no school work to be done, no playing of any games, no undue hilarity or noise, no sewing or knitting and so on. As I look back to those times I realize how meekly I accepted those prohibitions without question—although some still hold good to this day. For years after I left school, I didn't drink alcohol, attend a dance, or see a film at a cinema, as these were considered to be unacceptable worldly pleasures that could lead you along 'the downward path to corruption'!

Every Sunday, come rain or shine, we walked in silence, two by two to the local Gospel Hall in Cowleigh Road, Malvern, where we attended morning worship. This was not a set service, but taken by elderly men who prayed and gave short messages as they felt appropriate. There were silent pauses between these, broken only when a hymn was chosen, which was always sung unaccompanied by any instrument. Sometimes the tune chosen didn't fit the verses of the hymn, and when this happened and the singing faded out during the first verse, we found this highly amusing but had to keep straight faces under the ever-watchful eye of the headmistress who was always present. Reverence, respect and self-control were important Christian attributes that had to be learnt and put into practice.

After the service we returned to the traditional cold lunch of silverside of beef, mashed beetroot and potato, followed by coffee mousse. School meals usually followed the same pattern each week, so we knew what we would be served on any given day. One of the first lessons learnt was, 'Waste not, want not', so we were never allowed to leave any food on our plates at any meal. The school grew all its own vegetables organically, which meant they were not treated with insecticides. Consequently we were sometimes served cabbage or lettuce with greenfly and the odd slug. Patricia particularly hated the bugs in the over-stewed soggy cabbage, but was made to remain at the table for ages, with tears running down her cheeks, until she had eaten every last morsel. She still dislikes cabbage.

During those early days at the school, I also found mealtimes difficult to cope with and dreaded them. Having enjoyed appetizing food always beautifully prepared and served at my home in India, I found the school food tasteless, monotonous, and repetitive. Knowing we were required to eat everything we were given made it worse. The first time I saw doughnuts for tea, I was horrified because they reminded me of the cow dung balls used in India for fuel, which were stuck on walls outside village huts to dry in the sun. These doughnuts had a nauseating rancid smell, so I left mine. Matron in charge of our table noticed this and ordered me to eat it at once, but I ignored her command and rose to join the girls leaving the dining room.

'Sit down at once!' she thundered. 'You will stay here until you eat your doughnut, and I will remain with you until you do, no matter how long it takes.'

I was determined that I would **not** eat it, so began a battle of wills. I sat there looking at it in silence, whilst she lectured me about being cooperative and warned me that my stubborn attitude would cause trouble in the future. I listened, but was still determined I would not be bullied by her. We continued to sit there as the minutes ticked by. Matron was equally determined that she wouldn't relent either and became increasingly impatient. She had already given me a broken rule for refusing to obey an order, so by continuing to defy her, I felt I had nothing to lose. We sat there for almost an hour, and it wasn't until she reminded me that the longer we sat there, and the more prep time I was missing, the less free time I would have as I would have to do my homework then. As I valued my free time I reluctantly capitulated, almost choking with every mouthful. It was a hard lesson that I had to learn that day, and I still can't stand the sight or smell of a doughnut.

As we entered the dining room for breakfast one morning, there was a permeating smell of burnt egg, which we were served and knew we were expected to eat. I noticed how some of the girls were already disposing of it in a rather unusual way. We always carried a clean white handkerchief in the pocket of our thick navy woollen bloomers. With this spread out on my lap I managed to scoop some of the egg off the plate into the hanky, whilst pretending to eat small mouthfuls. Before leaving the table, I carefully folded it into a parcel, stuffed it into my bloomer pocket and hurried to the rubbish chest in the boot room to dispose of it. Once there I found it was already full of burnt scrambled egg. I admit that I resorted to this method of food disposal on more than one occasion. Should I leave any uneaten food on my plate nowadays, I still have a twinge of conscience.

On Saturday afternoons we gathered in our house sitting room for a session called 'Windows'. Appropriately named because it was a time when we learnt about the lives of other people, some of them great, and some quite ordinary, but who have left their mark on society or the world by their example or achievements. We listened as a teacher read to us about them, while we knitted or sewed garments to be sent to various missions to distribute amongst needy people at home and abroad. These sessions were always interesting and often inspiring, as they transported me out of the humdrum routine of school life to a vision of wider horizons. Some of those girls may also have been inspired by what they heard, because I know that, after they left school, several trained as missionaries and went abroad to various parts of the world where they worked amongst suffering, needy people.

I always found the letter writing periods difficult because as the years passed, the vision of my mother and father had faded into the past and no longer meant anything to me. In fact, I had forgotten what they looked like or how it felt to be loved by them. Sadly during this time I loved no one, and felt no one loved or even cared about me, so I found it difficult to say anything to them, especially as I knew my letters would be inspected and corrected by a teacher before being sent. Would they want to know about my escapades or misdemeanours? I didn't think so! Years later I discovered that my-end-of-term school reports, which they received in India were not very good, especially when one ended with the words; 'Justine's work has improved slightly this term, but she is still a trifle truculent'.

With no one to turn to when I found myself in trouble, I gradually became more self-assured and independent. Besides, being the elder sister, I felt it my duty to be responsible for my sister who was often homesick and upset by her classmates who were sometimes unkind to her. When this happened I did my best to comfort her because I had got used to being away from my parents, so instead of feeling homesick, I felt a sense of rebellion at having been left at school for so long.

One day, not long after we started school, we were assembled in the classroom, sitting at our desks awaiting the entry of our teacher Miss Chapman, for a history lesson. She was a lady of large proportions with long black hair, which was plaited and coiled around each ear like earphones and kept in place by numerous hairpins. Just before she entered, a classmate had so upset Patricia that she had burst into tears. Feeling angry at what had happened, I retaliated by pinching her arm just as the teacher entered. Unfortunately she saw me do this, and without stopping to enquire the reason for such behaviour, ordered me to return to my dormitory to stay there for the rest of the day. I had nothing to read or do, and wasn't even allowed to join the other girls for meals, so lay on my bed gazing at the ceiling while pondering my wrong doings and wondering how to avoid them in future. But the more I thought about this punishment, the more I was convinced that it did not fit the crime, and as a result felt even more rebellious and disgruntled.

When I returned to England from India after the war was over, I paid a short visit to my old school and was greeted by the deputy headmistress who genuinely seemed pleased to see me again after all those years. As she opened the door, I mistakenly greeted her with the words, 'Hello Miss Snog!' which was her nickname when I was at school. Admittedly, that was not a great introduction to my visit, and I hoped she didn't think I was intentionally being disrespectful. Honestly, it was a genuine mistake. However, the meeting went well. As we talked about the days when Patricia and I were pupils there, she surprised me when she told me that I had been the subject of more staff prayer meetings than any other pupil that had ever attended the school. I must admit that it shocked me, because I hadn't realised at the time, that I had caused them so much trouble and still feel that I cannot be regarded as an example of the efficacy of staff prayer meetings. Maybe, had I been shown a little more tolerance and understanding during those difficult days, it might have proved to have been more effective.

But there were also happier memories of my time there when on special occasions whole school went in a convoy of charabancs for a picnic to some beauty spot. One pleasant outing was to the romantic baronial castle of Eastnor near the ancient 15th century town not far from the Malvern Hills. It was a sunny Saturday in March as we drove through the park to the magnificent castle. Here and there we saw herds of deer grazing peacefully by the lake or lying in the shade of giant trees whose new leaves were the brightest shade of green, and all around us was a carpet of wild daffodils. I had recently learnt Wordsworth's poem 'Daffodils', and as I gazed upon them wondered if he had seen such a scene as he wrote those words.

> 'I wandered lonely as a cloud
> That floats on high o'er vales and hills,
> When all at once I saw a crowd,
> A host of golden daffodils,
> Beside the lake beneath the trees
> Fluttering and dancing in the breeze.'

After our picnic amongst the daffodils we were asked to pick them. Permission had previously been granted in order for them to be taken to the Mildmay Medical Mission, where they would be distributed to poor people in the slums of the East End of London, some of whom may never have seen a daffodil.

There were other outings to places of interest like the Royal Worcester Porcelain Factory where we watched a very old man with a long white beard painting exquisite fruits and flowers on delicate bone china. Another place visited, which was always a popular venue for the girls, was to The Cadbury's Chocolate Factory where everyone was given a small tin of chocolates at the end of the tour. On one occasion a fruit farm had a bumper crop of Worcester Permain apples and we were requested to harvest as many as possible to take back to school. There were also educational visits to the beautiful Worcester Cathedral where we learned about its history and the lives of famous people buried there, and a particularly enjoyable visit to the Zoo where we were able to ride on an enormous very hairy dromedary. I looked forward to these outings, which helped to make school life bearable.

We were delighted when the school allowed Patricia and me to keep two fluffy young pet rabbits as a special privilege. They were both gentle cuddly creatures. We loved them dearly and they gave us much pleasure, except on the night they escaped when we were worried that they might have been taken by a fox. After searching for hours, we found them contentedly eating the cabbages in the school's vegetable garden. I mention our rabbits because the keeping of pets at school had never been permitted before and because this rule had been relaxed for us, it started a string of complaints from the other girls who felt that they should also to be allowed to bring their pets to school. So the ban had to be lifted and the girls brought various small animals with them at the start of the following term. A problem soon arose from this concession when a girl's mice escaped from their cage and disappeared into the woodwork where they were impossible to find. As they were left to multiply, this meant that forever after, mice of various colours were often seen scampering around the school in the most unexpected places causing disruption and hilarity whenever they appeared. Because they were such cute little creatures, no one made any effort to try and get rid of them.

Gardening was introduced into the school curriculum, which I was keen to take part in. We were each allocated a small plot, which we could design and maintain, and there was a competition to see who could create the most original garden. My weekly pocket money was six pence, so I decided to buy some flower seeds and a little pottery garden gnome with a fishing rod that I had seen during a visit to Woolworth's, when at that time everything in the store sold for 3d or 6d. I found an old enamel basin lying in the hedge and set it into the ground with a ring of stones around it. Then I filled it with water from the village pond and sat my little gnome on the edge of it. I hadn't noticed that it had some frogspawn in it, so was surprised when after some time I discovered tiny tadpoles swimming around in it. Of course these soon turned into frogs, and I was very unpopular when they did and the girls found them amongst the plants in their gardens, especially when they stepped on one. Nevertheless I was pleased to see my flowers blooming and filling my little garden with a mass of colour.

What an expression!!!

Imagine my surprise and delight when at the end of term prize giving; I was awarded a silver trophy for the best most imaginative and well-kept garden.

There was an orchard at the end of the school garden where we used to play and climb apple trees in our free time. On the other side of the boundary hedge was another orchard belonging to an old lady whom we nicknamed 'The Old Witch,' because she looked like one in her long black clothes and battered old straw hat as she hobbled about amongst her apple trees. One day during break-time we were playing with a ball there, when it accidentally went into her orchard. I climbed through a hole in the hedge to retrieve it and, finding the ground covered in windfall apples, decided to gather a few to take back to my classmates. As I was collecting them, I was unaware that this old woman who must have been hiding behind a tree when she saw me come into her orchard, was intent on catching me. The first I knew was when I felt a hand grab the collar at the back of my neck.

'Got you!' she shouted as she tightened her grip. 'I've caught you stealing my apples and I'm going to take you to the police station to report you for theft.'

I panicked as I heard the school bell ringing for us to return to the classroom to resume lessons and pleaded with her to let me go, because I knew I would be in trouble when it was discovered that I was missing. She ignored my pleas as she marched me out into the road, pushing me along in front of her whilst prodding me with her walking stick. As we were getting further and further away from the school, I realised she fully intended to carry out her threat, so had to find a way of escape. Summoning all my strength I ducked suddenly, twisted around and gave her a violent shove, which threw her off balance and sent her crashing to the ground where she lay there shouting abuse at me, as I raced back to the school, terrified at what had happened.

We were never permitted outside the school grounds alone, but as I had to return via the main gates, I knew I would be in further trouble if a teacher saw me. Unfortunately, as I ran through them, it was my bad luck to have been seen by the deputy headmistress, who escorted me to her study for questioning. When I told her what had happened, she was furious and gave me a broken rule and I was subjected to a stern lecture. But this was not the end of the matter, because the headmistress then summoned me to her study and proceeded to give me yet another lecture.

She told me that I had broken at least two of The Ten Commandments, then reeled off all the crimes that I had committed.

"Thou shalt not steal, and thou shalt not covet thy neighbour's goods', and as you were caught in her garden, it could mean that you may also have to pay a fine for trespassing, should she decide to take the matter further. You were out in the street alone when you should have been in class, and I have just heard that you also used violence against this lady. For such serious offences you will be severely punished, and given extra detention periods during your free time to make up for those lessons you missed."

For what had started out as an innocent escapade, I now felt like a criminal as I listened to her listing all the crimes I had committed and wondered what punishments lay in store for me. I was soon to discover.

There were ninety boarders at the school whilst I was there, and a strict routine was followed for entering and leaving the dining room at mealtimes. When the bell rang, we assembled in our classrooms and waited there until the second bell, then made our way to our seats in the dining room through the long hall past the headmistress's study. To my horror, I discovered that one of my punishments that day was to sit on 'the stool of repentance' outside this room under the gaze of every girl as they filed past on their way to the dining room for the evening meal. They would all know that I must have done something dreadful to be administered such a punishment.

As I look back to the shame and embarrassment that I suffered then, is it any wonder that such incidents sowed seeds of resentment that still remain clearly imprinted on my mind? When something like this happened, I couldn't complain to anyone but just had to suffer in silence whatever punishments were meted out to me, and as an eleven year old I found this hard to bear.

The prolonged separation from my parents had helped to make me more independent and self-assured during those years, and I believe hardened my attitude towards people in general. It was many years before I felt able to understand the true meaning of the word 'love'. Possibly due to the unpleasant experiences during the most formative years of my life, I turned my affections in another direction. Throughout my life I have had an interest in nature and an affinity for all God's creatures. Having seen so many animals suffering whilst living in India, I had compassion for them. The satisfaction of being able to help or rescue an animal in distress, whenever the opportunity arose, was always a rewarding experience.

CHAPTER 13

THE HOLIDAY FROM HELL!

In an age when children who are at boarding school in England can now fly anywhere in the world to be with their parents within a few hours to spend their school holidays, no one can understand the deprivations we endured during some of those holidays, because we were unable to visit them. The only route to India then was by sea via the Suez Canal, which took three weeks each way. As it was not possible to spend school holidays with our guardian and we had no relatives or friends in England who could take us, there were occasions when we had no option but to spend them rattling around the empty school in charge of a rather disgruntled teacher who had been assigned to take charge of my sister and me. I hated such holidays, because there was nothing to do or to amuse us. In the nineteen-thirties, television, videos and mobile phones had not been invented. We had no radios, comics, newspapers or magazines either, neither were we allowed visits to any cinemas. Consequently there was no way of knowing what was going on in the world outside. Sometimes we listened to a classical record or two on the gramophone, play a game of Snakes and Ladders or Monopoly or read a book from the school library, otherwise there was nothing to amuse us, so the days were long and life was incredibly boring.

I can recall one memorable holiday, which Patricia and I had to spend at school because no one had been able to arrange for us to go anywhere. It was memorable because it was so incredibly boring and unpleasant, especially as the person who had been allocated to look after us was a teacher I detested called Sally J who was our geography and maths teacher. I was hopeless at maths so was constantly in trouble with her over this, because I seldom got my sums right and couldn't understand algebra and geometry at all (and for that matter, still don't.) Even though we were meant to be on holiday, she was still strict with us and never took us on any outings or made any effort to give us a good time.

Poor Sally J was a strange looking woman who always wore long woollen skirts and crimson bloomers that came down to her knees. Her black hair was scraped back into a low bun and her large nose, which was usually bright red, seemed to match her bloomers. How do I know about the kind of bloomers that she wore? Because whenever she wanted to blow her nose, she would lift up her skirt in front of all the girls in the class, take out her hanky from the pocket in them, blow her nose very loudly, and afterwards return it the same way.

During a maths lesson one day, the girl sitting at the desk next to me was annoying me, so I 'swore' at her and said 'Go to **Jericho!**' (I knew the word '**Hell**' was a forbidden word). Sally J had heard and called me to come to the front of the class where she scolded me in front of the girls.

'You will **never** swear again, and so you will remember this, you are to write out—'**I must not say "go to Jericho"**, one hundred times during your free time, and I will also give you extra maths for detention.

So that afternoon, when my class were enjoying themselves in the playground, I sat in the classroom writing out the lines. I numbered the lines in my note book, 1 to 100 and wrote out the word 'I—I' one 100 times, 'must—must', one 100 times and so on. Then spent the rest of my detention time trying to do the difficult arithmetic she had given me. Yes, I hated her **and** the maths, and could not easily forgive her for this.

In contrast to these holidays, we did once enjoy a very pleasant holiday in Switzerland during the summer of 1937, when Nella Selby, our junior matron, took pity on us and invited us to stay with her family in their villa on the shores of Lake Lugano. Her brother Raymond joined us at Basle where we had to change trains, but as our train from London was late, we had to run to make the connection. As we did so, Patricia fell and her case shot to the edge of the platform as the train was about to leave. Luckily Raymond managed to grab her and the case, and bundle her on to the train as it moved off. Because it was so crowded Raymond lifted us up onto the luggage rack, where we spent a very uncomfortable night trying to sleep with the wooden slats sticking into our ribs, but in the morning we were rewarded with stunning views of lakes and ranges of snowy mountains as we passed through pretty villages with their little Swiss chalets.

By the shores of Lake Lugano with mischievous Bruno

Our destination was a large rambling house near the waters edge amongst pine trees, where we spent carefree days with her family, sometimes taking trips across the lake in their boat to visit a little taverna for a meal in a quaint village whose ancient colourful houses appeared to rise out of the lake and cling to the steep mountainside.

It was during this holiday that I almost drowned. We had gone to a sandy beach along the shore for a picnic and a bathe. Whilst I was standing on a low jetty watching some of the family swimming, Nella's young brother Bruno playfully pushed me into the lake, not realizing that

I couldn't swim. The water was deep, and I went right under. As I came up and shouted at him, he thought I was joking, but when he realized I wasn't, dived in to rescue me.

There was another holiday in particular that I can never forget because I remember it as the **Holiday from Hell!**

For the Christmas holidays the school arranged for us to go to a poultry farm near Ilfracombe in North Devon where they took paying guests. It sounded like a good idea, and we were looking forward to it. The farm was run by a middle aged couple and their daughter. It was soon after our arrival that we encountered problems when we discovered they belonged to a strict religious sect and had some rather strange and unusual ideas. Their large rambling house stood in the middle of a pinewood. As there was no electricity, the only lighting was by paraffin oil lamps, which we were not permitted to use. Every evening we were given just one lighted candle to prepare for bed, and once that had burnt out or blown out we had to manage in the dark as best we could. There was no heating in the house. Even though there was a fireplace in every room, the only fires that were lit were in the breakfast room and sometimes in the lounge. Our cold and draughty bedroom was sparsely furnished with an iron double bedstead with brass fittings and a lumpy feather mattress. Patricia and I had to share this, but as we had never slept in a double bed before this caused problems.

Feeling rather apprehensive on our first morning, we entered the breakfast room to be greeted by a nod from Mrs B and a welcoming smile from her husband. Ruth their daughter sat between them looking embarrassed. After grace was said, there was an uncomfortable silence throughout breakfast as Kitty their young maid waited on us. (We later discovered that Kitty was only 12 years old and had come from an orphanage to live with them and be trained as a domestic servant.)

After the meal we went to the lounge for morning prayers. When Mrs B saw that we hadn't brought our Bibles with us, she warned us that should we have to go upstairs again to fetch them, we could remain there as we were not permitted to use the stairs more than twice in a day as it would wear out the stair carpet. This sounds incredible, especially as we were paying guests.

One day when we sat down to high tea, Mrs B noticed that Kitty had forgotten to lay the table correctly, so angrily summoned her. The poor girl stood there trying to remember what it was. Losing patience with her, she made her fetch a stepladder and sit on top of it until she remembered. We felt embarrassed and sorry for her as sat up there being humiliated in front of us. All she had forgotten was the salt and pepper.

We grew very fond of Kitty during our stay there. She was the same age as I was and Patricia and I befriended her. She had a jolly outgoing disposition, and I can picture her now with her pretty features, cherubic expression and a mop of black curly hair. During the day whilst she performed the household chores, she dressed in a blue overall with a white mop cap, but before she served afternoon tea she had to change into a black dress with a starched frilly white apron, and a frilled white band across her hair. She had to work very hard for long hours without a break, yet we never heard her complain. Because she had no family or home to go to, I think she felt grateful for somewhere to live, other than the orphanage. Late every evening we could see her disappearing through the dark pine forest with a little light in her hand. It was not a torch but a small paraffin oil lamp, even smaller than a teacup, so the light couldn't have lasted for very long. We discovered that she slept in a small, sparsely furnished, unheated room some distance from the house. It was located up a steep track in the disused tennis pavilion where all the incubators were stored. She must have felt very lonely there. Early every morning we heard her cleaning out the fireplaces and relighting the fires before preparing breakfast.

One morning when we came down for breakfast, Mrs B handed us each a toasting fork and told us to make toast by the fire. After we were seated and I went to help myself to a slice, she surprised me when she told us it was only for the grown ups. The same thing happened when I helped myself to some jam on another occasion. As I recall this it sounds crazy, even laughable, but at the time I found it hurtful and embarrassing. We were certainly not being treated as paying guests, and both Patricia and I were puzzled by her attitude towards us.

We were awakened early one morning by piercing screams coming from the kitchen. We crept downstairs to investigate, and as we peeped through the kitchen door, we were horrified to see Mrs B chasing Kitty around the kitchen table trying to hit her with a broom handle. We desperately wanted to intervene but dared not. When we came down to breakfast, the table was bare. We discovered that Kitty had run away. She must have been very scared to do such a thing. We never discovered the reason for this, and were very upset about what had happened, because we never saw her again. This disaster did nothing to improve our relations with the family and made us feel even more resentful at the way in which we were also being treated. Kitty had told us she wasn't paid any wages, but worked in return for her keep. We discovered that she had precious few belongings, and being wintertime we were worried as to how she would survive. Mrs B didn't appear unduly worried about her disappearance, just very angry that she had dared to run away. Her poor husband kept silent, possibly shocked at what had happened. Now Ruth had to take over Kitty's duties until another girl was found. Mary arrived a few weeks later. She was about fourteen years old, possibly from the same orphanage, but as she always looked sad and withdrawn, we found it difficult to make friends with her.

We were surprised one day when Mrs B and Ruth suggested they would take us to the beach in their old car, which we called 'The Tin Lizzie', because it rattled so loudly whenever they went out in it. Ruth drove us to Sandy Bay just a few miles away, through the pretty village of Lee with its thatched cottages. There was a strong gale blowing when we reached the beach, and as it was too cold and windy to walk on the sands, we returned to the farm. As we got out of the car we were amazed when we were each asked for 2s 6d towards the cost of the trip, which was the total amount of our weekly pocket money. We decided that in future we would prefer to stay and clean out the chicken houses.

The family had a lovely little mongrel dog called Roy who we used to take for walks. He had been taught not to chase the chickens, but one day when he was caught eating chicken droppings he was beaten and shut up in the cellar where he howled pitifully for a long time. This so upset us that we took him food and water and remained with him until he was let out.

Mr B had a delivery of eggs to make in the village, and we were delighted when he invited us to go with him. He parked the old 'Tin Lizzie' on the top of a steep hill outside the shop facing forwards, and I helped him with the baskets of eggs. Patricia decided to remain in the car with Roy who was sitting on the back seat with her. As we were returning to the car we were horrified to see it rolling down the hill gaining momentum. Mr B started running after it shouting 'Pull on the brake!' but I don't think Patricia heard him. Horrified, I stood there transfixed to the spot as I realised that there was nothing that either of us could do to help her. There was a white wall at the bottom of the hill across the T-junction, and the car was heading straight for it. I just hoped she would have the presence of mind to lean over from the back of the car and try and pull on the brakes. As I asked God to help her, the car skidded to a halt just before it crossed over the road to hit the wall at the bottom. She must have managed somehow to reach and pull on the brakes and when we reached her she looked shocked. Poor man Mr B was full of remorse and probably worried that he would be blamed for what happened. In the nineteen thirties, there wasn't any requirement for cars to have tests for road worthiness, such as we do now, and it was a common sight to see rusty old cars rattling along the roads, just like Tin Lizzie, so was it any wonder that the brakes or gears gave way on this occasion?

Towards the end of the holiday we were looking forward to returning to school, because the tension that we felt had gradually built up to such an extent that we were unhappy there. Patricia and I had frequently experienced problems over sharing the double bed because our sleep was often disturbed when we kept rolling into each other during the night. We had never found it easy to get to sleep throughout the whole time we were there, and things erupted one night when just as I was going off to sleep, Patricia turned over in bed and accidentally rolled into me. With nerves already frayed, an argument ensued over how much room each of us should have. As neither of us could agree, tempers erupted and I am ashamed to say I picked up the porcelain chamber pot from under the bed and threatened my poor sister with it. As I waved it about angrily, it accidentally hit the brass knob on the bedstead and shattered. Thankfully it was empty. The noise brought an angry Mrs B to the scene, and I had to confess to having had an 'accident.' As my pocket money wasn't sufficient to pay for a replacement it was put on our account and sent out to my parents in India. Years later when I told mother what happened she said she had always wondered why she had to pay for such an unusual item.

As Christmas approached our parents sent us some extra pocket money to buy ourselves some presents. At Ruth's suggestion we were taken to Ilfracombe to do some Christmas shopping. She suggested a pipe for her father, a plaid car rug for her mother, also a wooden wall plaque kitchen reminder with the words 'Home Sweet Home', and a fitted sewing basket for herself. By the time we had purchased all these items there wasn't any money left to buy ourselves anything. On Christmas day her parents gave us each a small jam jar filled with some coloured bath crystals that I had seen for sale in Woolworths for 3d. Ruth's gift to us was a table napkin envelope, which she had sewn together from two pieces of linen and embroidered our names on them. I wonder why I have remembered this holiday in all its detail, yet have forgotten about the other holidays we spent during the years we were at school.

CHAPTER 14

LAST HAPPY TIMES

Storm clouds were gathering over Europe in 1939 and my parents were becoming increasingly worried about what might happen to us if war was declared, so they decided that mother should come to England to visit us. We were delighted at the prospect of seeing her again after such a long separation. She planned to rent a furnished house near the school for several months so we could stay at home with her and attend as day pupils. When she eventually arrived from India, I remember feeling embarrassed at our first meeting when she kissed me calling me 'darling' as it was many years since I heard anyone call me that. I also found difficulty in calling her 'Mummy' and it took me some time before I could feel part of a family again. She brought our five-year-old sister Claire with her, whom I didn't remember as she was only a year old when we came to school in England in 1936.

Mother rented a large house called Wellfield near the school in Malvern, and felt it necessary to find someone to help her to run it. A friend recommended a pleasant young lady called Kathleen Cozens whom she employed as housekeeper and nanny for Claire but, as mother couldn't cook, she still required someone to do this and the housework. A jolly young girl called Monica applied for the post and was accepted. She was the daughter of a chimney sweep and proved to be an excellent cook and housemaid. The average weekly wage for a living in job at this time was 17 shillings 6 pence, but she was delighted when she received 25 shillings instead.

Having endured school life for so long, it was a wonderful experience as I began to relax and feel part of a family once more, and enjoy the comforts of home. Gradually those feelings of resentment that had been building up within me for so long, gave way to a sense of well-being and happiness and, as a result of this, the quality of my school work improved as I took a greater interest in my studies.

Next door to us was an impressive house with a tower, called Link Tower Lodge. It was the home of a retired clergyman, Rev. Percy Weston, his wife Margaret and their four children—three middle-aged daughters, Dawn, Miriam and Stella and their younger son Denis, who was nineteen years old. He was an impressive young man, tall, well built, and very good-looking. Having completed his schooling at Monkton Coombe College in Bath, he was studying at an agricultural college near Malvern in preparation for emigrating to Southern Rhodesia (now Zimbabwe) to set up a farm there. We became very friendly with this delightful family. Denis often called at our home on his way back from college to see us and help me sometimes with my maths homework, which I always found difficult. Although he was six years older than me, we had much in common and became good friends, in fact he was just like a big brother to me. We both loved nature and wildlife, and sometimes went for walks or cycled together in the countryside. He knew all about nature and the names and habitat of the various birds and animals that we encountered. As we walked through the woods on one occasion, I was delighted when he showed me a sleepy dormouse (now sadly a rare sight) curled up asleep in a hollow at the foot of a tree, and took me to watch a family of badgers at play around their set. Denis had an amazing labelled collection of different varieties of wild birds' eggs, which I learnt to identify, in fact all I learnt from him then has remained with me throughout my life, and even though I am old now, I still take great pleasure in observing birds and wildlife, planting flowers and gardening.

One day he called to tell us that he had found a jackdaw's nest with a newly hatched batch of chicks and suggested that they would make interesting pets for us. So he constructed a large aviary in our garden, and when they were ready to leave their nest, brought us three of them. This was a decision that we later came to regret, because as they matured, they woke us at dawn every morning, as they called to each other with their loud 'tchackertchack'! They became so tame that we often let them out of their aviary into the garden, where they amused us with their antics, and we were surprised that they never attempted to fly away.

Denis knew that I loved horse riding, and when a friend of his asked if he knew of anyone who could take his show horse to the local Horse Show to compete in a showing class, he suggested that I might like to do this. I was delighted and eagerly accepted the invitation. The owner kitted me up in the correct riding habit and I set off for the stables with Denis. When I arrived and saw this beautiful animal restlessly walking around his stable, I began to have my doubts as to whether I could manage him, so asked if I could try him out first in their menage before leaving for the show. When he reached it he started leaping about and was so excited that I found him difficult to control. Suddenly he bucked, swung around and bolted back to his stable, almost decapitating me as he raced through the door. I was very embarrassed by what had happened and had to admit that he had been too strong for me to manage after all.

Sometimes during the school holidays when it was a wet day and there wasn't much to do, Denis would invite me to play a game of Monopoly with him. We would climb up to the lovely room at the top of the tower of his house where there was a view of the beautifully kept garden full of flowers, with great cedars casting their shadows across the lush green lawns. I loved to visit that room because it was so peaceful up there. Sometimes we just sat there and talked, like me, he was a great talker. He loved to hear me tell of my early life in India and the escapades that I got up to while at schools I attended, and I enjoyed listening to him tell me of his plans to settle in Southern Rhodesia, after he had finished his studies at college. At other times we would while away the time by playing a serious game of Monopoly, which he invariably won.

One summer's day I answered a knock on the door and saw Denis standing there with his bicycle. He had come to ask whether I would like to go for a cycle ride with him in the country. I readily agreed, but after we had been cycling for about half an hour, I suggested we stop for a rest at a beauty spot where there was a lovely view across the rolling countryside to the distant mountains. As we were standing there admiring it, he unexpectedly put his arm around my shoulders and asked if he could kiss me. I was shocked by this request, as we were just good friends, and he had never shown any sign of affection towards me before, so was taken completely by surprise. In fact I was so embarrassed that I angrily pushed him aside, ran back to my bicycle, and peddled away from him as fast as I could. Naturally he was surprised at my unexpected reaction and called after me to slow down, but I was cycling so fast that as I came to a sharp bend in the road and applied my brakes too sharply, the cycle skidded sending me flying over the handlebars into a ditch full of stinging nettles.

Denis was following, and when he saw this happen, jumped off his bike to pull me out, but I was so flustered that I refused his help and scrambled back up through the stinging nettles by myself and cycled off again, with Denis close behind. When I reached home exhausted, mother and Kathleen were horrified when they saw me and wondered whatever we had been up to. Leaving Denis to explain, I rushed upstairs to immerse myself in a bath of cold water hoping this would relieve the stinging sensation.

Denis had left by the time I came down to tell mother what had happened. From her persistent questioning I realized she was still puzzled by his explanation, and wanted to know how I came to be covered in a stinging nettle rash. I couldn't understand why she kept asking me if he had done anything to me. 'Done what?' I wondered. At the time I had no idea why she should have been so concerned about what could have happened that day, and she had no idea why I should have been so worried about him wanting to give me a kiss.

The following morning Denis called to see me with a bunch of wild flowers that he had picked for me and apologised for having upset me so much. I felt stupid and embarrassed at having reacted so unreasonably to what I now realized was just an innocent show of affection. Even though I forgave him, he never dared ask or attempt to kiss me after this, though we still remained firm friends.

Denis was the first man I had met, and having never had anything to do with the opposite sex before I adopted an aloof attitude towards him. My irrational behaviour might be explained when I record the fact that I was brought up at a time when children lived in 'the age of innocence' for much longer than they do nowadays. The fact that sex education was not taught in schools may have had something to do with it. Because I had parted from my parents at such an early age, it was obvious that they must have thought it unnecessary to inform me on such matters, so I knew nothing about the facts of life then or even at the time of the unfortunate episode with Denis, and I was still in ignorance about this until I was well into my teens.

When I was almost twelve, I was walking in the school grounds with my friend on a cold snowy day. There were icicles hanging from the creeper at the side of the path and I broke one off and put it in my mouth. When she saw me do this, she suggested that it might be dirty and make me ill with diphtheria. I had no idea what disease this was so, when I started to haemorrhage that evening, I was sure that was what I was suffering from. Worried, I went to see Sister at the clinic, who casually told me not worry because it was a natural occurrence for girls of my age. This did nothing to allay my fears, so I spent a sleepless night. The headmistress called me to see her in the morning, supposedly to enlighten me on the subject but, after listening to her clumsy explanation, I was left even more confused and still in ignorance of the true facts. From what she said, I actually thought that it could be possible to have a baby by being kissed by a man. How could anyone have got it so wrong? But this fear was in my mind when Denis asked if he could kiss me. So was it any wonder that he couldn't understand my violent reaction. I was far too embarrassed to discuss this with him, but ours was an innocent friendship, and we never mentioned 'the stinging nettle episode' again.

There were happier memories when our family joined the Weston family for a wonderful holiday at Criccieth in North Wales. We spent many happy days on the beach and went for picnics in the countryside, made all the more enjoyable by Denis's exuberance and mischievous good humour. He was gifted with a beautiful singing voice and loved to sing romantic or comical songs, which kept us amused. Always the perfect gentleman, he was kind, considerate, gentle-natured and caring. He loved joking with me, or playfully teasing me, and invariably I would respond by giving him 'the cold shoulder', or frustrate him by pretending not to be amused by his jokes. I **was** really quite fond of him

A happy day on the beach with the Westons—1939
Left to right. Denis, his mother Margaret, and sister Dawn, my mother, his sister Stella with my sisters Patricia and little Claire and the author.

but didn't know the meaning of true love, or how to express my feelings, so found it difficult to respond to the affection he showed towards me.

While we were holidaying in Criccieth, we stayed in a guesthouse on the seafront and the Weston family stayed in the one next door. Patricia and I shared a room on the first floor overlooking the garden and because it was so hot we slept with the windows open. Early one morning we were awakened by the sound of a man singing beneath our window. I looked out to see Denis with his arms outstretched looking up at me as he sang some verses from The Donkey Serenade, a song made popular at that time by the American singer, Perry Como. Could it have been that he chose to sing this particular song to me because it reflected my attitude towards him?

> There's a song in the air,
> But the fair senorita
> doesn't seem to care

for the song in the air.
So I'll sing to the mule
if you're sure she won't think that
I am just a fool
serenading a mule.

There's a light in her eye,
Tho' she may try to hide it,
She cannot deny,
there's a light in her eye.
Oh! The charm of her smile
so beguiles all who see her,
that they'd ride a mile
for the charm of her smile.

This was the crazy kind of thing he would do, and although he had such a lovely voice and I was enjoying listening to him, I was worried that he might wake up the other guests in the house, so put my finger to my lips to hush him up, but he ignored this gesture and just continued singing. He was always filled with 'joie de vivre'. I'm sorry to say that I don't think Patricia appreciated it or approved of his behaviour, which I am sure she found rather embarrassing, especially when one of the guests remarked upon his antics at breakfast!

On the last day of our holiday he took me to Criccieth Castle. It was a glorious sunny day as we wandered amongst the ruins, while Denis read from the guidebook telling me the interesting facts about its ancient history. Afterwards we enjoyed a picnic as we sat high up on the cliffs overlooking Tremadog Bay and watched a glorious sunset. Those were wonderful carefree days filled with happy memories. Little did we know then how soon a war was to change all that.

During our time there, a Christian voluntary organization called The Children's Special Service Mission; (CSSM) was holding a crusade on the beach for children on holiday there. They were known all around Britain for the crusades that were being held on the beaches of many of the big seaside towns. Denis's sisters had volunteered to help with the one in Criccieth. It was interesting to watch the many activities that attracted large crowds of children and their parents. A pulpit of sand, beautifully decorated with shells, was created on the beach, and a lively informal service conducted from it. Everyone joined in the singing of hymns and choruses and listened to stories from the Bible about Jesus and his teachings, and afterwards, games and competitions were arranged with prizes awarded at the end of the day.

That summer of 1939 was the happiest time I had ever spent with mother and the family. After all those difficult years at school when Patricia and I were without anyone to turn to when we were in trouble or who seemed to care about us, I had felt a great responsibility towards her, being the elder sister. Because she had a mild and timid nature and was easily upset when she was often bullied by some of the more aggressive girls, I would always go to her rescue and try and 'sort out' anyone that upset her. Unfortunately this invariably got me into trouble and punished for my actions. Now mother was home with us again, I felt relieved of this burden.

With all that young people have to amuse themselves nowadays, we had to make our own amusements by playing games, reading, doing jigsaw puzzles or having a singsong around the piano. One day Patricia and I found the trunk that contained some of mother's ball gowns, and we amused ourselves by dressing up in them. I can't imagine why she had brought them to England with her because she must have realized that she would wouldn't be attending any Balls, so had no chance of wearing them. When she saw us she was quite surprised at the transformation, and took this photo. I was surprised to see that I looked like an elegant young lady instead of a girl aged 13 years.

We had an old wireless set, and the highlight of our day was to listen to Uncle Mac's Children's Hour Programme on the BBC. As mother listened to the daily news bulletins she became

increasingly worried about what she heard. We were too young to take an interest in politics so couldn't understand her concern. When she told us about a man called Hitler who was causing problems in Europe by invading neighbouring countries, we didn't understand the significance of this, or that it might involve Britain in war. Politics was not a subject taught in school.

On Sunday September 3rd, 1939 we had attended Morning Worship in the Gospel Hall and were walking back home for lunch. As we passed a man in the street he called to mother—'**We are at war!**' Little did I realize then the meaning of those four small words, or how soon they would change the course of my life.

After the Christmas school holidays, Mother had planned to return to father in India with Claire, but now she was faced with a dilemma. After they had exchanged several cables, it was decided that she should remain with us until the political situation

became clearer. There was some discussion about us returning with her to India but they were reluctant to disrupt our studies, so for the time being we continued our schooling and enjoyed the comforts of home for a little longer.

When we lived in Calcutta, our family were close friends with the Golder family and often went on outings together. They left India at the same time as we did, and we continued to keep in touch with them here in England, so when the air raids began in London, mother offered to take their little son Peter, who was the same age as Claire, to live with us in Malvern. Hundreds of children were leaving their homes in the big cities that were targets for German bombing, and being evacuated to 'safe' places in the country to live with any strangers willing to take them in. It was a sad time for everyone and caused the break up of so many families, but this was only one of the many tragedies during those terrible years of the war.

CHAPTER 15

WAR DAYS

The news on the wireless was full of the threats of air raids and warnings about spies being dropped by parachute all over Britain. All signposts were removed and should anyone stop to ask the way to a particular place, they were to be regarded as potential German spies. Air Raid Precaution Wardens (ARPWs) were appointed for every road, to ensure strict 'black out' procedures were observed by every householder. Instructions were issued as to how every windowpane was to have masking tape stuck on it to prevent the glass causing damage in the event of bomb blast. The curtains had to be lined with thick black cloth, so that no light was visible from outside, should German bombers fly over us. All streetlights were extinguished, so walking back from school in the blackout on dark winter's evenings proved difficult, especially when there was a thick fog. Everyone burnt coal, anthracite, coke or wood in their fireplaces, which often caused thick foul-smelling smog. There were no governmental controls about such emissions in force then but, because of the problem, the government later introduced The Clean Air Act in 1956. Until then, we had to endure what were called **Peasoupers,** when it was impossible to see even a foot in front of you, and the foggy air that was filled with thick, acrid sulphurous fumes that could choke you. I remember seeing a bus conductor walking along in the gutter in front of his bus in one of these, with a flaming torch to guide the driver as it crawled along the curb. I once had a nasty experience myself when I went to post a letter in one of these peasoupers. Even though the post box was only a few yards from the house, I became totally disorientated because the fog was so dense, and spent ages groping around until I found our front gate again.

Soon the undulating wail of the air raid sirens could be heard at night and we had to hurry downstairs to squeeze into the tiny cupboard under the stairs, which we had been advised would be the safest place if we didn't have an air raid shelter. The pulsating drone of the German bombers on their way to the munitions factory at Hereford were often heard, and whenever there was a full moon, these bombing raids were more frequent. There was a scare that the Germans might use poisonous gas on civilians, so we were all issued with gasmasks and instructed to carry them with us at all times.

Young men all over Britain were being called up to enrol for active service and were responding in their thousands as they flocked to the recruiting centres. There was a great feeling of patriotism in Britain at the time and everyone wanted to do their bit for their country. Many young lads keen to join up were too young, so lied about their age and were accepted into the forces. It was a very sad day when Denis called to say good-bye because he had received his 'call up' papers, and had to leave at once for the training centre. He wanted to train as a pilot so joined the Royal Air Force (RAF). We had enjoyed so many happy days together and now I was going to miss him.

Mother received several cables from father because he was becoming increasingly concerned about the news of the escalating situation of the war in Europe. There was the threat of a German invasion of Britain, as well as the Blitz on London and the bombing of many of our major cities. Because of these dangers, he wanted us to return to him as soon as possible. Due to the hostilities, the shorter route via the Suez Canal was closed, so the only alternative was a six to eight week voyage around the cape of South Africa. There was no aeroplane passenger service to India then, apart from the Sunderland Flying Boat, which took about four days because it had to touch down to refuel en route in several countries. Father had decided that he didn't want us to return to India on the long sea voyage because of the dangers, so instructed the travel agent Cox and Kings to obtain tickets for all the family to fly out to India on this flying boat. As our wardrobe consisted mainly of school uniforms, mother took us to Daniel Neales in London, to purchase suitable outfits for this prestigious flight. Our outfits consisted of smart fitted cream Shantung silk coats, matching gloves, silk stockings, smart brown bar shoes, and to complete the ensemble, hats of fine cream coloured straw with a garland of silk flowers around the crown.

We were packed in readiness to depart when a message was received from the agents, telling us that the flight had been cancelled due to the intensity of the bombing on London and that our only alternative route was to join a convoy of troopships. So we would have to make that long voyage around the Cape after all. The British government in conjunction with the military had commandeered all passenger liners that had been converted to carry troops out to the Far East. With difficulty, passages were obtained for us on a troopship that had reserved some cabins for civilian passengers, and would be leaving Liverpool for Bombay shortly. I was worried at the thought of travelling on such a long voyage with all those men on board.

When our friends the Golders heard that we were leaving and would be travelling back to India by sea, they decided to join us because the bombing had become so intense in London, that they also felt it wasn't safe to continue to live in England any longer.

The date fixed for our departure was the Saturday of August Bank Holiday weekend in 1940.

Denis in his RAF uniform

We were sorry to say goodbye to all our friends at school and especially to Kathleen who had become part of the family whilst she had been with us. She wept as we left, knowing that she might never see us again. The dear Weston family came to Malvern Link station to see us off as we boarded the train, where there were fond but tearful farewells. I was thrilled that Denis had been able to come too, but felt very sad that the time had come for me to say goodbye to him. Being the first young man that I had ever met I had always remained aloof, but we had enjoyed each other's company because he was always so cheerful and amusing. I realized now that I was going to miss him because our friendship had blossomed and I had grown very fond of him. He had joined the RAF and was soon to train as a pilot and as he stood there smiling at me, I thought how stunning he looked in his smart blue-grey uniform. The last precious memories I have of him are as he came over to give me a portrait photo of himself that he had made especially for me. The family were boarding the train and as I turned to follow them, he took me in his arms and hugged me. As we stood there embracing each other, he bent down and kissed me tenderly on my forehead and whispered in my ear; '**Please promise to come back to me after this war is over and marry me, because I do love you**'. His plea was so sincere, that I promised him I would. He was reluctant to let me go, but the guard was blowing his whistle so I had to board the train. I was overcome with emotion and stunned by what he had just said. The train pulled out of the station and as Denis ran beside the carriage waving to me, I shouted a tearful 'good-bye'. He blew me a kiss and called out, '**Not goodbye. Only until we meet again**'. I leant out of the window and waved until he was out of sight, then burst into tears.

I missed him, and wondered how long it would be before I would have the joy of seeing him again. We kept in frequent touch with each other by letter, and he always ended them with the words; 'Your loving Denis', followed by a PS. 'I **still** think the same', by which I knew he meant that he still loved me.

Some months later, when I returned home from school for the holidays, mother broke the sad news to me that Denis had been killed in an air crash, but she didn't have any further details. She had withheld this news until then for fear of it upsetting me during my studies. I had been wondering why his letters had stopped, but wouldn't allow myself to think the unthinkable, that he might have been killed. I was heartbroken when I heard it, and for years wondered how it had happened. It's only very recently that I have been able to discover this and where he is buried.

He joined the RAFVR on 11 Jan 1941 to train as a Pilot Officer and after training at Ampthill (Beds) and qualifying after only four months, he was flying his Wellington bomber back to base when it went out of control and crashed at 2.25 am on the 29th of May 1941, just 2 miles SW of Cranfield Airfield. Sadly he was killed, but mercifully the remainder of the crew survived. He was only 21 years old, and is buried in St Peters Churchyard in Malvern Wells. Inscribed on his

In Memory of
Pilot Officer DENIS MARK WESTON

60070, Royal Air Force Volunteer Reserve
who died age 21
on 29 May 1941
Son of the Revd. Percy Moss Weston and Margaret
Ellen Weston, of Malvern Link.
Remembered with honour
MALVERN (MALVERN WELLS) CEMETERY

THEIR NAME LIVETH
FOR EVERMORE

beautiful white marble tombstone is the emblem of the RAF- spread eagle's wings-and at the bottom, a brief poignant biblical text from Exodus chapter 19 verse 4: "**I bare you on eagles' wings and brought you unto Myself**". He is also remembered on the War Memorial in Holy Trinity Church Malvern, where he worshipped with his family.

What a tragic waste of a young life that had so much to offer and still so much to live for, but that was the case for so many fine young men as the war dragged on.

After the First World War, King George V visited the Flanders Battlefield in France in 1922 and said of the tragic loss of life then:

'We can truly say that the whole circuit of the earth is girdled with the graves of our dead…and, in the course of my pilgrimage, I have many times asked myself whether there can be more potent advocates of peace on earth through the years to come, than this massed multitude of silent witness to the desolation of war'.

It was Dr John McCrea, a Major in the Canadian Expeditionary Force, who fought and tended the wounded on the battlefields in France during the First World War and saw all the carnage there, that led him to write this famous poem that so poignantly echoes those words of King George V and expresses the thoughts of the thousands of people who like me, have visited the many War cemeteries in various parts of the world and seen those white crosses and memorial headstones row upon row, disappearing into the far distance.

In Flanders Fields.

In Flanders fields the poppies blow
Between the crosses, row on row,
That mark our place; and in the sky
The larks, still bravely singing, fly
Scarce heard amid the guns below.

We are the Dead. Short days ago
We lived, felt dawn, saw sunset glow,
Loved and were loved, and now we lie
In Flanders fields.

Take up our quarrel with the foe:
To you from failing hands we throw
The torch; be yours to hold it high.
If ye break faith with us who die
We shall not sleep, though poppies grow
In Flanders fields.

This poem ensured that the poppy became the lastin symbol of remembrance.

These same fields are **still** covered in poppies. I have seen them there in full bloom looking like a red carpet, and from time to time the bodies of those soldiers are still being unearthed, then receive a full military re-burial with honours.

It was only about twenty years after these words were written, that thousands more were to die in the cause of freedom as World War 11 spread over the globe bringing with it such desolation, suffering, hardship and grief.

As I look back to those early days of that war, I thank God that I was able to leave England then and return to India where I was able to live in more peaceful surroundings. But we still kept in touch over the wireless with the news of those terrible events as they unfolded from day to day in Britain and Europe, and listened to those marvellous speeches of that great man Winston Churchill, which helped to encourage the members of the forces and the people of Britain to '**keep going**' throughout those dark and difficult days.

CHAPTER 16

RETURN TO INDIA

The train on which we were travelling in August 1940, on that hot summers day, was very crowded with troops on their way to Liverpool to join their ships there, and it was a tedious and uncomfortable journey for everyone. We left Malvern at 1pm and were due to arrive at Liverpool at 6pm, travelling via Hereford where we had to change trains but, because we were nearly two hours late, we missed the connection and had to wait on the platform for three hours for the next train, in complete darkness because of the black-out restrictions.

Stella Weston, Denis's younger sister, had kindly offered to travel with us as far as Liverpool to assist mother with little Claire and Peter whom we had brought with us to join his mother on board. We were very grateful for her help because she was also able to assist us with the vast amount of luggage that accompanied us, which had to be loaded and unloaded from the trains.

When we finally reached Liverpool, an air raid siren was sounding. Eventually we managed to find a taxi and reached the hotel quite exhausted around midnight. A pall of smoke lay over the blacked-out city from fires started by an earlier bombing raid on the docks. By the time we had completed the hotel formalities it was 1 a.m. and we were just settling down to sleep, when the air raid siren sounded once again. This brought all the hotel staff banging on the bedroom doors urging every one to hurry down to the cellars. Just as we reached there it sounded as though all hell had been let loose. I was terrified as bombs were exploding all around us shaking the whole building, and the sound of the anti-aircraft guns pounding away as they tried to shoot down the bombers was deafening. After the two hour long air raid the 'all clear' sounded so we made our way back to our beds again, only to have to repeat the whole procedure an hour later. In spite of such a disturbed night, we still had to be ready early next morning to go to the docks and endure the long procedure of embarkation before boarding the ship. There had been a delay in obtaining our passports before we left, so we were anxiously awaiting the arrival there of Peter's mother Mary, whom we hoped had been able to collect them in London for us and bring them with her.

Fortunately we didn't have to wait too long before we saw her and she was able to give them to us. While we had been waiting, we tried to find out more about the ship on which we would be sailing to India, because details had to be kept secret due to the tight security restrictions that were in force.

When we reached the docks, the sight that greeted us was awesome. We realized then, the cause for all the bombing on the previous night. There were giant silver coloured barrage balloons all over the docks to discourage low flying enemy aircraft. Liners packed with troops were moored along the dockside in every direction. Because of the strict secrecy required due to the fact that we would be travelling in a convoy of troopships, it was only then that we discovered that the ship we were to sail on was called the SS **Orion**.

The **Orion** was classified as a luxury liner whose peacetime route was normally to transport immigrants from England to Australia. The Duke of Gloucester launched her in 1934 by a unique radio link from Brisbane in Australia. A button was pressed which transmitted signals around the globe to ultimately activate the launch process. Now she had been painted Admiralty grey and commandeered along with all the other liners and fitted out to carry 5,000 troops to the Far East, with some First Class cabins reserved for civilian passengers.

(I've since discovered that she was fitted out to accommodate 7,000 troops when later she took part in 'Operation Torch' in October 1943, when she landed two groups, each of 5,000 men on the coast of North Africa. During the war years she carried 175,000 soldiers and civilians and steamed 380,000 miles on her various voyages. Since she was launched in 1934 she had carried altogether the vast number of 500,000 passengers to various parts of the world. So she did her bit to help to win the war and was a very lucky ship to have survived, especially when she steamed in treacherous waters for so many years.)

Having thankfully got our passports and completed all the boarding formalities, we made our way to the ship. To mark this occasion, we dressed smartly in the outfits we had bought for the aborted flying boat trip. As we walked up the ship's gangplank, the soldiers that were lining the decks watching us exploded into a loud chorus of wolf whistling and shouting, which I found very embarrassing and set me wondering if this was what we were to expect during the long voyage ahead. I was told that the **Orion** was carrying just a few civilian passengers to the Far East, and I believe I was the only teenage girl amongst them.

We were shown to our spacious well-appointed cabins, and relieved to find that we had been allocated our own deck area where we could relax away from all those troops. She was a lovely ship and as we found our way around her, I marvelled at the fine décor and sumptuous furnishings with gleaming chromium fittings everywhere. There was a beautifully appointed dining room and an enclosed gallery right around the deck where you could walk on windy days, also a small swimming pool. I felt greatly privileged to be travelling in such style and comfort and, after unpacking and settling in, I felt happier about the prospect of the long voyage ahead.

Early the following morning the **Orion** pulled away from the quayside and steamed towards the open sea. I was intrigued to see a great boom being swung out in front of the bow of the ship with a strange contraption attached to it. Evidently this was a **Paravane,** a safety device that would cut the wire rope of any submerged mine with its saw-edged jaws before it could hit the ship and blow it up. We were told that all the other ships in the convoy had also been fitted with this device, as we would be sailing in dangerous waters.

Every ship in that convoy had been painted the same shade of Admiralty grey and the sight was awesome as we watched all the liners join, ship after ship, to make a large convoy in an impressive formation. Four destroyers headed the convoy, with an enormous battleship in the centre behind them, followed by **The Empress of Australia** and **The Duchess of York** sailing abreast of each other. Behind them in the centre came **The Antonia**, followed by the two ships **Oronsay** and **Georgic**, sailing parallel to each other. In the centre behind them came our ship the **Orion**, and completing the formation, following behind us were two more ships, **Samaria** and **Asteria**. Overhead several planes from an aircraft carrier circled constantly to protect the convoy from attack. As soon as we were away from the coast, all the ships increased their speed in order to get us out of the danger zone as fast as possible, because we were very vulnerable from attack by enemy submarines. The sight of the formidable naval escort all around us comforted us.

The Golder family and us

Soon after we left the docks, we were called to the Lifeboat Stations for lifeboat drill. The life jackets were cumbersome; eight six inch squares of cork sewn into thick canvas (four pieces in front and four behind.) This was pulled over your head and tied together by webbing tape under each arm. We were instructed to carry these bulky jackets around with us **all the time** for most of the voyage.

Mother kept a daily record in her diary of the voyage from Liverpool as far as Cape Town, so I will refer to it from time to time as I write about that eight-week voyage. The first entry reads:

'We were cheered to find that we were travelling in such a fast and important convoy, and it was all very exciting to watch, though we prayed that we would soon be out of the danger zone. Although it was comforting to see such a powerful escort, we realised that our safety lay in the protecting arm of God and our trust must be in Him.'

No sooner had she written these words, than we found that faith was about to be tested by a frightening experience, as she continues:

'After lunch when we were just clear of the Irish coast, there seemed to be a stir and a rustle of excitement on board all around us, with passengers rushing hither and thither calling out to each other as the ship slowly turned around in the middle of the convoy and we found that we were steering back the way we had come. How sad and heavy were our hearts as we saw the whole convoy steaming past us and we were left all alone in these treacherous waters going in the opposite direction.'

We were all very concerned as we watched the convoy disappearing over the horizon and were left wondering what had happened. Then the Captain announced that the ship had developed engine trouble and we were making for a port in Scotland for engine repairs, and that every passenger must keep their life jackets with them at all times and observe strict blackout procedures as we were now without any escort travelling in dangerous waters. To make matters worse, the seas became rough and the ship rocked and rolled, and I felt miserably sea-sick and very frightened that we were now so vulnerable to attack from the U Boats and mines all around us, and without any protection. At one point we were ordered to the lifeboat stations when a U boat was sighted and we saw the ship increase her speed and adopt a zig-zag course to avoid it, so we were very lucky to have escaped being torpedoed, possibly because we were an unarmed passenger ship therefore proposed no threat to it.

Onboard the Orion in 1940 with Patricia and Claire

Everyone was very relieved when we finally reached the safety of the port of Greenock in Scotland. It was very boring to be stuck there for a whole week while the repairs were carried out, especially as no one was allowed ashore, and tantalizing to see the purple clad hills and rolling green fields in the distance and have to remain on board when we wanted to go ashore and explore.

It was on Sunday the 11th of September 1940 that we heard cheering coming from the troops on board as the ships engines started up and the Captain told everyone that we would soon be on our way to join another large convoy. At 11am it was exciting to see a formidable battle cruiser steam slowly past us, and the **Orion** left its berth to follow her. This was the signal for the **Franconia**, who had been anchored close by, to join us. There were several other very large ocean liners also full of troops that had been waiting in port with us until our engine repairs had been completed. As we steamed towards the Firth of Clyde, other ships including battleships, destroyers, minesweepers and various other naval craft suddenly appeared from all directions, forming an enormous convoy of eighteen ships. What amazed me was the way in which every ship moved so smoothly into its allotted position with such precision to form a pattern like a gigantic chess board. It was comforting to see our convoy encircled by such powerful naval craft with planes circling above to protect it.

The sea was calm but it was cold even though the sun was shining as we steamed south past the lovely scenery of the west coast of Scotland, but when we reached the Irish Sea the weather changed and we hit a terrible storm. Mother describes it in this way:

'What a night we had. The ship seemed to be rocking about a lot and there was a great deal of creaking and groaning going on. It still continues today and I feel as though I am on a mad rocking horse or a switchback. It was quite interesting watching how the other ships were also being washed by the waves and the destroyers appeared to be submerged for most of the time.'

We sailed on down the east coast of Ireland and finally said goodbye to England as we passed Lands End and entered the Bay of Biscay, notorious for its rough seas. The storm continued for two more days, and we didn't go near the dining room, as we felt so seasick. I noticed that all the furniture had been chained to the floor and the rims around the tops of the tables had been raised to prevent the china and glassware sliding off. The waves were breaking over the bow of the ship right onto the deck and I wondered how much longer we would be subjected to this battering. Once in the Atlantic, we were relieved when we awoke to blue skies and a calm sea and were able to settle down for the first time to enjoy life on board as we sailed towards our first port of call, Freetown in Sierra Leone, on the west coast of Africa.

Throughout our voyage we were in constant risk of attack from the Nazi U-boat wolf packs that were following us all the way. We continued to travel under high alert conditions, which meant daily lifeboat drill and dragging those awful bulky life jackets everywhere and, at sundown, rigid blackout restrictions were still in force. All the windows and portholes in our cabins which were our only source of fresh air, had to have the heavy curtains drawn across them and as there was no air-conditioning in any ships at that time, we only had little fans, which were quite inadequate. An extract from mother's diary vividly describes those conditions.

'Monday 20th September 1940. It is beginning to get very warm and the awnings have been put up on deck. The weather is getting very unpleasant as it gets hotter and hotter each day. Last night, with the 'blackout', which gets earlier each evening, the lounges and cabins were stifling inside, so I took the girls up onto the top deck where we walked in the dark trying to find a cool spot. We are all hoping that we will arrive in Freetown tomorrow. It will be good to see land again, not having sighted any since the Irish coast.'

Freetown was still a British colony, which was the reason for such a concentration of troop-ships and naval craft in the area. This was the first port that we could safely enter since leaving the shores of Britain.

'Tuesday. September 21st. Whilst at P. T. (physical training) class this morning, land was sighted, and the class broke up as everyone excitedly ran for their binoculars. Now we are all hanging over the rails to get a closer look. It is very lovely. As we get nearer we can see that the hills are all covered with very lush green trees. There is a ship coming out to meet us; it is our armed auxiliary that has been escorting us all the way. We saw it go ahead to see if everything was alright for us to go into the harbour. We are passing a pretty cove where the sand is the yellowiest that I have ever seen, and it is fringed with palm trees. Sadly the Captain has just announced that no one will be allowed ashore, so we content ourselves with watching all that is going on. There are already a lot of troop-ships in the harbour, as well as some Dutch cruisers. We have just seen an oil tanker come alongside us to refuel our ship, and the children were very much amused by the antics of the monkeys that were climbing all over it. A number of African natives have paddled out to our ship in their very frail little dugout canoes, to try and sell the passengers some of their goods. There is a great deal of shouting and haggling by the passengers as they bargain for mangoes and coconuts and other odds and ends, which are pulled up and down to them in baskets. There are two Negroes who are diving for coins thrown by the passengers. They are like diving ducks because they stay under the water for so long, and then come up with the coin in their mouths. We left Freetown at 5.30 pm, having been there for 5 hrs, with a Dutch cruiser as escort. It was good to get out to sea and feel the cool breeze again after the stifling heat in the harbour.'

We continued to sail south along the west coast of Africa past the Ivory Coast and on into the Gulf of Guinea where, on the fourth day after leaving Freetown, we passed the Republic of Gabon, then one of the most prosperous states in Africa. Mother's diary continues:

'We crossed the Equator today and I felt the bump! There was the usual King Neptune (the Roman god of the sea.), crossing the Equator ceremonies on board when all kind of antics took place that were usually reserved for those passengers who were crossing the equator for the first time.

'The ceremony took place on the edge of the swimming pool where the 'volunteer' was seated. Someone dressed to look like King Neptune with the help of his followers then covered the poor unsuspecting victim with lather, then made attempts to shave it off with an enormous fake razor, after which they were tipped backwards into the swimming pool where the helpers helped to wash it off. Though everyone was highly amused by King Neptune's antics, I thought it was all rather ridiculous.

'As this was most probably 'a first' for all those troops on board, I am sure that they will all have got off lightly as there were far too many of them to be given the treatment that was normally kept for the newcomers. There was a great deal of noise coming from their decks, so it sounded as though they were having a good time.'

Sunday 26th September 1940. My fourteenth birthday! This was celebrated with a birthday cake at teatime when I had to blow out the candles as the waiters surrounding me sang Happy Birthday. In the evening we were invited to a concert put on by the troops in their quarters. At first I was apprehensive about attending, because I didn't like the thought of facing all those soldiers and possibly being whistled at again, but thankfully the soldiers behaved well and I very much enjoyed the programme which I am sure had been put together bearing in mind that young ladies would be present. The standard of those performing was remarkably high and there was a great deal of talent amongst them and also a lot of laughter coming from all the boys. We were invited to several more concerts after that, which we thoroughly enjoyed and which helped to break the monotony of the long weeks on board.

During those long hot days there was very little to do apart from trying to keep cool in the little swimming pool, so I spent much of my time lying on a lounger reading in a quiet corner of the deck reserved for civilian passengers. At the end of it was a barrier between our section and the area crowded with the soldiers. Sometimes when they saw me they would wave and whistle or call out to me, and I was too scared to respond, but one day, plucking up courage, I wandered over to have a chat with them. They were so closely packed on deck that I felt sorry for them and guilty that I was travelling in such luxury, especially when they told me that they were sleeping in hammocks below decks. On the occasions I talked with them, I found they were fascinated to learn that I had been born and brought up in India, and they wanted me to tell them all about it. As I talked to them and listened to their light-hearted joking amongst themselves, I was upset as I thought that this would possibly be a one way journey for so many of them. They had all been issued with tropical kit, which included a topee (pith helmet), and I was surprised to discover that they seemed to be unaware of their exact destination apart from knowing that they were going to the Far East. This was probably due to the strict security and high alert conditions that were in force throughout the voyage.

It was not long after my talks with them, that little notes started appearing under my cabin door. One read: 'Dear Miss, I enjoyed our chat today. **Please** meet me by lifeboat No.6 after supper tonight. I'll be waiting there for you. Love from John.' This puzzled me, as I had no idea who John was, there must have been many with that name, and being naive I hadn't any idea why anyone should want to meet me there. When I asked mother about this she was not forthcoming on the matter, and just told me to ignore them.

During the following weeks more notes from different soldiers appeared and I became increasingly puzzled as to what I should do about it and wondered who could be delivering them seeing our cabins were out of bounds to the troops. When one of them read, 'Dear Duchess, please meet me at the rendezvous I arranged. I have waited there for you every night and still you don't come, why? Love from Jim.' I was determined to find out what was going on.

Our cabin had been allotted a steward and a cabin boy, a rather saucy young man whose duty it was to care for our cabin and prepare our baths; a service I was not happy with because he was always hovering around me saying, 'Can I prepare your bath now Miss?' It occurred to me that he might have had something to do with the notes I was receiving. When I questioned him about them, he admitted he was responsible for delivering them. I was so annoyed that I threatened to report him, but he apologised and promised not to do it again. All the same, I felt sorry for those men who had been sending them. Obviously I couldn't do anything about their requests, but was curious to know why I had been nicknamed 'The Duchess'. Eventually I discovered this was because I often ignored soldiers who called out to me when I passed by their decks, which led them to think I was being aloof and unfriendly. Little did they know it was because I was scared stiff of all those strange men around me, and with five thousand of them on board, felt totally overwhelmed.

Claire reminded me of a tragedy that happened to one of the passengers travelling with us. This poor mother had five children including a baby to look after on her own and always appeared to be having problems keeping track of them, especially her eldest boy who could be seen climbing on everything. Claire was six years old at the time, and remembers joining them in the shipboard activities organised for the children. The distraught mother had evidently made an idle threat that if the children didn't behave themselves in the cabin she would push them out through the porthole. One day she had left them in the cabin with the baby for a short while, and when it wouldn't stop crying the children had pushed it out through the cabin porthole and it had fallen into the sea. One can imagine her horror when she returned to find her baby gone. Everyone felt desperately sorry for this grief stricken young mother, so some of the passengers rallied round to help her with the children.

Whilst sitting reading in my usual quiet spot on deck, I often saw a fine looking young sailor smartly dressed in naval uniform, smiling at me whilst sanding the ship's teakwood deck rails. He was about twenty years old, six foot tall and well built, with thick dark wavy hair and piercing blue eyes. I had always tried to avoid his gaze, but on this occasion I couldn't because he was working so close to me, so I said 'Hello'. He returned my greeting, and said his name was Jock Devine and that he came from Lanarkshire. He was curious to know how I came to be travelling to India on a troopship, so I told him and we talked about India. Having never been there before he was interested to know more about it. Since joining the **Orion,** its usual route had been between England and Australia, so for him this voyage was something of an adventure. After this meeting, he often sought me out and we talked about his life at sea, and he enjoyed listening to my tales about India.

As we travelled on towards our next port of call, Cape Town, we were closely escorted by, what mother referred to in her diary as '**our** Dutch cruiser.' Its constant presence over so many weeks had helped to give us a sense of security and comfort. Several days after leaving Freetown there was great consternation amongst all the passengers when a three funnelled ship appeared on the horizon, because no one knew whether it was friendly or not. As it drew closer we were puzzled as to why it steered such a circuitous route towards us. People were starting to fear that it might be an enemy ship after all. The tension mounted as the Dutch cruiser moved away and appeared to be steaming towards it. Could it be going to engage with it? We were still on a state of High Alert with blackout restrictions every night and knew we were still highly vulnerable from U-boat attacks at any time. As this huge ship came closer, I saw through my binoculars that it was a naval vessel with a seaplane on its decks. Everyone was relieved to discover it was a cruiser that had come to take over the escort duty of our Dutch one. We were sorry to see it sail away over the horizon after it had afforded us protection for so long.

Once the new escort had joined us, our speed increased tremendously and I wondered why, so asked a ship's officer. He informed me our ship was running behind schedule and the Dutch cruiser had not been capable of increasing its speed to enable us to catch up with the convoy that we had been travelling with at the start of our voyage, which was waiting for us in Cape Town. As I reflect on the enormity of the operation that was involved in getting that vast number of troops to the Far East in safety, I marvel that our voyage was completed with such efficiency and without a major incident. We discovered later that several of the other ships in our convoy had been sunk by the U-boats that had been trailing us all the way, in spite of the formidable naval escort, so we were very lucky..

Two days later heavy seas hit us again and it grew much colder as we journeyed south. There was no one on deck, as the other passengers would be found sitting around the fires in the lounge. We had certainly experienced the extremes of weather conditions on this trip, from steamy sweltering heat to freezing gale-force winds, and I wondered what lay in store for us, as there were still several more weeks to go before we reached our destination.

As we were nearing Cape Town and this would be the first time that we would be setting our feet on dry land after such a long time at sea, the troops celebrated the event with another concert to which we were invited. I sensed an air of joyful anticipation and relief amongst them, which was reflected in the various acts that were performed, some of which were hilarious and greeted with roars of laughter from the

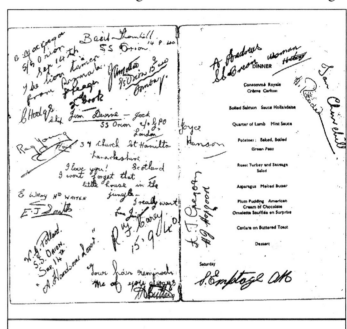

Menu signed by members of ship's crew

boys. There was one skit that I still remember entitled 'The Little Green-eyed Goddess from Kathmandu', with one of the boys dressed like a Nepalese goddess and the other like a peasant, which must have been based on some poem. The dialogue was so amusing that it was almost drowned by the laughter that it produced. Following that we were treated to a beautiful rendering of Mendelssohn's Moonlight Sonata played by a very talented pianist. To end the concert we all joined in the lusty singing of some of the wartime songs such as, 'We'll meet again', and 'Wish me luck as you wave me goodbye'.

After the concert, the Captain invited us to a special 'Landfall Dinner'. I have kept that evening's menu, signed by some of the ship's officers and crew as a memento of that special occasion. After dinner most of the passengers danced to a live band but I preferred to walk on deck in the cool of the evening.

I was up very early the following morning and went up on deck to find there was great excitement on board as the distinctive shape of Table Mountain in Cape Town came into view. As we approached the port, I was amazed to see so many naval ships moored alongside great ocean liners packed tightly with troops. We steamed slowly past them to our berth, to loud cheering and frantic waving as they welcomed us.

Because of our delayed arrival, we were told to our great disappointment that we would only to be allowed to spend half a day ashore. The ships that were in our first convoy and had steamed away leaving us alone to return to Scotland, had been in Cape Town for a week awaiting our arrival and enjoying the hospitality of the folk there who had held street parties for them and welcomed them into their homes, and a great time had been had by all. We were given the choice of either going up Table Mountain or taking a tour around the Garden Route and visiting an ostrich farm. Seeing that the mountain had its famous tablecloth of cloud on the top so there would be no panoramic view, we chose the tour.

It was a lovely sunny day, and good to be on dry land again after all those weeks at sea. As we were driven through the city, we were amazed by the way in which it was decorated to welcome the troops. Everywhere were flags, bunting and banners with welcoming slogans. We were quite disappointed to have missed all the celebrations that had been laid on by the local people who had turned out to greet them. The following day it was time to depart and once again we watched all those ships manoeuvring into their positions in our convoy in preparation for the last stretch of the voyage to Bombay.

We steamed out of the harbour into the South Atlantic, around the tip of South Africa and into the Indian Ocean and passed the port of Durban where some of the convoys had been diverted, to avoid congestion in Cape Town. I heard later, that all the troops that had gone ashore there had also enjoyed a similar welcome from the inhabitants.

A lovely lady who lived in Durban called Perle Sielde Gibson and was an opera singer, came down to the docks each day to welcome all the troop and hospital ships with her wonderful singing. She came to be known as the Lady in White to the many thousands who passed on their way to the eastern battlefields. Standing on a fifty foot high platform, she sang to them through a loud hailer, nostalgic songs such as 'We'll gather lilacs in the spring again' and patriotic songs like 'There'll always be an England' and 'We'll meet again, don't know where, don't know when...' amongst others. It is said by those who heard her, that these hardened soldiers were often so moved by her beautiful singing that some of them were reduced to tears as they thought of their loved ones and realized that they

'The Lady in White'

might never return to their homeland to see their loved ones again. She was a great morale booster and was idolized throughout the Armed Forces. Perle was reputed to have sung to a thousand troopships and three hundred and fifty hospital ships during the war. In recognition of this, Queen Elizabeth unveiled a statue of her in 1995, on the same jetty where she had sung to them. In those days there was a tremendous spirit of patriotism wherever one went, and a great sense of camaraderie amongst the troops.

After the excitement of Cape Town, life on board became rather mundane as we sailed away into the Indian Ocean out of sight of land. I spent a lot of my time looking over the deck rails watching the parting of the waves at the bow of the ship and always found it very exciting when the porpoises came to join us and travel for quite long distances before suddenly disappearing. At other times I often saw shoals of Flying Fish leap out of the water and skim across the surface of the waves before diving back into the sea again.

Sometimes when we got bored, Patricia and I used to look through the large picture window of our cabin that opened at the same level onto the sailor's recreation deck and watch them as they played games and amused themselves. Whenever Jock caught sight of me at the window he would come over and sit on the deck beneath it and talk to me. He loved to hear me tell of my early days in the mountains of Kalimpong and Darjeeling and my descriptions of the sunsets on the magnificent Himalayas that could be seen from Ahava, and stories about the laughing hyenas and the leopard. I think they so captured his imagination that when I asked him to sign my souvenir Landfall Menu at the end of our voyage, he wrote on it "I love you and I will never forget that little house in the jungle. I really won't! Love Jim".

One of his sailor friends was a musician who sometimes joined him to entertain us by playing his accordion. This often attracted the attention of some of the other sailors who would come over to us and join in singing some of the nostalgic war songs that we all loved to sing together during those dark and difficult days. Mother was aware of this and we were thankful that she approved with the proviso, 'As long as this is always conducted strictly through the window'.

As we passed Madagascar and sailed up through the islands of the Seychelles and past Mombassa, soon to cross the Equator for the second time and enter the Arabian Sea, it started to get very hot again. Throughout the voyage we had experienced total extremes in the weather conditions, but from now it would be continually hot. I felt very sorry for all those soldiers who had never experienced such heat and would be suffering great discomfort in their crowded quarters. Because of the short time that we had been in Cape Town, they probably hadn't even been allowed ashore. Whenever we closed in on any of the other ships in our convoy, they all appeared to be as tightly packed with troops as ours but the rousing cheers that came from them as we passed, showed that they were still in good spirits in spite of suffering such cramped conditions.

We were now on the last leg of our journey and there was an air of excitement on board as we neared land, especially when we passed several ships coming in the opposite direction, possibly from Bombay, the port we were heading for.

As it was to be our last night on board, the Captain arranged a farewell dinner for us. Afterwards, the ship's officers and some of the more important members of the crew came in to be introduced and thanked for their excellent care of us on what had been a long and hazardous voyage. Then we toasted each other with champagne, after which we all linked hands and sang Auld Lang Syne. After bidding farewell to the other passengers, I returned to the cabin. Feeling tired but exhilarated, I packed away my belongings and went to bed.

Early the following morning as I looked out of the porthole and saw all the sailors bustling about on their deck, I was puzzled when I caught site of Jock sitting on a coil of rope with his head in his hands. He looked dejected, and because I was concerned to see him like that, I called to him. He came over and as he looked up at me, I noticed his blue eyes were full of tears, so asked what was troubling him. I was very surprised when he told me that he had fallen in love with me and was heartbroken because he couldn't bear the thought of never seeing me again. I was lost for words, as I hadn't realized he felt like that about me. I had always kept my personal thoughts and emotions to myself and wasn't conscious of having given him any encouragement to think I might care for him. I had only shown friendship towards him and his mates. I felt sad at leaving him so distressed, so we exchanged addresses and I told him I would write to him. As I said goodbye and offered him my hand through the window, he grasped it and held it to his lips reluctant to let it go. It was a poignant memory, and I hoped he might soon forget me, but as time passed it proved that he didn't.

Although I was only fourteen years old at the time, people often mistook me for being much older than that, possibly because I was an 'early developer', and being head and shoulders above my sister who was only eighteen months younger than me, I always acted like her big sister.

Having packed the last of my belongings, I was preparing to leave the cabin when there was a knock at the door. I said 'Come in', and the saucy young cabin steward who had given me such trouble over the 'Duchess' notes, entered.

'I've come to say goodbye to you Miss, and I can't let you go without telling you how much I have enjoyed looking after you throughout this voyage, and I am going to miss you.'

This outburst took me totally by surprise, and I was shocked and indignant when he came up to me, supposedly to shake hands, but instead took me in his arms and kissed me passionately. (Being kissed by a man was the one thing I still dreaded!) Before I could recover my composure, he was gone and it was too late to do anything about it, because the rest of the family were already waiting for me in the lounge. As I joined them, mother noticed that I looked flushed and upset so asked me what was the matter, but I was far too embarrassed to tell her.

We heard noisy cheering coming from the troop decks as they saw the wonderful sight of the Great Archway of India coming into view. As I gazed upon it, I was reminded of the day in 1936 when I had sadly watched it receding into the distance as we said goodbye to India and sailed away to England to be left in a boarding school there. But now this same sight thrilled me. I was returning home again, though apprehensive about meeting my father after being away from him for so many years, and worried because I couldn't remember what he looked like.

As the ship was being tied up at its berth with everyone on board crowding at the rails, we saw a large military brass band resplendent in red and gold uniforms with their white helmets, waiting on the quayside to greet us. As they played rousing marches, Land of Hope and Glory, and There'll always be an England, and other nostalgic songs, I was overcome by emotion as I joined in the singing with the soldiers.

Mother had difficulty in spotting father amongst the crowds that thronged the quay, so it was a while before she caught sight of him. Suddenly I saw her waving frantically and calling, 'Arthur, Arthur!' as she pointed at someone in the crowd.

'Look girls, there's Daddy. He's wearing a cream suit and a brown Trilby hat. Can you see him?'

Having described him to us, I caught sight of him and waved. He had seen us and was waving back. As he was walking along the edge of the quay looking up, he failed to see a large metal bollard in front of him and tripped over it. As he lay sprawled across it, we watched as he picked himself up, and bowed to it. The soldiers who had seen this happen roared with laughter, but he appeared quite unperturbed as he looked up and waved to them. Poor father! At least he appeared to have a sense of humour.

After the gangplank was lowered, father made his way towards it and waited there to greet us. Meanwhile there was frantic activity amongst the soldiers who had donned their khaki topees and slung their kit bags over their shoulders in readiness for disembarkation. As I watched them, I was amazed to see a group of them being swung over the side of the ship by a crane, clinging to the net covering an enormous load of luggage. At the other end of the ship, cranes were also unloading our baggage, so it was a while before we could join my father. When the call finally came to disembark, we made our way down the gangplank where he greeted me with a kiss and a hug. I remember feeling very uneasy and embarrassed because I couldn't think of anything to say to him.

Once we had located our luggage, he organized a horde of coolies to carry it to our carriage on the boat train. We were delighted to find that he had reserved a first class air-conditioned compartment for us, a luxury that had not been available when we left in 1936. So this time the 40-hour journey to Calcutta would be a comfortable one.

During the trip we learnt that, while we had been away in England, father had moved house to a much larger place with a large garden, which he described to us in detail. It was located in Harrington Street, a quiet road just off the main Chowringhee thoroughfare within walking distance of the

My father in Sept 1940

large grassy area of the Maidan, and from his description it sounded ideal and I was looking forward to being able to call it my home.

When we finally arrived at Howrah Station in Calcutta, I was surprised to see a welcoming party of staff from father's office with garlands of marigolds and sweet smelling jasmine flowers, which they placed around our necks as we alighted from the train. They took care of our luggage and arranged for coolies to carry it to the cars that awaited us. I had forgotten what India was really like and that it would be so crowded and noisy. The heat was stifling as we drove over Howrah Bridge through the congested traffic and crowded streets to reach our home. In spite of this, I was thrilled to be back to a place where we could all live together as a family again. As we drove up to the front door we were welcomed by Trixie, my parents little fox terrier, and the servants who had lined up to welcome us with 'Salaams' as they put their hands together in greeting.

As I entered the house, I was delighted to find it to be so spacious and beautifully furnished. The furniture was of teak and all the furnishings were of bright colours. From the hall you entered a very large lounge with lofty ceilings which led on to a covered verandah. Three bedrooms led off the lounge each with an en suite bathroom. The dining room had a massive highly polished table that could seat twelve and an impressive carved sideboard. Several electric fans (punkahs) hung from the ceilings in every room, because air conditioning was a luxury that came some years later. Outside was a large well kept lawn marked out for a game of tennis, and there were numerous flowering shrubs and beds full of colourful flowers. I knew at once that I was going to be very happy in my new home, though I realized now that I would have to become used to a completely new lifestyle.

CHAPTER 17

TOGETHER AGAIN!

That evening was memorable as we sat down to supper together for the first time as a complete family after so many years of separation. It felt strange to be waited upon by servants who served us an excellent three-course meal tastefully presented on silver salvers, with crystal finger bowls for each of us to rinse our fingers after we had eaten. So this was how we would dine in future and I'd have to adapt to these new customs and learn the local language soon as none of our servants or any of the locals spoke English.

It was hot and humid as I climbed into bed and I felt stifled under the mosquito net. The electric *punkah* whirred noisily overhead and I found it difficult to sleep. Strange noises were coming from outside my bedroom window, so I got up to find out what they were. By the light of the full moon I could see a horde of bat-like creatures hanging from the branches of a tree. Some were squabbling, whilst others were landing or taking off with a loud whirring of wings. It was like a scene in a horror movie. Their cries disturbed me

The whole family united at last!

throughout the night and thankfully by dawn they were gone, but unfortunately they returned every night until the tree was stripped of all its fruit. These were fruit bats, sometimes known as flying foxes. Because of their red furry bodies and pointed muzzle they looked like foxes with wings and I was told that the adults weighed about 2lbs and had an average wingspan of up to 5ft. I was particularly relieved to hear that they were harmless. As dawn broke the raucous cawing of hundreds of crows awakened me. Ah well! This was India and just another of the many sounds and sights that I would have to get used to once again.

I was concerned when I realised that we were now exposed to the multitude of diseases that surrounded us, no matter how hard you tried to protect yourself from them, you were still always at risk. We'd had all the necessary jabs before leaving England, but you couldn't guard against malaria, because if you had constantly taken the drug mepacrine or quinine, which were then the only recognized prophylactics for this disease, they could turn your eyes and skin yellow.

Shortly after we arrived home, Patricia suddenly went down with a fever. Her temperature shot up to 105F! The doctor suspected typhoid when she became delirious and the high fever continued for over a week. A second opinion was sought and, as the two doctors were trying to make a right diagnosis, the fever broke. A bright red rash spread all over her body, which confirmed the diagnosis of the second doctor, which was Dengue fever. This disease like malaria is caused by a mosquito bite, but with malaria the repetitive attacks though violent, are short lived. Patricia's illness continued for a long time, and the muscles of her face became paralysed. As she slowly recovered, all her hair gradually fell out and it was several weeks before she was strong enough to take even a few steps.

In view of Patricia's illness, I counted myself lucky because I only contracted jaundice, dysentery, and amoebic dysentery. But I felt a constant fear of catching some other deadly disease, especially as there were no antibiotics available in those days.

We were fortunate to have a car with our own driver always waiting to take us anywhere we wished to go, so we often went to the Calcutta Swimming Club for lunch and a swim. It was the only place to keep cool when the temperatures rose to over 100 degrees Fahrenheit. In the afternoons we often drove out of the city to the beautiful grounds of the Tolleygunge Golf Club for afternoon tea and at the weekends, father would join us there to relax and play a round of golf.

Mother in 1940

The New Market was a wonderful place to buy materials with its enormous selection that could be purchased for just a few rupees. Mother employed a full time durzi (an Indian dressmaker) who sat on the floor of the verandah with a small Singer sewing machine, making clothes for all the family. Magazines such as The Lady, Needle Woman and Vogue, were sent to mother from England so that she could keep abreast of the latest fashions. In spite of the dust and heat she was very fashion conscious and dressed immaculately in lovely clothes. With her striking features, lovely figure and dark wavy hair, she looked so young that she was often mistaken for our sister. Because she was petite and her shoes were only a size two, she had them specially made for her. One pair was made of real cobra skin, which fascinated and amused some of the boys in the forces who visited us later on when my parents opened their home to them. They jokingly referred to her as 'The little lady in the snake skin shoes'. She was vivacious, kind and welcoming to everyone she met, and a great raconteur with a sense of humour who kept them and us spellbound by her tales of the days when she first came out to India. We had parted as children and returned as teenagers, so were now able to appreciate her fine qualities and the motherly love and caring she showed towards us. I felt a sense of guilt now for the resentment I had felt towards my parents at having been separated from them for so long.

We loved looking through the new Vogue magazine when it arrived, so we could choose a dress for our durzi to copy and make up from the lovely fabrics that we had bought. It was fascinating to see him create these wonderful dresses as he sat on the verandah floor whilst holding the material taught between his fingers and toes and running up the seams on the rickety old Singer sewing machine. The dresses we chose were in the height of fashion and he skilfully

A tennis tea party

managed to reproduce exact replicas of the designers of the day. For a minimal cost, the end result was truly miraculous.

Sometimes tennis parties were organized for friends and members of the forces, when after several games, afternoon tea with cakes and sandwiches would be served on the lawn. This was often a rather hazardous affair because of the Red Kite Hawks (commonly referred to by the troops as 's—hawks!'), which circled overhead constantly, waiting to swoop down and grab your food in their talons just as you were about to eat it. I had an experience of this on more than one occasion, in spite of the *jemadhar*, who stood by waving a flag on a long pole to try and deter them.

During the prelude to Christmas, it was the custom of father's office staff to call on us bearing gifts for all our family. For my sister and me, beautiful saris, and for my parents, intricately carved ivory ornaments and an alabaster model of the Taj Mahal that lit up inside. Other gifts included a variety of engraved brassware inlaid with colourful enamel, and a beautiful Persian carpet. Another unusual gift that mother was not too pleased to receive, was a pair of very large full grown Norfolk turkeys. As these birds were not usually available in India, we wondered where they had come from. They wandered around the garden and became so friendly and domesticated that they would visit us in the house, particularly during mealtimes.

One day we discovered that the hen was sitting on a clutch of about a dozen eggs, and the prospect of little chicks running around the garden didn't please my parents at all, but the problem was resolved when we later found her dead on her nest, for no apparent reason. The cock turkey was so upset that he attached himself to Claire and followed her everywhere, which seemed rather strange behaviour for a turkey. Our car was usually parked in the drive by the house, and it was amusing to see him displaying to his reflection in the large chromium-plated wheel hubcaps. He must have thought that his reflection was a rival.

As Christmas day approached mother reminded us that the turkey had been given to us to eat on that day. We were horrified at the suggestion because we had grown quite fond of him, so were surprised that she could think we could eat such a lovely creature. Faced now with a dilemma as to how she could dispose of it without upsetting us, she contacted a friend for advice. We refused to have any further discussion on the matter. A few days later he disappeared and in place of him was a six-foot Christmas tree in the lounge for us to decorate. Seeing we were living in the centre of the city and Christmas trees grew far away up in the mountains, we wondered how she had obtained it. When we asked her about the mysterious disappearance of our turkey and how she had been able to find the tree, she just told us to be content with this substitute. It was a couple of months later that we eventually found out what had become of him. We were invited to visit friends of my parents, who were in charge of

A beautiful sari for me

the Botanical Gardens on the banks of the Hoogli River. As we disembarked from the launch they met us and we followed them to the house where we were greeted by their little daughter and our turkey. Mother had given them our turkey in exchange for the Christmas tree that had been cultivated in the gardens. They had planned to eat him for their Christmas dinner, but because he was such a friendly bird and had attached himself to their little daughter, they couldn't bring themselves to do this.

CHAPTER 18

HEBRON SCHOOL

Since our arrival in India, our parents had been trying to find a suitable school where we could continue our education and prepare for the examinations that had been disrupted by our departure from school in England. Friends of theirs had recommended a school in South India situated in a beautiful area of the Nilgiris hills, so they sent for a prospectus. From this they found that Hebron was a multi-national school, which also catered for children of missionaries. It was founded in 1899 as a school with Christian principles and its motto was 'DEO SUPREMO' (God Supreme). It aimed to give its pupils a high level of education and training in a wide variety of subjects and sports, and to illustrate this I quote a paragraph from their prospectus, which states 'Hebron's Aims':

'Our aim as a school is to educate our students so that they have a considered and balanced world-view. A vital part of this is an understanding of the teachings of Christ as revealed in the Bible, with their implications for individual and community life. We regard every student as a valued person whose mind, body and spirit all need nurturing within a loving and caring environment. Our desire is that such an environment would challenge the students to work out the focus and direction of their lives and prepare them for life after school within the international community'.

As I read these noble sentiments, I felt sure that it was a school where I could be happy, and was pleased when my parents decided to send Patricia and me there to complete our studies. I couldn't help wondering why we had been 'banished' to a boarding school in England when we were so young and where I was so unhappy that it brought out all that rebellion and resentment in me, the memory of which still lives with me to this day. Strangely as I think about it now, I never put this question to them, but at the time meekly accepted whatever they decided was best for us.

Hebron was situated up amongst the mountains amidst tea gardens in Coonoor, and enjoyed a pleasant climate throughout the year. This was not far from the well known hill-station of Ootacamund, founded in the early nineteenth century by the British who had built their houses there to resemble 'a little bit of England.' Because of the beauty of the location and the ideal climate, many of the maharajahs had also chosen to build their summer palaces there. It was also the location for the summer residence of the government of Madras, which was housed in a magnificent colonial building built by the British who left their legacy of wonderful architecture right across India.

Because it was such a long and difficult four-day train ride to get there, I was glad mother decided to accompany us to see us settled in, but before this she had to take Claire to Darjeeling to leave her at a private school called Hilltop. Poor mother continually had to travel here and there to see us settled in one school or another and kit us out in various new uniforms. Now we had to be fitted for the uniform of Hebron, and trunks packed for the long nine-month term. Yet once more we were forced to accept that we would not be seeing our parents during this period.

As there was no direct express train to Madras we discovered that we would have to travel an arduous and circuitous route stopping at many stations along the way. We boarded the train at Sealdah station and even though we had a first class compartment, it didn't have air conditioning, so mother purchased a large block of ice (a *maund*—80lbs) to place in a tin tub in the centre of the carriage to keep us cool, because it was obvious the small fan would be totally inadequate. In spite of the ice block, the stifling heat was unbearable. We found out that the train didn't have a restaurant car, so we had to alight at various stations en route to have a meal in the station restaurant whilst it waited for us. So no wonder the journey took four days. The service in these restaurants was usually very slow, and at one station whilst we were still eating our meal, we heard the guard blowing his whistle and saw him waving his green flag to signal the train to move off. As it did so, we rushed out onto the platform shouting for it to stop. Fortunately he saw us and quickly waved his red flag. Mother was so angry that she scolded him for not first checking that we were aboard. She insisted then that the train must wait until we had finished our meal, which it did. This sounds incredible and could not have happened anywhere else in the world, except in India.

Whilst we were waiting at another station along the route, our carriage stopped in front of a tea tent on the platform crowded with locals. Suddenly a little pariah puppy came flying through the air to crash on the ground in front of my carriage. As it lay there howling in pain, I jumped down from the carriage and rushed into the tent shouting for the man who had kicked it. Mother pleaded with me not to leave the train as it was about to move off, but I was so incensed I ignored her warning. While I was telling them what I thought of their cruelty, I heard the whistle blow and rushed out to find that the train was moving off. Poor mother was hanging out of the carriage door, frantically calling to me, afraid I might be left behind when we were still two days from our destination. Seeing this I raced along the platform and leapt into our compartment like John Wayne. Mother was not amused and scolded me for giving her such a fright.

When we finally reached Madras this was not the end of our journey, as we still had to travel on the Nilgiris toy train up into the mountains to Coonoor where the school was situated. This little train with its blue and yellow carriages was similar to the one that we had travelled in so long ago when we went up into the mountains to the convent in Darjeeling. The Blue Mountain Railway was a twisting narrow-gauge track on which the train climbed up through magnificent dense forest and tea plantations, crossing two hundred bridges and crawling through sixteen tunnels over a distance of forty-five kilometres. The unique feature of this line is the toothed central rail which the locomotives lock onto on the steeper slopes. Also what is quite unique is that the little engine is at the back pushing, rather than pulling from the front. A brakeman sat on a platform at the front of every carriage, and we were amused as we watched the performance every time we pulled away from a station as each man had to wave his green flag when the carriage was ready to move off. The dramatic scenery was quite as spectacular as the Darjeeling railway, as we looked down into the gorges along the route with the numerous waterfalls cascading into the deep ravines below.

After a spectacular journey, we alighted at Coonoor station, collected our luggage and boarded the school bus that awaited us. We drove through the town, then out into the jungle, climbing ever higher until we reached the area of the tea gardens where we got our first glimpse of Hebron, an impressive building situated on a high ridge overlooking them. At the entrance of a long drive was an unusual half-moon arch with a motto inscribed on it. It was called The Moon Gate, and if I remember correctly after 60 years, the motto was Deo Supremo (God First).

When we reached the school, we were greeted by the friendly staff who showed us around. The relaxed atmosphere impressed me, which was in such contrast to the previous schools we had attended. After seeing us settled in, mother was driven to the Missionary Guest House close by where she had planned to stay for a while. We were glad of this, because we were allowed to visit her whenever we had free time.

There were several houses situated in the extensive grounds of the school, and we found that we were to be in the senior dormitory of Chaplin House, which we would share with two girls that were identical twins, Joan and Dorothy Ward. This proved to be most confusing, as you could never be sure which one you were talking to, and the teachers were even more confused during the lessons when they tried to identify them, which caused us some amusement. Even though we were with them throughout the nine-month term, we still didn't know which one was which.

Every day after breakfast we assembled for school prayers when we often sung the school anthem. I can still remember the words and the tune.

> Deo Supremo our motto;
> Deo Supremo our aim,
> Of Hebron our Alma Mater,
> Hebron the school we acclaim.
>
> Up in the hills so charming,
> Up on the mountains height.
> On—in the realms of learning;
> On—in the paths of Right.

Amid the subtle temptations
Of Pride and Selfishness;
To learn the true preparation
For Victory and Selflessness.

On Sunday mornings we walked in file to the Union Church in Coonoor, which was always full. I remember one occasion when three of us who were in the school choir, had to sing in harmony the anthem, 'God is a Spirit, and they that worship him must worship him in Spirit and in Truth', during the taking of the collection. I hoped that our singing was so appreciated that it resulted in a more generous amount for the church and not vice-versa.

Because I was missing all my pets, I was allowed to buy two Abyssinian guinea pigs, which were kept on the lawn in a large hutch and run that the school carpenter constructed for them. It was not long before I had the pleasant surprise of finding that they had produced a litter of six babies. Unlike rabbits, they were born with their eyes open, and they were quite lovely with their little bodies covered in silky fur rosettes. Within minutes of their birth they were running around the run, and were fascinating to watch. Sometimes I carried them around with them peeping out of my blazer pocket, but when I took them into the classroom one day and they started squeaking during the lesson, they gave everyone a fright and caused a disruption which got me into trouble. Sadly one of them died and after burying it I tried to make a little cross out of bamboo to mark the place, but as the knife slipped it almost severed my thumb and I bear the scar to this day.

Another concession granted to me was that I had a dovecote of carrier pigeons. As seniors we were allowed to roam the hills and jungles in pairs or small groups at the weekends, so I used to take a pigeon out with me and send it back with a message to my friends.

My special friend was a girl in my class called Judith, who came from the Outback of Australia, so she was quite at home in this wild area. Sometimes we went for walks in the jungle, which was quite safe during daylight apart from poisonous snakes that we kept a sharp lookout for. One day we saw one at the side of the track and as Judith thought it might be venomous, decided to kill it. I was impressed when I saw the expert way in which she did this. Finding a forked stick she pinned its head to the ground, then with the knife she always carried, thrust it through the head and brought it back to school suspended on the end of the stake, where she skinned it and pinned it out on a board to dry. She was so pleased with the result that she proudly wore it wrapped around her topee as a trophy.

A new dormitory wing was being constructed adjacent to the one in which we slept. We had watched the Indian labourers building it, as they climbed the flimsy bamboo scaffolding carrying bricks and buckets of cement on their heads. After several months it was nearing completion. In the early hours one morning we were awakened by a loud rumbling noise and our beds were shaking violently. Naturally I assumed it must be an earthquake, but as I looked out of the window I saw the new dormitory extension tumbling down the hillside in an avalanche. It was quite terrifying as I had visions of our dormitory also being swept away with it. It was lucky that it

Hebron School's Centenary Badge showing the motto with the eagle

happened before the dormitory was occupied and the builders had commenced work that day, otherwise there could have been a tragic loss of life. The accident was obviously due to poor construction, inadequate foundations and several days of rain. I couldn't help feeling worried that this disaster might have caused some damage to the foundations of the dormitory in which we slept, and that we too might disappear down the hillside, seeing that it was also perched on the edge of a ridge.

During my first term at school I enjoyed the measure of trust and freedom that we were granted, and as I look back across the years to that time, all the memories of my stay at Hebron are happy ones.

Hebron School celebrated its centenary in 1999 when 500 pupils from all over the globe attended to share in a week of celebrations and reunion. Unfortunately it was not possible for me to be present, but regional annual reunions are held in different parts of the world wherever there are groups of Hebronians residing, which are also able to link up through a newsletter, The Hebron Alumini.

The only disadvantage of being in Coonoor was that we had to make the long tedious return journey to Calcutta, but as this was in the company of some other girls whose parents also lived there, we were able to have fun together to brighten that hot and uncomfortable train journey which seemed to take forever, and we were all relieved when we finally reached our destination to spend the three months Christmas holiday period with our parents.

When I returned home I discovered quite by accident, that whilst I'd been away in Coonoor, cables had been arriving for me from the sailor Jock Devine that I had said goodbye to on the **Orion**. Mother had decided not to forward them to me at school because she felt it was pointless to pursue a friendship that could never be continued because he would always be at sea. I found out about this one day when the bearer brought me a small yellow envelope addressed to me. I knew it was a cable and was surprised to read the message from Jock. 'HAVE SENT YOU MANY CABLES AND LETTERS FROM EVERY PORT SO WHY NO REPLY STOP PLEASE WRITE SOON STOP I LOVE YOU STOP JOCK'.

This upset me very much, because he must have thought me to be heartless to have ignored them for such a long time, which was far from the truth. So I wrote to explain the reason for not having done so. As years passed he continued to write me loving letters, and in one of them asked me to marry him saying he was prepared to give up a life at sea and take a job on land if I wanted him to. Even after I became engaged to someone else some years later and wrote to tell him so, he was still reluctant to give me up. It puzzles me whenever I think of it, why he should have loved me and continued to persist for so long, when on my part, though I liked him very much and enjoyed his company, I had never given him any encouragement and thought ours was just a casual friendship.

CHAPTER 19

HOME FOR CHRISTMAS

It was wonderful to be home again for the long Christmas holidays. Since mother's return from England she had taken over the duties of running the home again. Whilst we had been away my parents decided to open their house as a 'home from home' and offer hospitality to any servicemen who wished to visit them. Calcutta was full of troops at this time awaiting transfers to the various war zones and they were seen aimlessly wandering around the streets because there was nowhere for them to go. It was not long before word got around that any of them would be welcome in our home, regardless of rank. Every evening mother had food prepared and the table laid for twelve people, even though there were only five of us in the family. This practice was continued for the duration of the war. Those places at the table were soon filled and after the evening meal we often gathered around the piano for a singsong. There was a lot of talent amongst those that visited us. Sometimes they would stay chatting with us late into the evening reluctant to leave because they enjoyed being amongst a family once again.

When there was a good English film showing at the local cinema, we used to invite some of them to lunch and afterwards take them to see the film. On one occasion the film showing was 'South Pacific', and it was the first time that I had ever heard Hawaiian music played on a Hawaiian guitar. I enjoyed it so much that I wanted to learn how to play one. I mentioned this to father and was delighted when he found one for me. It was black, inlaid with exotic mother-of-pearl butterflies, and after I learnt to play it, we enjoyed some happy musical evenings with the lads.

Many of them wrote us grateful and affectionate letters after they left to move on to various war zones. I have kept some, and re-read them from time to time and reminisce about those nostalgic days. One such letter was from Pilot Officer Harold Barnes in the RAF, who often came to our home when he was stationed in Calcutta in 1945. He was a very talented musician and entertained us with his songs and piano recitals. The Military Authorities discovered his talent and he was called upon to give troop concerts and record musical programmes that were broadcast on All India Radio. I quote an extract from the last letter that he wrote to us on 29th May 1945, because it expresses the sentiments of many that visited our home. As a family, we were just thankful that we had been able to make their time with us so memorable and worthwhile, and they in return, had given us the pleasure of their company.

'My dears, 'Thanks for the memory' might be a fitting song for this moment. It appears that I shall be denied the privilege of seeing you all again for I have had my marching orders at long last. Have said a sad farewell to you and the piano upon which I last played a few 'Songs without words' of Mendelssohn's—not appropriate I think, you will remain with me in spirit…When I left you and turned to give you one last look, I couldn't help feeling sad. I somehow felt that I had come to the end of a lovely book, the chapters of which had thrilled me but had left me wishing that the conclusion had been different…So now I leave you and again I tender my grateful thanks for all the loving-kindness you so graciously bestowed upon me…My love to you all. Harold.'

Sadly we never saw or heard from him again, so were left wondering what became of him, as we did about so many of those who visited us. But some of them became so much a part of our family that they stayed in touch with us throughout the war and long after it was over. Others were sadly missed when we heard that they had been killed or wounded in action.

Amongst all those members of the forces that visited us, there were some that wrote heartrending letters to me telling of their loneliness and asking me to write to them. One lad who was in the RAF wrote to say that he had received the sad news that his wife had been killed in an air raid on London, and when he saw me on his first visit to our home, he thought I looked so much like her. Another soldier who had visited us was so depressed when he left, that he wrote asking if I would write to him and if I didn't grant his wish, he would feel constrained to jump off the Howrah Bridge.

Those Christmas holidays were the happiest that I had ever spent, especially with all the unexpected visitors coming and going, there was never a dull moment. Christmas day was special because we held a big party for any of the lads that could come. The weather at this time of the year was very pleasant with warm sunny days and cool nights, so we hired a launch and took them down the Hooghly River to the Botanical Gardens for a picnic under the great Banyan Tree by the lake where they had fun playing games and one of them fell into the lake. Then whilst we ate we played music on our portable gramophone. It was wonderful to see them enjoying themselves and it made all the effort worthwhile.

So those that visited us could enjoy a new sport, we acquired an archery set and arranged competitions amongst various members of the forces who showed considerable skill in hitting the bull's-eye from about fifty feet away. I enjoyed watching their fun, but considered it to be a man's game. One day I was invited to have a go, and after being shown how it was done, I placed the arrow in the correct position, pulled back the bowstring and let fly the arrow that was way off course. Unfortunately there was a coolie painting the servants godowns at the end of the lawn, and I just missed killing him as he was climbing a bamboo scaffold with a bucket of whitewash on his head. He heard our cries of alarm as we saw the arrow flying towards him, and turned sharply to look, tipping the whitewash all over him. Luckily the arrow embedded itself in the trunk of the palm tree in front of him, which saved him, or else I could possibly have faced a charge of manslaughter.

When I went into my bedroom one evening there was a terrible smell in there. As I entered the bathroom, I surprised a wild civet cat in the bath, which disappeared through a hole in the mesh that covered the window. My guinea pigs cage had been broken into a few days previously, and several of them had been killed and mutilated, so I was convinced that this civet cat was the culprit.

I hurried into the lounge where a group of the boys were enjoying an after dinner drink, to tell them about the civet cat and ask for their help to get rid of it. As we made our way outside I saw father's golf clubs in the hall, so armed with these and torches we went in search of it. It was sitting on a window ledge two stories up just below the parapet of the flat roof, so we rushed up there to try and trap it. As it was unable to climb back down, it came up onto the roof where one of the boys managed to corner it, and with a swing of his golf club, kill it outright. John was the hero of the moment, but he had used such force that the head of the golf club had flown off. We were relieved to be rid of this menace, especially as civet cats are known to be such ferocious creatures that it would probably have killed again.

One day I heard the pitiful bleating of a lamb coming from our garden and went to investigate. There was a lady at the front door with a tiny black and white lamb in her arms. I was surprised and curious to find out where she found it as we were living in the heart of the city. She told me how she had been shopping in the New Market and was passing the butchery area when she heard the pitiful bleating of a little lamb. Its owner had evidently sold the ewe for slaughter but no one wanted her newborn lamb. Without thinking of the consequences, she had picked it up, given the man some money and taken it back to her flat. She didn't know what to do with it so contacted a friend who suggested she should bring it to us as we had a large garden. When we heard this we couldn't refuse to give it a home.

He was tiny with long dangling ears, and his little body, was half black and white, covered with soft curly fleece. We decided to call him Larry. Mother wanted to know where we planned to keep him, and when I suggested he might live in the house with Trixie, she was horrified, and insisted he would have to stay in the garden. We tried this, but his continuous loud bleating upset everyone, so we had to make a bed for him on the verandah in the house so that he could be near us. So dear mother had to put up with him running around after us, but once Trixie became accustomed to her strange companion, they became great friends.

Larry loved to cuddle up to you.

He soon grew fat and healthy and started acting like a dog. Whatever Trixie did, he tried to do. If we were going out for a drive they seemed to know and were already lying on the back seat of our open-top Pontiac car waiting for us. They especially loved to drive with us to the beautiful grounds of the Tolleygunge Golf Club where they amused everyone with their antics as they chased each other up and down the hillocks and around the sand bunkers on the golf course. They accompanied us wherever we went, even shopping in the large British departmental stores of Hall and Anderson or The Army and Navy Stores, where they caused a sensation amongst the shoppers. Larry could be quite mischievous at times when he would come into the lounge, put his feet up on the sideboard and eat the flowers out of the vase, or race on to the verandah whilst we were enjoying our tea and pull the lace doyley from under the plate of sandwiches, scattering them all over the floor so he could eat them. Sometimes he crept up behind to butt me, and then race off to hide in the bushes. At other times he could be very affectionate and cuddle up to you should he find you in bed or resting on a lounger in the garden. When the boys from the forces came to visit, he kept them amused playing 'head-ball'. When they threw him a football, he would jump up and butt it back to them. He was certainly a most unusual pet and endeared himself to everyone.

At the end of the holidays when we had to return to Hebron, there was a problem that had to be resolved before we left. What could we do with Larry? As mother didn't want to be left to care for him, she contacted the Principal of Hebron to ask if he could return to school with us. We were surprised when we were informed that he would be welcome there. But when we thought about the practicalities of such a decision we decided that it would be unwise. The long four-day train journey, and because he would want to be with us all the time, would have caused too many problems, so there was no alternative

Larry enjoyed butting me!

but to leave him behind with mother. She wasn't very pleased about this, but as she knew we were so fond of him, agreed to give it a try.

Not long after we had returned to school we received a letter from her telling us that since we left, Larry had caused several problems. Because he was missing us so much, he just wandered around the house and garden looking for us and bleating continuously. Keeping him tethered in the garden had proved to be an unwise decision because it had made him frustrated and aggressive. Feeling sorry for him one day, mother went over to pet him but, as she walked away, he broke loose and butted her so violently that she was thrown off her feet—and this was in front of the servants. Now he was fully-grown he had developed sharp horns, so mother had also suffered nasty bruising. After this incident, she realized that he would have to be found another home. This news distressed us because he had always been so gentle and affectionate, so this aggressive behaviour was quite out of character. But it was quite apparent that he would have to be allowed his freedom again. So she contacted our friends at the Botanical Gardens and was relieved when they agreed to take him.

CHAPTER 20

EVACUATED TO DEHRA DUN

W e had been at Hebron just over three months when the House Mistress awoke Patricia and me early one morning to tell us that we had to pack up our belongings and be ready to catch the train that same day. They had received a call from our parents asking them to arrange for us to travel at once to Dehra Dun in the Punjab Province, where mother would be meeting us. Shocked at this unexpected news we wondered what had occurred to necessitate this sudden decision to take us away from school in the midst of our studies again. We discovered that there were rumours of a possible Japanese invasion of Colombo or Madras to create bases there, which would cut off South India and prevent us from returning to our home in Bengal. So little is known about what would have been a disastrous catastrophe for India with far reaching results, that I will give brief details of that amazing story which I heard many years after the event and, which again, changed the course of my life.

On the 2nd of April 1942 Squadron Leader Birchall of the Royal Canadian Air Force arrived in Ceylon with his Catalina flying boat and a mixed crew of six RAF sergeants, a British RAF officer and a Canadian navigator. Their duty was to patrol an area 550 kilometres south east of Ceylon. The following day they set off at dawn and having seen nothing, were just about to return to base when the navigator spied some specks on the southern horizon. As the specks grew in size and number, binoculars revealed a vast armada of Japanese warships, including three aircraft carriers. (It was the same fleet under Vice Admiral Chuichi Nagumo that had blasted Pearl Harbour.)

Birchall flew over the convoy to identify and count the ships in order to inform his base. But as he did so, the Japanese sent up Zeros from the carriers to attack him. As his wireless operator hastily sent a coded message to the Royal Navy Base at Colombo, six Zeros struck the plane from above, with their cannons blazing. Birchall tried desperately to shake them off with the Catalina's twin machine guns firing back, but the shells had badly damaged his plane, injuring and killing some of his crew. Whilst the message was still being transmitted, the Catalina crashed into the sea. Sadly the plane sank with three of the wounded crew. The other members of the crew though injured, managed to get out and were hauled out of the sea by the Japanese crew and flung onto the deck of one of the destroyers, where they were questioned as to whether they had sent any messages about the fleet to their base. Birchall lied about this saying that the Zeros had shot them down before they could do so, but just as he said this, a Jap wireless operator appeared saying that Colombo was on the air calling for a repeat transmission from them. For that, Birchall was severely beaten and, even though they were all suffering from their serious injuries, they were thrown into a small, damp, dark lock-up where there was not enough room for them to lie down.

Meanwhile Birchall's brief coded warning was enough to produce a quick response, which enabled 118 merchant ships to flee from the ports of Colombo and Calcutta, and the Royal Navy's Eastern Fleet to race for a safe haven, thus saving them from being attacked in the ports as the Japanese had done in Pearl Harbour. With Birchall and his wounded men aboard, the Japanese fleet continued steaming towards Colombo.

On the following morning, 125 Japanese planes from the aircraft carriers attacked Colombo, but were surprised when 50 Hurricane aircraft and heavy ack-ack fire met them. Though our planes were greatly outnumbered and outgunned, they kept the attackers so busy defending themselves, that their bombers did little damage to the city. So Birchall and his crew had actually succeeded in saving Ceylon, and subsequently Southern India, from an invasion by Japan.

Sadly, Birchall and the remainder of his crew were kept in inhumane conditions in various prisons where they suffered torture at the hands of the Japanese until they were released in 1945. When he returned to Canada and people heard his story, he was called 'The Saviour of Ceylon'. His crew that survived with him echoed the feelings of the many prisoners of war whose cause he had championed in those prisons, when they said, 'There are many alive today who would not have survived without Birch'. In 1947 Winston Churchill paid tribute to him when he declared that Birchall's courage in helping to foil the Japanese invasion of Ceylon was 'one of the most important contributions to Allied victory'. So what happened then in Ceylon, was the specific reason for our rapid departure from Hebron that day, and was also the cause of the unpleasant train journey that we had to make to reach Dehra Dun.

One of the reasons that it turned out to be such a terrible journey was because April to June is the very hottest time of the year when the temperatures in the cities of the plains, soar to 125 degrees Fahrenheit. Mother had chosen for us to stay in the hill station of Dehra Dun, because, with its altitude of 700 metres, the weather would be pleasantly cool then. We would now have to find another school where we could complete our education.

The journey down the mountain from Coonoor to Madras on the Blue Mountain railway was as before, a very pleasant one, but the nightmare started when we boarded the main Northern Line train that stopped at every station along the route from Madras to the foothills below Dehra Dun, a journey of four days, covering almost the full length of India. As no one was able to escort us, we had to make the journey alone, which was a daunting prospect, because it was not customary for young English girls to be travelling on an Indian train unescorted. So with instructions from the guard to keep the carriage door locked at all times and the shutters closed at every station, and never leave the train to partake of meals at the platform restaurants, we set off wondering whatever lay in store for us.

As usual, the carriage had inadequate facilities to cope with the intense heat, and we found the only way to keep cool was to wet a small towel and place it on the rexine leather cloth surface of the bunk to lie on. Normally we would have had our own bedding-rolls, which we always took with us, but because of the unexpected departure, no arrangements could be made. We managed to survive on curry and rice ordered by the guard to be passed through the carriage window as we stopped at the various stations. An additional problem was that drinking water was in short supply. On the third day when we reached Agra, we saw a man on the platform followed by a coolie pulling an enormous metal container with a *maund* (80 lbs) block of ice in it, and hoped it might be for us. We were delighted when we realised it was, and that father, who had been aware of the discomfort we suffered, had arranged it for us. Because there was no air-conditioning, this helped to make the rest of the journey bearable.

When we finally arrived at Dehra Dun mother was waiting for us on the station platform. She told us about the lovely house called Rushmi she had been able to rent from a maharajah, and we were relieved that at last we would be able to enjoy some comfort after the horrendous journey that we had just endured. As we drove through the area I noticed that it had the look of an English town, with all its colonial buildings and pleasant houses in tree lined streets and gardens full of flowers. The Botanical Gardens in Dehra Dun were well known for their great variety of rare trees and The Forestry Commission also had its centre there. It was surprising to learn that, even though this was a hill station, it was also famous as the centre for Basmati rice.

In 1932 a prestigious Military Academy was founded there and it is still India's equivalent of England's Sandhurst Military Academy. At the entrance to the building there is an engraved plaque in the hall which reminds cadet officers who train there of their duty. It reads:

> *The safety, welfare and honour of your country come first—always and every time.*
> *The safety and welfare of the men you command, comes next—always and every time.*
> *Your own welfare and safety comes last—always and every time.'*

On Sundays we went to the Cantonment Church with mother. After the service one morning, we met three young officer cadets there from the Military Academy, and mother in her usual friendly way invited them to tea. They introduced themselves as John, Peter and Bill. Peter was a great sportsman, having obtained four Blues during his time at Oxford and John was a talented artist. But it was Bill especially, that caught my attention. He was tall, well built and strikingly handsome, and made a great impression on me. When they arrived that afternoon and we talked together, I discovered that on completion of Bill's training, he was applying to be commissioned into a Gurkha regiment. When they left, they expressed appreciation of our hospitality, and told mother it felt like 'a home from home', so she invited them to visit at anytime.

While we were there, my parents were trying to find us another suitable boarding school. They had heard about a finishing school that had recently been opened in Simla, a hill station in the Punjab, to meet the particular needs of the many young girls of our age group, (I was nearly sixteen) who were scattered all over India. They obtained a prospectus and after having satisfied themselves that it was a suitable school, they decided to send us there. A new term was about to begin so we hurriedly packed again and set off for Sherfield School where we were to spend two terms, each nine months long, studying for our final exams.

When Peter, John and Bill heard that we were leaving they came to see us off. They had often visited us during our short time at Rushmi and as Bill and I got to know each other better, I grew fond of him, so was particularly sorry to have to say goodbye, knowing that I would probably never see him again. I wondered why my life so far seemed to have been made up of so many sad partings.

Although we had no idea of this, of these three wonderful young men, only Bill was to survive the War. Peter was killed in action in Italy while serving with the Rajputana Rifles and John succumbed to poliomyelitis. Such was the tragic cost of war.

CHAPTER 21

SIMLA and SHERFIELD COLLEGE

As Simla was only a day's journey away by car, it would not be necessary for mother to accompany us to the new school, as Patricia and I could easily make the trip together to the foothills at Kalka, where we would be able to complete the final part of the journey on what was called The Viceroy's Toy Train. This was yet another narrow-gauge single line railway similar to those at Darjeeling and Conoor.

The Viceroy of India, Lord Curzon, had undertaken the building of this railway with its 96 km line winding back and forth across the mountainside. It was completed in 1897 and had 103 tunnels, 24 bridges and no less than 18 stations. We were lucky to be able to travel the seven-hour journey to Simla in the first class glass-sided rail car, which was hauled along at a leisurely pace by a tiny blue and white engine through stunning scenery. It was built as a single-track railway, with an ingenious safety system to ensure that there were no accidents between trains using the same line but travelling in opposite directions. It was called Neal's Token System, whereby the guards exchanged leather pouches with station staff strategically placed on the platforms. These contained small discs, which the driver then slotted into special machines to alert the signals ahead. I mention this 'fail-safe' system because since it has been in operation there has never been an accident. (The railways in Britain would do well to learn something from this little vintage railway.)

Of all the hill stations, Simla was by far the most glamorous, unlike any other place in India. It was set against the side of one of the lower ranges of the Himalayas, one ledge above another, with narrow paths everywhere and sheer drops into the valleys below.

Christchurch Cathedral perched on the ridge above the steep mountainside

Because Simla is situated at an altitude of 2,159 metres, the climate is always cool and pleasant, and for this reason in 1864 it became the Supreme Government of India's official hot-season headquarters. The outcome of this was the building of a steadily increasing number of splendid colonial buildings and residences that are still standing today. Everything about Simla was so unmistakably English. This lovely cool green place with its immaculate gardens filled with English flowers, also attracted the elite of the Raj's top brass and legions of 'grass-widows', whose husbands had to remain in their jobs in the cities to sweat it out all through the hot weather season. With its magnificent views and the pleasant climate, it soon became famous for the social lifestyle that these summer residents enjoyed, when there was an endless round of garden parties, balls, formal dinners, bridge parties, concerts, plays in the Gaiety Theatre, fashion shows, gymkhanas or races on the Allendale Racecourse. When Patricia and I arrived there in 1942 we were invited to some of these special functions. Sometimes we went to listen to the brass band playing in the bandstand on the Mall as the residents promenaded there in the cool of the evening. There was a nineteenth-century atmosphere about the place, probably due to the absence of the motorcar because of the steep slopes, so either you walked everywhere, went by rickshaw, or hired one of the many horses that were available from the 'horse rank' where they waited with their *syces*.

Most people preferred to travel by large rickshaws which seated four persons, with a team of four or five coolies, two men behind to push or act as brakemen and two in front to pull, with the fifth man acting as a relief. Some of the resident families of Simla had their own grand rickshaws with their personal rickshaw *wallahs* dressed in colourful individual livery. You could always hear the patter of bare feet as they ran past you at full speed down the Mall.

Sherfield School—Simla

Sherfield was a pleasant country style house, quite unlike the schools that we had previously attended, and at once I sensed a family atmosphere amongst the staff and girls. Because the house was not large enough to accommodate

An aggressive Rhesus monkey

all forty pupils, several other houses had been acquired nearby for use as dormitories and additional classrooms. Patricia and I slept in a house with a corrugated tin roof, which was about a ten-minute walk from the main schoolhouse through a dense pine forest full of monkeys. It was the male Rhesus monkeys in particular that always frightened me with their shrieks and mock charges every time I walked past them. We were told that if we avoided eye contact and ignored them, they would be less likely to attack us, but this wasn't easy because there were so many of them and they were unpredictable. As this was the only way to the main school building, we were forced to brave them. Apart from the danger from monkeys, we could wander anywhere in Simla without fear in complete safety, such was the respect that the locals had for the British. In fact that could have been said for anywhere you went in India at that time.

Much as I loved living in Simla, those monkeys always caused me problems. I went back to my dormitory one day during break time to get some roasted peanuts I had bought from the bazaar, which were stored in a tin under my bed. To my horror, a group of monkeys had got there before me. They were enjoying themselves as they sprawled all over my bed and one was sitting on my pillow. They had emptied the contents of the tin onto the bed and there was a terrible mess of the peanut shells everywhere. One of them had torn my sewing box apart and unravelled the cotton reels. I shouted at them hoping to scare them away, but they became aggressive and threatened to attack me, so I made a hasty retreat and went to find the *chowkidar* (watchman) who came and managed to chase them away using a large cane.

They left behind a terrible smell, which lingered in my room for days, and especially in my bed. After their visit, we had to have wire mesh fixed to all the bedroom windows, which wasn't entirely

successful as they still managed to find a way into the house. One came into the bathroom one morning to steal something off the shelf while I was having a bath. There was nothing I could do except to pretend I hadn't seen it. These were rhesus monkeys, but there were also other monkeys called langurs. They were about two foot six inches tall with grey fur and black faces. Though not quite so aggressive towards humans they were still a menace, especially night when our sleep was disturbed by a troupe of them scampering across the tin roof of the dormitory, sounding like a loud rumble of thunder.

Sherfield had a varied and extensive curriculum for its pupils and was lucky in having successfully recruited a team of excellent teachers and staff to equip young ladies to embark on a wide range of careers. The school soon gained a good reputation under the direction of the talented and experienced headmistress, Mrs Harvey. I remember one teacher especially because she was so quaint. She always dressed in long full-skirted black dresses with big lace collars. She obviously thought she was a reincarnation of Queen Victoria and acted as such, and in fact looked much like the queen in her later years. Whilst she was knowledgeable in the subject of History, the girls found her presentations rather boring. Whenever anyone sighed during class, she always said, 'Don't sigh, it shortens life'.

One of the subjects that every girl was required to take was the St John's Ambulance Association course in First Aid and Home Nursing. After we passed the exam, we were awarded the certificate and the uniform of the Association, and, dressed as nurses; we posed for a group photo along the school drive.

Dressed in our First Aid uniforms

While I was at Sherfield, I developed a verruca on the sole of my foot, which in spite of treatment, refused to heal. Because this made it difficult for me to walk the half-mile to school each day, the doctor arranged a visit to the local hospital to have it attended to. I arrived there having enjoyed a hearty meal, expecting it to be treated under local anaesthetic, but discovered to my amazement that I was to be given a general anaesthetic instead. I explained that I had just eaten so couldn't have the operation yet, but they told me that as it was only a small one which wouldn't take long, everything would be all right. The next thing I remembered was lying on the operating table and being told to start counting…one…two…three…When I came to, I was feeling terribly sick, and as I opened my eyes I was surprised to see a young man in pyjamas leaning over me applying a handkerchief soaked in cooling Eau-de-cologne to my forehead, and wondered how he came to be there. He explained that he was a patient in the next room, and because I had been groaning so loudly, he felt he had to do something to try and relieve my agony.

Because I had eaten just before the operation, the medical staff were concerned when I had tried to vomit before regaining consciousness, which could have had disastrous results had I been choked by it. Now my leg was even more painful than before, so I couldn't walk at all. This posed the problem of how to get to the school, but was solved when a kind girl in my form lent me her own horse, which she had been permitted to bring to school with her.

Although the school had rules that had to be observed, we were given the freedom to go anywhere during daylight hours. I loved horse riding, and as cars were not permitted in the town because of the steep terrain, and as rickshaws were too expensive for me, I rode everywhere. Patricia and I often hired horses from the local horse rank, where there were many to choose from. I was aware that all horses were unpredictable, and should be carefully chosen when ridden for the first time, but it wasn't always possible to get this right.

Once I chose a fine looking black horse whose name escapes me, but an appropriate one for him would have been 'Satan'. Riding along the mountain tracks through the forests with breathtaking views of the snowy ranges in the distance, was always a memorable experience, but the ride on this occasion was memorable for a different reason. This particular horse appeared to be very docile, unresponsive and sluggish for most of the ride until we reached The Ladies Mile, a long level track on the mountainside, when unexpectedly he gave the most enormous buck which unseated me, and as his feet touched the ground again, he bolted whilst I was still hanging on to him for dear life. I couldn't throw myself off because he was going too fast, but as I hung upside down underneath his neck, I was able to clasp my hands behind his ears and lock my legs at the base of his neck, so he was forced to slow down. Had anyone had a camera, I think that it would have made quite a spectacular movie sequence.

Patricia was following me some way behind, and must have been horrified as she turned the corner on to the Ladies Mile and saw me disappearing in a cloud of dust. As it couldn't continue galloping with my weight around his neck, it slowed down and I had the presence of mind to fling myself off to the side to avoid being trodden on. Now free of me, he galloped off again, so Patricia had to go after him. I limped after her and was relieved when I saw she had managed to catch him. Remounting, I followed her back to the horse rank at a more leisurely pace, and when I handed him back to his *syce*, told him what I thought about his horse and was careful never to hire him again.

As pupils of Sherfield were not required to wear a uniform, we were allowed to dress in fashionable clothes. All of us were in our teens, so attracted the attention of the boys from Bishop Cotton's, another boarding school in Simla for young gentleman. Sometimes they hung around our school gates in the hope of 'chatting up' the girls. There was one boy in particular, named John, whom I saw there from time to time. He was the son of General 'Bill' Slim, who commanded the 14th Army in Burma and later became Field Marshal Viscount Slim. These boys invited the girls to their school to see a musical they were performing called The Mikado, in which John played the role of Nanky Poo.

Sometimes we met up with them on the Mall for a chat, and on one occasion they invited a group of us to go with them to a late night movie, Walt Disney's The Reluctant Dragon, showing in the local cinema. It was strictly forbidden that any girl should be out of school after dark, so we decided the only possible way to do this was for us to disguise ourselves in the boys' school uniform. Somehow the clothing was smuggled into our dormitory and we successfully dressed up to look like boys. I had thick hair down to my waist so had great difficulty in stuffing it into the peaked cap. We set out to meet them at the prearranged rendezvous and tried to make ourselves as inconspicuous as possible as we entered the cinema. During the film, everything was okay, but when the lights came on during the interval and we saw some of the teachers from our school sitting two rows in front of us, we kept our heads down, and thankfully were never noticed. After the film, one of the boys who were escorting us back to our dormitory, asked me if I would like a cigarette. When I told him I didn't smoke, he suggested I should try one. Foolishly I agreed and he lit it for me. As I tried to inhale I started choking violently much to my embarrassment and the amusement of my friends. It was a good thing I found that experience so unpleasant because it put me off smoking for life.

In Simla on Sundays, everyone dressed up in their best clothes and went to the service in the imposing Anglican Christchurch Cathedral. In 1857 the Victorians built this at the end of the Mall in the style of a church in an English town, with its Tudor belfry. In the tradition of Victorian Christianity, its bells were cast from the brass of cannons captured during the Sikh wars. At that time, when the church was so overcrowded and there were not enough pews for the congregation, the minister appealed to the ladies to reduce the size of their crinolines.

Every Sunday when we attended morning service there, the church was always packed to capacity with ladies and gentlemen dressed in outfits which would have been in the height of fashion at Royal Ascot or a Buckingham Palace garden party. Outside was a guard of honour awaiting the arrival of the Viceroy of India, Field Marshall Sir Archibald Wavell and the Viceregal party. They always arrived in a convoy of magnificent red (the exclusive colour for the Viceroy) coach-built rickshaws, each bearing the Royal Insignia on its doors, with four liveried runners dressed in red and gold to control each one. It was a most impressive sight, and my memories of it are as clear as though it happened only yesterday. The entire congregation had to be in place before they arrived, and as they entered we all stood in respectful silence whilst they walked up the aisle to their reserved pews as the beautiful music from the organ filled the church.

Forty years later in 1962 I was able to return to Simla when I was touring India with my husband and a party of veteran officers from his old Gurkha battalion. Four of us went into that same church for a Sunday evening service that was taken by the Indian pastor. Our friends sat in the Viceroy's pew and my husband and I sat in the Commander-in-Chief's special pew just behind them. The church was empty except for us and six other Indians who were not wearing any special clothes for the service. It was such a drab scene, without even a vase of flowers to brighten it. I have to admit that I felt quite tearful as I recalled the days when as a teenager, I was able to be part of those glorious days full of grandeur, pomp and ceremony, and felt truly privileged that I had the opportunity to have been there to witness such pageantry.

A tragic sight! Sherfield in ruins.

While in the area we decided to go in search of my old school Sherfield, and after a few false trails we found it. The sight that met my eyes was even sadder than my experience in the church. That lovely place where I had spent so many happy months, lay in ruins. The roof had collapsed and growing out of the middle of the house was a large pine tree. As we wandered around, an old man came out to speak to us. He had been the watchman from the days when I was at school, and told me that he remembered the time when all the girls were there. When it closed after the partition of India, and there was nowhere for him to go, he had stayed on there all those years, to watch over the place.

It was 1943 when Patricia and I returned to Sherfield for the second and last nine-month term to study in earnest for the final school leaving exams. My parents had warned me that if I failed, I would have to return for a further term to retake them, which I didn't want to do. As I was almost seventeen years old, I felt that it was time for me to study very hard and plan a career for myself

Unfortunately just about a week before I was due to sit my finals, I developed a high

He was still watching over
Sherfield

temperature and went down with dysentery. In spite of being told by the principal that I must stay in bed, I managed to persuade her to let me attempt to sit them. Even though I was feeling so ill, I was so determined that I managed to walk to the convent where the exams were being held. All through the exams I was embarrassed as I had to keep asking the Nun in charge for permission to visit the toilet, and each time had to be accompanied to make sure that I didn't cheat. I was very relieved when I heard later that I had passed all of my exams with good grades.

Just before the end of term as we were preparing to return home to Calcutta for good, I was doing some shopping in the Mall, when I saw a scruffy little white terrier running around. It looked as though it was lost so I watched it for some time before approaching. When I finally went over, it greeted me excitedly and appeared relieved that it had found someone at last. It had no collar and was very dirty and in such a poor condition that I guessed it must be a stray. As I was leaving Simla shortly, I was faced with the problem of what I should do with it, as I knew I could not just walk away and leave it to its fate.

There were literally millions of stray and semi-wild dogs as well as the pariah dogs all over India, and any welfare societies that there might have been, couldn't cope with such an enormous problem, so I felt that I had to take care of it myself. It followed me all the way back to my dormitory where I gave it a bath. The dog was a bitch, and because after bathing her, the soft coat looked like pale straw, I named her Thatch. I told the principal about her and the problem I faced in contacting my parents to ask for permission to bring her home with me. As it was the end of term and I would be leaving in a few days, she kindly cabled them with my request. I was relieved when the reply came, and I was told that they would welcome her. Sadly our dear little dog Trixie had died and they were grieving over her loss. Thatch had such a wonderfully friendly nature, that they were sure to love her, and I hoped she would help to fill her place. She turned out to be quite the cutest, fun loving, most adorable little dog that I have ever owned, and continued to give us so much pleasure throughout the time she was with us. She never caused us any problems and always appeared to enjoy her travels with us wherever we went.

When the time came to leave Simla, it was with mixed emotions. I had enjoyed my time there amidst such beautiful surroundings, and whilst it was good to be going home again, it would be to a hot, crowded, noisy city and to an unknown future. So my sister and I set off on the tedious return journey to Calcutta with Thatch, who was no trouble at all and took a great interest in everything. When our parents met us at the journey's end they were quite delighted when they saw her. It was amazing how quickly she settled into the daily routine of life at home just as though she had always lived with us. Although she was a stray and had never been trained, possibly because initially she may have belonged to Indians in the bazaar,

Please take me home!

she soon learnt to respond to our commands and become house-trained. She was a great favourite with all the soldiers who visited us, because she was always so friendly and ready to enjoy a game of ball with them.

CHAPTER 22

SERVICE IN THE WVS

During the two terms that Patricia and I had been away in Simla, the war had escalated and Calcutta was filled with British and American troops in transit to and from the War Zones. The local hospitals were filled with the sick, wounded and dying soldiers. A large building at the end of our Harrington Street had been converted into an officer's hospital, which I often visited with other members of the Women's Voluntary Service (WVS) to do what we could to help the patients, who were always cheered by our visits. Since returning home I had been unable to find a suitable job, so decided to help the war effort by joining the WVS. As there seemed to be nowhere in the city where our forces could go for relaxation during their time off, a large house was acquired and converted into a recreation centre with a free canteen for them. It was so popular that it was always crowded, and I was asked if I would help there. This kept me busy as I hurried about serving the soldiers with drinks and trays of food. I enjoyed the work until one day a soldier pulled on one of my long plaits as I was passing, and cheekily said, 'Ding, ding! What about a cup of char, Miss?' I was so offended that I went home at once and cut them off, without even un-plaiting them. The result was disastrous. Throughout my life I had never had my hair cut, so it had grown very long and thick, right down to my waist, but because it was cooler, I wore it in plaits. Mother was quite shocked when she saw what I had done, because when I combed it out, it looked jagged. Seeing me so upset by what had happened, she did her best to trim it for me, but it took me some time to get used to my new look.

In spite of this, I returned to help at the WVS Centre. One day I heard our British soldiers complaining that since the American G.Is (General Issue) had arrived in Calcutta, the locals had put up their prices on everything, so on their meagre pay they were unable to afford to buy gifts to take home to their folks. I believe the BORs (British Other Ranks) were only paid

Dinner with some servicemen

about two shillings and six pence a day, whilst the American soldiers were paid much more. So I offered to organize a weekly shopping spree to take them down to the New Market and bargain on their behalf, for anything they wanted to buy. This idea proved so popular that as the word spread amongst the boys, there were several already waiting for me with their shopping lists when I arrived. Hiring rickshaw *wallahs* who could take two soldiers in each rickshaw, solved the problem of transport, so with me in front to lead the way, they ran behind me in a convoy. When I visualize the scene of a young English girl leading a convoy of soldiers through the congestion of the traffic down the main street of Calcutta, it must have caused some amusement to the locals as we passed by. It was a pity that no one was able to record that scene on film.

When we reached the market I told them to split up into small groups, then after they had decided what they wanted to buy, return to me and I would help them barter for the best price. Fortunately, I was able to speak Urdu fluently, so when the shopkeepers realized that I was a local resident and therefore knew the fair price, I was able to get bargains for them. These shopping sprees were greatly enjoyed by the troops and because they were so successful the convoy grew larger each time I took them.

Throughout the War, my parents continued to keep an open house with a warm welcome for anyone in the services, consequently we met many interesting people including women, some who were nurses in field hospitals in battle areas. One couple who met in our home got married in the Cathedral close by, and I was asked to be bridesmaid, and my father to act as proxy for the bride's father. The groom's brother Mark was given special leave to attend the wedding as best man, but afterwards he seemed to think that it was the prerogative of the best man to marry the bridesmaid, even though I had never met him before, and I had great difficulty in persuading him otherwise. Another frequent visitor was an RAF padre with a great sense of humour, who became a close friend of the family, and we all enjoyed his visits. His was a demanding job, when he was posted to an RAF base where he had to bring solace to men who were sick, wounded or dying. He wrote to tell me that he had been allotted a jeep, which he had named after me. Puzzled, I wrote to ask him the reason for what I hoped would have been an honour. He replied saying that it reminded him of me because; 'It was unpredictable, and had a mind of its own!' I was not too pleased and told him that I could have done without that dubious honour. All the same he grew fond of our family and kept in touch with us after the war was over. When the time came for him to finally leave, he wrote us such a heartfelt letter. It read:

> *'I'm afraid my good-byes are always inadequate, and the other day is no exception. I can never say all I want to, but I do want you to know how much I have loved being able to come to an 'open house' and appreciated all your kindness to me during these last few months. I shall miss you all a lot. Thank you very much for everything and how I thank the Lord for our happy times of fellowship together. God bless you all. If I weren't so shy, I would have given you all a 'holy kiss'…with love Morrie.'*

As a parting gift he gave mother his pocket New Testament with the RAF emblem with their motto **Per Ardua Ad Astra** embossed in gold lettering on the front, and on the first page, A MESSAGE FROM HIS MAJESTY THE KING which read:

'To all serving in my Forces by sea or land, or in the air, and indeed to all my people engaged in the defence of the Realm, I commend the reading of this book. For centuries the Bible has been a wholesome and strengthening influence in our national life, and it behoves us in these momentous days to turn with renewed faith to this Divine source of comfort and inspiration.' dated September 15th 1939.

I believe that there were many of our boys in the forces who carried a copy of this little book in their breast pockets in those terrible days during the War.

Sometimes when there was a full moon, we organized a moonlight picnic for the boys visiting with us at the time. There is a beautiful area outside Calcutta called the Dhukaria Lakes where we used to take them. I remember that the moonlight was so bright that we didn't need any lights as we enjoyed the picnic that was laid out by the waters edge. I can still visualise that scene with the reflection of the moon in the lake and the sound of the cool breeze rustling the fronds of the palm trees that lined its shores, and those boys stretched out on the grassy banks by the water, listening to the music we were playing on our gramophone. The scene was quite magical, and they loved it, and afterwards we received many warm letters of appreciation from them telling us it was an experience they would always remember.

We often arranged picnics for the troops because they enjoyed them so much. A favourite venue was in the beautiful grounds of the Victoria Memorial, just across the Maidan not far from the end of our road. It is a place that has always held many happy memories for me from early childhood. This magnificent marble building was an important symbol of British colonialism in India and was inaugurated by the Prince of Wales (later King George V) in 1921. Although it is such a spectacular building, I wonder why pictures of it are rarely seen nowadays. Possibly when India gained her

The Victoria Memorial

Independence, many may now wish to forget this era of British imperialism, when Queen Victoria ruled as Empress of India. It was surprising to discover that even though most of the streets in Calcutta that once had British names were renamed with Indian ones, the Victoria Memorial has kept its name and the various attempts by the authorities to change it over the years since Independence have come to nothing, so it still remains the pride and joy of Calcutta.

The Victoria Memorial was built during 1906 to 1921 with voluntary contributions from the Princes and Peoples of India, when Calcutta was a very important city of British India, and the Empire was at its peak. The whole of this vast building was constructed of polished white marble that was brought all the way from Makrana in the state of Jodhpur, and surmounting the great dome is a smaller dome with a dramatic bronze statue of an angel blowing a long trumpet, representing 'Winged Victory'. It is sixteen feet high, and even though it weighs three tons, it revolves on its base. It is amazing how they managed to place such a magnificent and heavy sculpture up there without the help of modern technology. It was Lord Curzon, who was later appointed Viceroy of India, that planned to have it built to commemorate Queen Victoria as Empress of India and as a worthy place to show a collection of exhibits and paintings of Indian history and especially that of the Victorian era. A British architect, Sir William Emerson, designed it in a Moghul-Renaissance style, which was reminiscent of the famous Taj Mahal. I was fortunate to have been able to view some of the wonderful exhibits on several occasions in the past and again when I revisited it on a recent visit to Calcutta. As I entered the great hall there was one particular statue that caught my eye. It was a full-size white marble sculpture of Queen Victoria at the age, when as a beautiful young girl, she ascended the throne. Someone had scattered fresh flowers around her feet.

One of the most enduring memories that I have of this place is when, as a teenager, I often walked on the Maidan in the cool of the evening with Thatch. There was a full moon, and as I looked across the grassy expanse and saw that beautiful white marble building glowing in the bright moonlight against the backdrop of the velvet starry sky, and reflecting in the lake, it took on an ethereal quality. This beautiful place later became very special to me, and still evokes nostalgic memories.

Late in 1942, the Japanese launched an air raid on Calcutta, which caused far more panic amongst the locals than was justified by the size of the raid. The majority of the local Indian population of Calcutta had no idea that the city was in danger of being bombed by the Japanese, so when the wailing sound of the air raid siren was heard for the first time, it created chaos over a wide area because the Indians didn't understand what it meant or what to do. When the bombs started to fall we could hear the explosions and the screams of these poor, terrified people mingled with the frantic barking and howling of the many pariah dogs which roamed the streets as they raced about the city in panic. The bombs that the Japanese dropped were of the anti-personnel type, which exploded at ground level, sending shrapnel over a wide area killing and injuring many hundreds in the densely populated parts of the city.

We had been warned of the possibility of air raids so had a shelter built below ground level in the garden, but when the air raid siren sounded and we hurried to take shelter in it, we found ourselves up to our knees in stagnant water swarming with a horde of mosquitoes which attacked us and made our stay in there extremely uncomfortable. We had taken our dog into the shelter with us, and I stuffed cotton wool into her ears hoping that this would help her from being alarmed by the sound of exploding bombs.

The Japanese paid dearly for their raid, because a young RAF fighter pilot named Sergeant Pring, gained fame by shooting down three of the bombers as they sought to escape, causing them to crash in the Sunderbans. This vast area of mangrove-covered islands form the delta of the Ganges as it debouches into the Bay of Bengal. It is also famous as the home of the Bengal tiger, now protected as a tiger reserve.

Many years later, by a strange coincidence, I discovered that it was Bill, (the same officer cadet in the Gurkha regiment that had visited our home in Dehra Dun) who was ordered to commandeer a river steamer and take his platoon to locate the planes after they crashed. For four days they searched through the maze of waterways until they finally found them, but were unable to find any survivors, just various body parts, such as a leg in its flying boot. It was assumed that the natives had rescued any survivors and buried the dead.

At this time India, was aflame with the British Quit India Movement, and Bengal was one of the most rabid anti-British parts of the country, so any surviving Jap would have found ready help to enable him to escape.

I was in Calcutta during this period and remember seeing groups of fanatic Indian youths shouting anti-British slogans, as they rampaged up and down Park Street throwing bricks through the windows of the shops owned by British citizens. During all the years that I had lived in Calcutta, the local Indians had always shown me respect, and I had been able to move around freely amongst them and cycle anywhere in the city without fear. Now I felt threatened by the changing mood amongst certain groups who would, before long, also be shouting slogans for their independence.

CHAPTER 23

THE BENGAL FAMINE

In 1943, disaster struck Bengal. There was a great famine over the whole of the state, and thousands of starving people made their way from their villages into the city of Calcutta in the hopes of finding relief. Very little is known about this catastrophe in which about 4 million people died, almost as many as died in the Jewish Holocaust, but this tragedy appears to have been deleted from history, but it will never be forgotten by me because I was there and witnessed some of those terrible sights.

The problem started in Bengal in 1942 when the rice production was poor, due to a fungal infection known as 'brown spot' and was exacerbated by the cessation of imports of rice from the rice-bowl of Burma, which had been invaded by the victorious Japanese. This, amongst other factors, caused the price of rice to more than double, so that the landless rural poor could not afford to buy it. Consequently they just starved to death or died of starvation-related illnesses; initially in their thousands, but later in their millions.

The famine greatly affected rural Bengal more than the urban areas. Because these densely populated rural regions were so badly affected, a steady migration of destitute people began surging towards the cities. Calcutta came to be **the** destination of the largest number of migrants in search of food. By October 1943 the number had reached 150,000. Unfortunately, whilst this disaster was escalating, there was a political crisis in Bengal when the British Governor was dislodged by devious means, and so was powerless to do anything about the situation. This left the Bengal Ministry to try and manage the worsening crisis, which appeared to be insurmountable. The Bengal government then became the target of attack for its failure to avert the crisis.

A politician in Calcutta by the name of Shaheed Suhrawady, earned millions of rupees by intercepting and selling on the black market, tons of relief rice which was destined for the starving refugees. He was a flamboyant, colourful character, grossly overweight, who went about the city dressed in silk suits and two tone alligator shoes. He also had a reputation for bedding high-class women of dubious character. It was known that he used public funds to maintain his private army of thugs, who terrorized his political rivals. Despite his terrible reputation, it seemed no one could or would, do anything about bringing him to book.

General Wavell, the Viceroy of India, was surprised at the complacency of the Bengal government, and in November 1943 he managed to persuade them to move these destitutes out of the city centre, where they were camped all along the main thoroughfare of Chowringhee and spilling out all over the Maidan and into the residential streets. This proved to be a gigantic and daunting operation. Wavell saw that something had to be done, and introduced a food-rationing scheme in an effort to avert further disaster.

He sent a message to Winston Churchill, the British Prime Minister, who summed up the whole situation: 'The Bengal famine was one of the greatest disasters that has befallen any people under British rule and the damage to our reputation here, both among Indians and foreigners in India, is incalculable'.

I was in Calcutta for part of the time during this disaster and can remember some of the shocking sights, which I find hard to describe because they were so horrific. We lived in Harrington Street, a residential road that led into Chowringhee opposite the Maidan. This large grass covered expanse, ran the full length of this street, and was bounded on the far side by the Hooghly River. The only trees on the Maidan were those alongside Chowringhee. It was under these that the refugees congregated to try and get some relief from the sun and the unbearable heat, as temperatures rose above 100 degrees Fahrenheit. The two small man-made water tanks on the Maidan were filled with stagnant water and was so impure that if the refugees didn't die of starvation, then they died from water-related diseases through drinking this polluted water. No wood or fuel of any kind was available, so the poor people couldn't boil water or prepare food, should they have been lucky enough to have had any. The sight of the poor, emaciated, starving children crying beside their mothers, was heartrending. The numbers of the dead were so great that the Calcutta Corporation just couldn't cope with the situation, so the dead bodies were left there causing further risk of disease. The most horrendous sight of all, were vultures circling overhead and fighting as they swarmed over the corpses, decomposing rapidly in the great heat. That terrible memory still grieves me because I was powerless to do anything help them.

There appeared to be no medical help forthcoming from anywhere, because I believe the problem was just too vast to cope with. This disaster happened before the days of International Relief Societies and the use of antibiotics, so there was no help available to feed them or treat the sick, and funds were in short supply. Some poor women gave birth on the pavement in our street and also outside our home. Most of these babies died because of the debilitated condition of their mothers. Some local organizations set up food relief centres in various parts in the State of Bengal, but these were quite inadequate to deal with the size of the problem, and in any case were too late to save the lives of the millions that suffered. My mother was so distressed at the plight of these poor people that she used to send out cooked food for any in our street who would accept it. She was so distressed when she found that they wouldn't eat it despite their hunger, because of their deep-rooted caste system.

The caste system is so complex that it is impossible for me to explain it in just a few sentences, but I'll attempt a brief outline, as it was closely linked to one of the many causes of the deaths during that dreadful famine.

In the year 600 BC, Varna (colour) became the standard means of classifying the fair-skinned Aryans from the darker earlier inhabitants of the land. Later this developed into the caste system that exists today. Caste membership is decided simply by birth and it remains an extremely important aspect of India's social structure. It also remains an explosive issue, especially when attempts are made to improve the social status of outcasts, who were the people Gandhi called harijans; which means 'the people of God'.

The migrants who had come to Calcutta in search of food were Hindus, not from the harijans, but from the Vaisyas caste, that is the class of traders and farmers. Every occupation had its caste (*varda*), splitting society up into a myriad of closed guilds into which a man was condemned by his birth, to work, live, marry and die. Linked to the caste system was the second concept basic to Hinduism; reincarnation. A Hindu believed that his body was only a temporary garment for his soul. Idolatry was to the Hindu, a natural form of expression, so he could worship God in any form that he chose, including spirits, natural forces, divine incarnations, water, fire, planets, stars, animals, and especially the cow. As a result of the latter it was estimated that in 1947 India had approximately 200 million beasts, and because they were so sacred they were unable to be eaten. These animals roamed freely across India through the villages, towns and cities, chomping through food that could have fed millions living on the edge of starvation. Every instinct of reason, of sheer survival, should have condemned those useless beasts. Yet so tenacious had the superstition become, that the slaughter of a cow remained an abomination to these poor Indians who were now starving to death. A caste Hindu would not touch food in the presence of a Moslem, and if a Moslem entered the kitchen of a Hindu he would then pollute it. So these Hindus dying outside our house in the street, refused the food that my mother offered them for fear that it may have been prepared by a Moslem cook or may have beef in it. Indeed it would have been similarly contaminated by contact with us Europeans. The only people who would have eaten it were the beggars or 'untouchables' that Gandhi spent so much of his life trying to help. Being at the very bottom of the pile, they were not at risk of 'losing caste'. The people now starving to death were not all beggars.

Even in the days before the famine, we had a family of beggars that lived on the pavement by the large communal dustbin not far from our front gate. They claimed it as **their** dustbin and spent all day scavenging in it for scraps of food, which they ate, or for bones, feathers, tins, and paper, orange peel that most probably went back into the food chain, in fact anything that they could sell for a few annas. This family consisted of an old man and woman, their son and his wife, several young children and a new baby that was born one night. I saw it lying there amongst all the vile rubbish when I went to take Thatch for her morning walk. We would send food out to them, although they never asked for any. They just appeared to accept this as their way of life, which could never be changed, because they were born into it. There were thousands of such families all over the city and it was where Mother Teresa had felt constrained to do something practical for these poor people.

A great deal has been written about Mother Teresa of Calcutta, so I will only mention her briefly. Born in 1910 as Agnes Bojaxhiu, she was an Albanian who came to the city in 1931 after joining the Irish order of the Sisters of Loreto. She was sent as a teacher to St Michael's Convent in Darjeeling, where my sister and I were pupils at the time, and it is quite possible that she taught us there. She became Teresa when she took her vows there before proceeding to Calcutta to teach in another school. It was in Calcutta that she saw the plight of the many destitute and dying people on the streets of the city, and her heart went out to them. She described this as a 'call by God', so was constrained to do something positive to help them. She sought and obtained permission from the Pope to put aside her nun's habit and wear a simple white cotton sari with a blue border, which became the uniform of her small group of helpers, whom we knew then as 'Sisters of the Poor', but later became known as 'Missionaries of Charity'.

She started her work by renting two rooms in a busy, noisy, overcrowded area known as Kalighat, near the famous Kali Temple, founded in 1602. This temple represents the heart and soul of Calcutta and is an important place in Hinduism. Thousands of pilgrims flock there, and many of the destitute choose to go there to die by the holy *tirtha* (a river crossing), and to make the transition from the mundane world to heaven. Because Mother Teresa was aware of this fact, she chose this site to start her work. No one had ever shown that they cared for these tragic souls

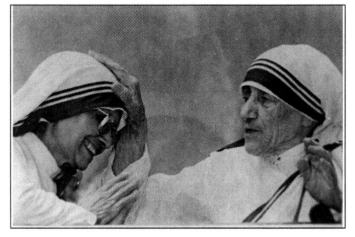

before. They were to be seen everywhere around the city. In the 1940s leprosy was incurable, and inevitably spread to other family members. It was a living hell for them. I saw one man, probably the children's father, being dragged along the pavement in a little wooden cart by them, as they rang a bell to warn people, so they wouldn't get too close to him as he was considered 'unclean'. This poor man was so disfigured by leprosy that he no longer looked human. Because of this terrible scourge, Mother Teresa opened a home for the lepers of the city, which required a great deal of stamina as well as courage, seeing that leprosy was highly contagious. Those who criticised her motives during her latter years, should have been in Calcutta at that time to see the terrible sights that I witnessed when I was living there. Sometimes the beggar women would actually disfigure their babies at birth, so that others might have pity on their plight and hopefully give them more money. It was only when I lived there, that I became painfully aware of this reality. Nowadays tourists are usually only shown the beautiful places and the wonderful things that this vast country has to offer, though sadly, beggars are still to be seen wherever you go.

On a recent return visit to Calcutta, we were stopped in the street by one of Mother Teresa's helpers and asked for a donation, which we willingly gave. We asked her about her work and was pleased to learn that, although Mother Teresa died on 5th September 1997, her group of dedicated helpers are still actively continuing the work that she started so long ago, and have expanded and set up more homes for the destitute, sick and dying. She was a saint in her lifetime if ever there was one, and set an example that hopefully future generations will follow.

CHAPTER 24

DAILY ROUTINE. A NEW LIFESTYLE

Now that we had finished our schooling days, we settled easily into the routine of our new life. I was amazed how smoothly mother managed to cope with the day-to-day running of the home. Because of the complex caste system it was necessary to employ many servants to look after our family, as each man would only do the work that his caste allowed him to do. At the end of the garden, there was a row of *godowns* (large brick built rooms) where each member of our staff lived with his family and was kept supplied with a daily ration of rice and *dahl* (lentils).

All the staff that worked in the house were smartly dressed in white jackets and trousers, with broad red and gold webbing cummerbunds around their waists and white turbans wound around their heads, and barefooted whenever they entered the house. The head bearer was in charge of the staff of the household and supervised them in the correct laying of the table, waiting at table, serving the meals, bringing us *chota hazri* (little breakfast of tea and fruit) first thing in the morning, as well as serving afternoon tea or drinks, and attending to the many visitors who called. A junior bearer called a *khitmagar* assisted him with these duties, such as clearing the table after meals, washing dishes and bringing all our meals to the house from the kitchen across the garden. These servants also made our beds, tidied our rooms and kept the house immaculate, and were always on call should we require anything.

Because the servants were always around, it was imperative that we behaved with decorum at all times, if we wished to keep their respect. They expected us to dress in clothes befitting a young lady, and that meant that we never wore low cut dresses, slacks or shorts or showed too much leg, and in those days we accepted this dress code as the norm. Even when we went to swim at the Calcutta Swimming Club, we never wore a two-piece bikini, but always swimsuits that covered our bodies adequately.

So that there would be no smells of cooking in or near the house, the one-roomed kitchen was situated at the end of the line of *godowns* across the compound, which was an area that was out of bounds to us. Because of this, I had no idea how to cook, boil an egg or even make a cup of tea.

All the family with Thatch in 1943

Everything was always prepared and served to us, so I grew up without any knowledge of even the basics of housekeeping, which inevitably caused problems later on.

We were lucky in having an excellent *khansama.* (cook). All the other servants held a good cook in high esteem, because no Indian could simply become a cook. It was an art that was passed down through generations from father to son. They were highly skilled men who created from their secret recipes wonderful gourmet dishes always attractively presented on silver salvers. Every evening our cook called on mother to be given the order for the meals that he was to prepare for the following day. Early every morning he would go the market to buy fresh food, then spend the whole day preparing our meals; breakfast, a three-course lunch, dainty sandwiches and cakes for afternoon tea, and a four-course dinner at the end of the day, when we would change into evening dresses if guests had been invited. Surprisingly, in spite of all this delicious food, none of us ever put on any extra weight.

Because of the cook's high status, he never washed the cooking pots or did any of these mundane tasks associated with cooking. This was always done by his *masalchee* (scullion), who would take no part in the cooking process, apart from preparing all the vegetables and keeping the open fires burning. The cook had neither a gas nor electric cooker, so I marvelled at the way in which he was able to produce wonderful food on such a primitive open hearth. Our favourite Sunday lunch was Mulligatawny soup, chicken *pilau*, and for dessert he created woven toffee baskets with great skill and filled them with delicious fresh mangoes and cream.

Since there were no dairies in India, our milk supply came from a cow that visited us every day with her calf. Mother used to have to watch it being milked, because had she not done so, water from the tap might have been added to make up the quantity required. Milk had always to be boiled. As there was no bottled water available either, every drop had to be purified by boiling. To sterilize all fruit and vegetables, they had to be washed in '*pinky pani*', (permanganate of potash). In order to avoid diseases from failure to take these precautions, mother always supervised this.

Another member of the household staff was the *jemadar* (sweeper), whose only task that he was permitted to do as he belonged to the lowest caste of all, was to sweep and wash the floors, keep the bathroom and toilets clean and look after the dog. The other servants believed that by touching a dog they would be defiled. The *jemadar* was dressed differently to the other house servants. He wore a long white muslin shirt over his *dhoti*; a long piece of cloth that was wrapped around his waist with the end pulled up between his legs and tucked into his waist in front. He was a pleasant man, always willing to do any task that was required of him. As I observed him as he went about his work, he appeared to accept his lot in life, even though he was such a lowly man, and be content with the secure job that he had with us, where he could live with his family.

Mother was such a caring thoughtful person and I believe that kind and fair manner that she always displayed towards the servants, encouraged them to be hardworking and loyal to our family. This was borne out by the fact they would never leave us unless they were retired because of old age, when they would be given a pension. In all the years I was in India, I never heard any of them complain about anything, no doubt because of the belief they held that whatever happened to them in this life, be it good or bad, was their *kismet* (fate).

Father had his own personal bearer. He was a very old man named *Hurree*. I'm not sure if that was his real name or whether it was one that father gave him, because he was rather slow and father was always saying '*juldi kurro* Huree' (hurry up.) I'm sure that he was the same loyal servant who had stayed with father throughout that terrible ordeal many years before when he nearly died of smallpox, before he met my mother. Hurree was very thin, barely five foot tall and slightly bowed, with dark brown skin that had the appearance of a walnut. He wore an enormous white, loosely wound *pugaree* (turban) on his head, which swamped his face. His large white moustache curled upwards across his face, and his twinkling eyes lit up as his face creased into a smile. He was smartly dressed in a spotless white shirt and trousers with a broad green and gold cummerbund around his waist. As he didn't want father to retire him, he remained with him for light daily duties such as running his bath, laying out his clean clothes morning and evening, helping him to dress, polishing his shoes, and seeing him off to the office in the car driven by father's *syce* (chauffeur). At the end of the day he was always waiting to greet him when he returned, and help him prepare for dinner or any other function that he might be attending with mother that evening.

No household was complete without the *mali* (gardener) who lived in his *godown* by the front gate and kept an eye on every one who passed through it. Even though he was an old man he was energetic and kept the lawns green and the garden full of flowers, which required a lot of watering, and every day he placed an arrangement of fresh flowers in each room.

Then there was also the *syce* (chauffeur). He was a Rajput from an ancient warrior caste that inhabit the northwest province of Rajputana (now Rajasthan), who were recruited by the British for service in two famous regiments—the Rajputs and the Rajputana Rifles. He was tall with a large black moustache that luxuriated across his face and curled up at the corners. Always smartly dressed in kakhi uniform with shining brass buttons and a turban with a high starched pleated plume, he was responsible to maintain the smooth running of our car, keep it highly polished and stay by it throughout the day in readiness to drive us anywhere at any time.

One afternoon whilst I was having a rest on the verandah, I heard a man shouting and the cracking of a whip in the street outside our front gate, so rushed out to see what was happening. I was appalled to see the driver of a cart shouting at two very large water buffaloes, as he lashed at them savagely with his whip. The poor beasts were struggling to pull an overloaded cart piled high with an enormous number of sacks full of coke. It was obvious that they were too exhausted to go any further because they were frothing at the mouth. The heavy weight of the load had caused the wooden yokes to press so heavily on their necks that their muzzles almost touched the ground. This sight so infuriated me that without stopping to think of the consequences, I rushed over to him shouting in Urdu, to stop beating them. Because he ignored my request, I grabbed his whip and threatened him with it. He was so startled that he ran away leaving me with his cart and the two buffaloes in the middle of the road. Realizing my predicament, that they must be released from their yokes at once, I awoke the *mali* from his afternoon siesta and asked him to help me. When he saw what I had done, he was horrified and stood there exclaiming, '*Bharperibaab Missahib!*' (A colloquial expression of amazement.) No doubt he thought that I had gone *tora pugli!* (a little crazy) and in hindsight, he was probably right.

Together we managed to lift the shafts and release the poor animals from their yokes and lead them through the garden to the water tank under the trees. Their bodies were dry and burning hot. These creatures were **water buffaloes**, and as such had to be submerged in water during the hottest time of the day. This was the law and every Indian was aware of it. To avoid being seen by the police, this man had sneaked up a residential road, and to make matters worse, had forced the buffaloes to pull a **double** load.

Our *dhobi* with his donkey.
A sketch by artist Sian Rosamund

We watered them and poured gallons of water over their backs to cool them. Then the *mali* cut some fresh grass, and left them chewing the cud contentedly in the shade. The large cart in the middle of the road was causing an obstruction and irate drivers were sounding their horns in the hope that someone would remove it. This noise aroused mother from her siesta and when she came to investigate the commotion and saw these two great beasts in her garden, she was horrified, especially when I told her that their driver had run away and left them.. By sundown, because the buffaloes were still in the garden, mother had visions of them being added to our list of family pets.

It was getting dark when I saw a man's face peering around the pillars of the front gate, so sent the *mali* to investigate. We were all relieved to hear that it was the driver of the cart who had returned in the hope of reclaiming the buffaloes. I went out to see him and scolded him for his cruelty to them, and when I threatened to report him to the authorities for breaking the law, he put his hands together in an expression of apology and pleaded with me not to, assuring me he would never do this again. It was too dark for them to continue their journey, so I told him they would have to remain in the garden overnight and be fed and watered, and that the cart must be moved at once. He assured me that he would do this, and when I went to check them before going to bed, I found him wrapped up in his dhoti asleep on the ground by them, The *mali* had been instructed that they were to be gone at sunrise, and we were relieved to find that they were.

There was another animal that visited our home three times a week. It was the *dhobi's* (washerman) donkey. Because there were five of us in the family, there was always a vast amount of clothing to wash, especially during the hotter months when we had to shower and change as often as three times during the day. The *dhobi* laid two large sheets on the floor in which he placed each item as mother ticked it off on her laundry list, then draped the two large bundles across the donkey's back and led the poor beast through all the traffic down to the *dhobi ghats* by the riverside. There he would beat each item on a stone using a bar of Sunlight soap, (detergents were unknown then) and although the clothes were washed in far from clean river water, they were miraculously returned the next day beautifully clean, starched and ironed. The ironing was done with a large metal iron with live charcoals burning inside it, but miraculously our clothes were never scorched. I always marvelled at this washday miracle.

Father knew that, like him, I was fond of animals, so had a very large aviary built for me in the garden, in which were all kinds of exotic birds and small animals, such as guinea pigs and rabbits. Sometimes one would see a vendor walking the streets with a wooden rod across his shoulders and two tiny cages suspended from each end filled with brightly coloured birds. The plight of these poor little creatures had always upset me, which was partly why the aviary was built. The next time I saw a man with these birds, I bought both cages and released the birds into the aviary. I didn't know what species they were, but after a few days I was puzzled when their colours started to fade. It was only then that I realized that I had been cheated, because all these little birds were just common sparrows whose plumage had been dyed, so I released them and was careful never to repeat my mistake. I was amazed at the cunning and ingenuity of the man that had so successfully conned me.

Amongst the other tropical birds in my aviary were genuine Java Spotted Sparrows, Red Wax-bills, Munias, a Hill Myna that could talk, a pair of Rose-ringed parakeets, several little green White-Eyes that looked as though they were wearing spectacles, and two beautiful Golden Orioles. Because I spent a lot of time in there with them, they became so tame that they would perch on my shoulders and feed from my hands. In the garden was a Dovecote with many lovely pigeons, which included white Dovetails, Pouter pigeons, Jacobeans, and several other exotic breeds. They were also quite tame and came readily to me to feed.

A friend called to see us one day with their small year old Australian terrier, a Sydney Silky, to ask us if we could give him a home as they were leaving for England and were unable to take him with them. Mother hesitated for a moment but we persuaded her to accept him because Thatch would enjoy having a companion to play with. We soon discovered that Timmy had an aversion to black shoes and especially to bare black feet. This caused many problems when he mischievously tried to catch the servant's toes as they walked, and attack the black shoes of our friends in the forces when they called to visit, which we found most embarrassing. We did our best to try and break him of this habit, but he was so mischievous and playful that we were unsuccessful, nevertheless he had great character and many other endearing ways, and we all loved him.

Thatch and Timmy became great friends and amused everyone with their antics. They would chase each other around, and you would often see them enjoying a tug of war with one of their toys when neither of them would give way, and this would continue for ages until one of them tired.

Everyday we used to take them for walks on the Maidan, which they thoroughly enjoyed. One day we passed a football match that was being played between two Army teams watched by soldiers who were sitting on the ground with their backs towards us. Timmy was running ahead with Thatch, and as there were no trees on the Maidan, he must have been desperate to pee, because I saw him cock his leg on several conveniently presented military backs clad in jungle green. In his state of acute need he could scarcely be blamed for regarding the inviting line of jungle green columns as surrogate trees. As he did so, some of the men felt their backs, but were so intent on watching the game that they never even looked around, so must have thought they were just sweating. I was so embarrassed but dare not call to Timmy for fear of attracting attention, so turned around to head for home, but he saw me and ran after me, no doubt feeling relieved and looking very pleased with himself.

One day we were concerned to find that Timmy was unwell and unable to get off his bed, so took him to the vet who examined him thoroughly but was unable to make any diagnosis. Antibiotics were unavailable then, so there was no treatment other than Bob Martin's products, which were for minor ailments. His condition rapidly deteriorated and it was obvious that he was dying because he couldn't move, let alone eat or drink. Poor little Thatch was so concerned that she just lay by his bed looking at him dejectedly, and we were at our wits end not knowing what we could do to save him.

As father had always treated us with homeopathic remedies, it occurred to him that possibly those same remedies might help Timmy. So he gave a homeopathic doctor full details of his symptoms, and sent the bearer around to collect the remedy he had prescribed. To our great relief and delight, after taking the remedy for three days there was a dramatic improvement in Timmy's condition, and he went on to make a full recovery. Later on that same year he was so full of life and so adaptable, that he was able to make the four days journey to Kashmir and enjoy a wonderful holiday with us there. Everyday we went out riding and even though he was so small, he chased after Thatch and managed to keep up with us.

Sadly his exuberance and tenacious character was eventually his downfall, because we heard from our friends who had given him a home when we left India, that, in spite of being so very tiny (about half the size of Thatch) he had run out to challenge a large pariah dog that had entered their garden, which had grabbed him by the neck and killed him. The family were devastated by his death because, like us, they had grown to love him dearly.

CHAPTER 25

BILL RETURNS

One day in November 1943, I was alone in the house when a young officer called to visit. As I entered the lounge, I recognised him immediately. It was Bill, the same handsome young officer that I had been so enamoured of in Dehra Dun. I was surprised to see him and asked how he had managed to find us again. Apparently he and his two friends had continued to visit Rushmi after we had left for Simla, and before mother left to return to Calcutta, she gave them our address there with an invitation to call should they be passing through. I thanked God that he had kept it safely and that the military had posted him near to Calcutta, which had made

it possible for him to visit us again. Mother had not realized that I had a secret interest in Bill, so had not mentioned the fact that he was visiting our home there on his weekend leaves, while Patricia and I were away in Simla. Bill told me that after he had finished his training at Dehra Dun, he joined the 9th Gurkha Rifles and that, instead of being posted to their Regimental Centre at Birpur as was usual, he was sent direct to the 3rd battalion stationed at Jhikargacha Ghat in Bengal, not far from Calcutta, which could be easily reached by train, so had been able to visit our home quite often and get to know my parents better.

During those two years since I last saw him in Dehra Dun, he had been sent to the Arakan, the coastal part of Burma, where there was fierce fighting with the Japanese who had invaded and conquered Burma and were now threatening to invade India. To meet this grave threat, in March 1943 Bill's division which was the 26th Indian Division, was sent there to counter their advance, but the Japanese defences were so strong that Bill's division suffered heavy casualties. He had recently returned from this operation and considered himself lucky to have got out of that bloody battle alive.

Sadly this short leave was about to end and he was due to return to his battalion, but was quite unaware that he would shortly be sent on operations with General Orde Wingate's Chindits, and spend five terrible months fighting the Japanese behind enemy lines in the hell of the Burma jungle.

I was pleased that he was going to be able to spend the rest of his leave with us, which would give us the opportunity to get to know each other. Every evening I took Thatch for a walk across the Maidan and, as I was about to leave, Bill asked if he could accompany me. Of course I was delighted. As we talked together about the war and how it had brought us both out to India, I was surprised to discover how much we had in common. I sensed that he had a kind gentle nature so was puzzled why he had joined a Gurkha regiment when they were known to be a fearless, fierce fighting race, so asked him about this. He told me that he had joined the Territorial Army when he was only eighteen years old; a year before War was declared, and because he was a conscientious objector on religious grounds, chose the Royal Army Medical Corps. While serving with them, as a teenager, in France and Belgium in 1940, he was at a place on the coast called La Panne, in Belgium, about eleven miles from Dunkirk, when it was decided that because of the close proximity of the Germans and the certainty that they would all be taken prisoner by them, the unit should be evacuated back to England.

There was a call for volunteers, and Bill with four others, volunteered to stay behind to help look after the wounded in their care. Eventually, with the Germans just down the road from them, the major in charge decided that of the twenty five volunteers (including those from other units), only eight needed to stay to continue looking after the wounded and be captured by the Germans. He therefore put 25 pieces of paper in his hat, eight of them numbered, and as it was passed around they all took one. Those who picked a numbered piece of paper had to stay behind, but the remainder had a chance to make a dash for Dunkirk and freedom. Bill was lucky because he drew a blank. About 340,000 troops had already been evacuated and Bill managed to get away from the hell of shelling, bombing and strafing, with the very last batch of 5,000 men near midnight on Sunday 2nd June 1940, so his escape was a very close run thing.

As a result of the horrors that he witnessed, and the savagery he saw from the Germans, including the bombing and strafing of defenceless civilian evacuees, his way of thinking had gradually changed, and he decided he wanted to hit back at the enemy. He was later recommended for a commission and decided to opt for the infantry.

During that short time we were able to spend together, we grew fond of each other and were sad that he would be leaving us so soon. A couple of days before his departure he asked if we could take Thatch for an early morning walk in the grounds of the Victoria Memorial as he wanted to tell me something before he left. It was while we were sitting there by the lake watching the sunrise, that he told me he had fallen in love with me and wanted me to marry him. Surprised but thrilled, I promised that I would. When we returned home, Bill broke this news to my parents and asked for their permission. They were delighted but told us that, as I was only seventeen, they felt that I was too young to become engaged, especially as Bill was about to be sent in to front line operations and might never return. We were upset at this but understood their concern for us. In

Bill asked me

spite of this, Bill decided he wanted to buy me an engagement ring, and agreed to my parent's suggestion that they could keep it safe until my eighteenth birthday, when should he return, we could get engaged and celebrate with a party. So he took me to choose a beautiful diamond ring and a lovely pearl necklace to wear as a token of his love for me.

I said 'I will'.

When the time arrived for him to go, it was with very heavy hearts that we had to part, especially as we both knew there was a possibility that we might never see each other again. Before he left, we visited the photographer to have our portraits taken, which we exchanged to remind each other of this special occasion. As we parted, we promised to write to each other, but after his departure I missed him terribly and worried about him constantly as I knew that he would be sent into the thick of the fighting once more. All I could do was pray fervently that God would take care of him and hope he would be comforted by the verse that I gave him from psalm 23 in the Bible. 'Though I walk through the valley of the shadow of death, I will fear no evil, for Thou art with me, Thy rod and Thy staff they comfort me.'

I had never before experienced the meaning of true love. I had grown fond of people, but never allowed myself to express my innermost feelings, in fact I felt I was incapable of loving anyone. Now I was overwhelmed with this new and thrilling emotion, which made me want to be near him, so when he left I suffered a great sense of loss. I wrote to him every day, and he wrote me wonderfully loving letters whenever he could. I treasure them still and when I re-read them sometimes, I'm reminded of those amazing days so long ago when I felt the thrill of my first love and the heartache I suffered from fear of Bill being killed, captured or wounded.

Bill with the rank of Major in 1944

Justine aged 17 years

CHAPTER 26

HOLIDAY IN KASHMIR

Bill left to rejoin his battalion, and, as I later found out, to leave his old division and to become part of a special airborne force, later to become renowned as the **Chindits.** I felt so sad at having to say goodbye to him that my parents decided we all needed to be cheered up by a visit to Kashmir. We'd heard of its beauties but never been there. It has been called 'The Paradise on Earth' and is steeped in ancient myths, and from the earliest times suffered under various rulers that involved the country in bloody wars. The earliest settlement in the whole of India dating back 3000 years has been unearthed near Srinagar, its capital. Its beauties were enhanced when the Mughal emperors designed and built wonderful gardens like the Shalimar Bagh, with its pavilions, lakes, fountains and orchards. The more we discovered about it, the more we looked forward to our holiday there.

My parents planned for us to stay there for three months during the hot season, but, before we left, mother had to take Claire back to her school in Darjeeling, where she would remain until the Christmas holidays. Because we were all going to be away for so long and they didn't want to deprive the members of the forces who visited us the hospitality they had enjoyed, my parents arranged for friends to stay and run our home so they could continue to come there.

When all the arrangements had been made, we embarked on what proved to be a fantastic holiday. I felt privileged to have been able go to a place of such outstanding natural beauty in a peaceful era, long before it was on the tourist trail. When India became independent in August 1947, Kashmir became the bone of contention between the new states of Pakistan and India. And because the majority of the people were Muslims ruled by a Hindu maharajah who couldn't make up his mind which side to join, the Pakistanis invaded Kashmir, then when he sought help from India later on, it was too late, so the long running dispute has never been resolved. Now, tragically, it is still difficult to visit there and one wonders if the dispute will ever be settled amicably.

It was a four-day journey by train to Rawalpindi (the same place where mother and father had first met twenty years previously) with a further whole days journey by a winding, tortuous route into the mountains by car to Srinagar, where we were to stay on a houseboat.

Waiting to load our 26 pieces of luggage onto the train.

I'm pleased that mother kept a diary, which I am able to refer to, to refresh my memory of it. She writes:

'We boarded the East Indian Railway Steam Express at Howrah station in Calcutta on April 27th 1944, with our dear little dog Thatch and twenty six pieces of luggage. (I can't imagine why we needed so much.) We had first class air-conditioned compartments, which made the journey quite pleasant for the first two days. We were due to change at Ghaziabad Junction onto the Punjab Mail, which was to have taken us via Delhi on the rest of the journey, but unfortunately our train was running two hours late. The Punjab Mail had waited for us for an hour, but it had to leave, and with it our reserved first class air-conditioned compartments. We had no choice but to try and find some other way to continue the journey. It was past midnight when we alighted from the train and, with our enormous stack of luggage, we found ourselves stranded on the platform. Father told us to try and find seats in the ladies waiting room whilst he stayed with our luggage, but when we reached it, the whole place was full of Indian women lying asleep all over the floor and every bench was filled. We returned to him to hopefully work out another solution. He managed to find the stationmaster, and when he told him of our plight, he was most obliging. He suggested we could spend the rest of the night in a compartment on a train in a siding, but warned us we would have to vacate it by 6am, or else we might find ourselves hitched onto a different train and be travelling to another part of India.

'When we finally located it in the dark and tried to load all our luggage into it as well as ourselves, we found that there were no lights in it, so by the light of a torch, we had to clean the layer of dust off the whole carriage before disinfecting it with Lysol and spraying it with the Flit can (mother always carried one of these on our travels) to kill all the mosquitoes and other crawling creatures. By now it was 2 am and we were so exhausted that we just lay on the bunks without bothering to unroll our bedding rolls, and tried to get some sleep. Thankfully the fan was working, but not for long, so despite the risk of being worried by mosquitoes, we had to open the windows. We were dozing off to sleep when some workmen came by hammering the wheels, couplings, nuts and bolts, to check that everything was in order, so we were disturbed once more. Just as we settled again, there was a yell from Patricia that she was getting wet. Water was shooting through the windows as the cleaners were hosing down all the carriages. The water helped to cool us, but we spent a very uncomfortable night, or rather what was left of it.

'So the night wore on with numerous other disturbances, but dawn comes even after the darkest nights, and here we are this morning in the same carriage, waiting for the train to start. We felt ourselves being shunted in the middle of the night but had no idea where we were going and, by 6 am when we were due to leave the carriage, we found that we had been attached to the train that was to take us on the rest of our journey. We were thankful that at least the stationmaster must have had pity on us, and had arranged this for us. Because of all the upheaval we were without food or water, so were glad when we reached a small station called Demel, where we alighted and went to the station restaurant to have lunch and buy some bottled water whilst the train waited.

Imagine my joy and surprise when I discovered that the label on the bottle said 'Malvern Spring Water' from the very same spring that Justine and Patricia had drunk from when they used to walk there on the Malvern Hills when they were at school there all those years ago.'

'When the train stopped at Lahore station at midnight, we were all delighted that one of father's distributors was on the platform to greet us with an enormous basket of delicious tropical fruits. The gallon of iced lemonade, which he had also brought, was most welcome. We were then able to leave the train briefly to have a good meal of curry and rice'.

As I look back to those days it seems that 'time' in India didn't really matter as life went on around you at such a slow pace. The attitude there was summed up by the word '*kal*', meaning 'tomorrow'. What with the intense heat and the noise and the crowds around all the time, it was easy to adapt to that way of life yourself. So picture us sitting around a table at one o'clock in the morning tucking into a hearty meal as the train waits for us to return to our carriage to continue its journey. Mother's diary continues:

'We still had at least one more day and nights travel before we reached Rawalpindi. The stifling heat was bearable during the day when we were moving and could have the windows open, but when we stopped at stations during the night, we had to close all the windows and shutters or else other Indian passengers would try to clamber through them into your compartment, in the pandemonium that erupted at every station. Anyway, they still banged on the shutters, even when there was a notice saying it was reserved. Whenever the train stopped at any station, day or night, there was always a cacophony of sounds with vendors shouting '*paan, biri*, cigarette' and '*garam chai*,' (hot tea) and '*Mussulman pani*, and '*Hindu pani*,' (water for Moslems and water for Hindus) and so on. If those that had been waiting, some possibly for several days, couldn't get into the train, then they would just clamber on to the roof or hang on to the sides, seemingly oblivious of the danger. There were so many people who travelled like that, without tickets, that the railway authorities were powerless to do anything about it.

'Eventually we arrived at our destination and found a large Chrysler car waiting to take us up through the mountains to Srinagar. As we commenced our onward journey we noticed a plane dropping parachutists who were landing quite close to us. They must have come from the military base at Rawalpindi. The road narrowed as we drove up into the mountains, with a sheer drop on one side of hundreds of feet to the floor of the valley below. As we rounded a bend we caught our first glimpse of the snowy mountain range in the distance and the raging torrent of the Jhelum River below. The road followed the course of the river for most of the way except when we climbed up into the mountains to the hill station of Murree at 8,750 ft only to drop down to 2,300 ft an hour later where we joined the river again. As we followed it, we saw great logs being floated down and, at various bends where they were piling up, men were perilously walking on them as they tried to free them to send them on their way.

'We were enjoying our scenic drive, when suddenly the car zigzagged from side to side on the narrow mountain road, then skidded to a halt on the very edge of a precipice. We thought our last

Our Shikara named—"I for you, you for me, we shall be happy together"

moments had come, and that we were about to go over the edge. It looked as though the steering wheel had broken, but when the driver examined the car he found that the front axle had cracked. We had to help unload our entire luggage so that the driver could get to his tools and, as we did so, the heavens opened and we all got drenched. By now the temperature had dropped dramatically, so we got back into the car and waited in the hope that another car would come by with someone who might be able to help us. As we still had a further fifty miles to go, we were worried in case we were still stranded on this dangerous mountain road when it became dark. Fortunately it was not too long before another car came by and the driver proved to be most helpful. Together the two men managed to clamp the broken axle and we were able to continue our journey. All our worries over the mishap were forgotten as we were driven through the most breathtaking scenery. The road levelled out as we reached a plateau at 5,765 ft and continued through fruit orchards, alpine meadows and lakes, which mirrored the snowy mountains in the twilight. As we neared Srinagar we drove along straight avenues of beautiful deodar trees by the shores of the lake and on towards the town'

Srinagar, at an altitude of 5,200 feet is situated on the banks of the Jhelum River, and lies in one of the most beautiful regions of India. The Mughal rulers were always happy to retreat from the heat of the plains to the cool green heights of Kashmir. These rulers developed their formal garden-style art to its greatest heights and many of their beautifully designed and tended gardens still remain. During the days of the Raj, the British, who were just as fond of the cool climate and the beauties of Kashmir as these Mughal rulers, also travelled here but were prohibited to buy land. So they adopted the superbly British solution of building houseboats, each one creating a 'little bit of England' as it floated on the tranquil waters of the Dal lake. This lake with its backdrop of snowy mountains is 6 km long and 4k km wide with two small islands in the middle and an intricate maze of waterways with the beautiful houseboats moored around its shores.

Once in the town we picked up Ahmed Joo, the owner of the houseboat we were to rent. He wanted to take us to it himself so we would not have to search for it amongst the many others alongside the island where they were moored. As we reached the Bund (lakeside boulevard) we noticed many pretty little shikaras (small gondola type boats) moored along its edge. These were water taxis used to take people to their houseboats, or just for a trip along the many waterways.

Ahmed took us to a magnificent shikara that was richly decorated in brightly coloured Kashmiri embroidered drapes. I was amused as I read its rather unusual name; 'I for You, You for Me, We Shall Be Happy Together.' This shikara was for our personal use as it belonged to the houseboat, so we climbed in and two boatmen paddled us over to it. I think this was the highlight of the long journey for Thatch who was quivering with excitement as she leant over the edge of the shikara, trying to catch the silvery fish as they darted past in the crystal-clear water. She had been wonderful throughout those long hot days and nights in the train and during the car journey along the winding mountain road. I think she sensed that there were exciting days ahead.

When the houseboat came into view we were enchanted with its beautifully carved façade. The sign over the entrance read 'The Pintail.' It was constructed of light natural deodar wood, and as we mounted the steps from the shikara and entered the lounge, we were amazed to find that all the walls and ceilings were decorated with embossed carvings of birds and flowers, and hanging from the ceiling was an enormous sparkling crystal chandelier. Persian carpets covered the floors in every room, and in the centre of the dining room was a large oval table with six beautifully designed, deeply carved chairs. The whole place was full of the wonderful fragrance of the cedar wood panelling. It was clear that these Kashmiris were skilled and gifted people to be able to produce such amazing objects.

Our beautiful houseboat—PINTAIL

That night we were so exhausted that we went to sleep early, soothed by the peaceful sound of the gentle lapping of the water on the sides of the houseboat.

Mother records our first day on the lake:

'May 1st 1944. This morning we awoke to brilliant sunshine and the loveliest view of snow clad mountains. I think our arrival had caused a stir amongst the locals because, when I went out on to the verandah, there were many little boats surrounding our houseboat, all waiting to know if there was anything we would like to buy from them. The flower boat was a picture, with all kinds of lovely English flowers such as lilies of the valley, pansies, peonies, anemones, sweet peas and roses etc. and there was a vegetable, as well as a fruit boat, full of exotic tropical fruits. There was another boat with stores and medicines, one full of furs, and one boat that particularly caught my eye was filled with sparkling gemstones and jewellery. Another one was full of exquisitely embroidered housecoats and Pashmina shawls, in fact there was no need to go into town for anything. I can see that we are going to arrive back from this holiday penniless.

'May 2nd. Though this is a lovely place to be moored, I can see that there is going to be too much going on around us, so we must ask Ahmed if we can go and look for a more isolated spot. Thankfully he was pleased to oblige, so we set out in our shikara to look for the ideal place where we would have the whole world to ourselves. As we drifted along through the beautiful waterways and canals with just the sound of the gentle rhythmic splash of the paddles as our two men rowed us along, we saw many little shops right on the waters edge and were amused at some of their names. Two signs read, 'Suffering Moses-Pashmina shawls', 'Jolly Joe—Woodcarver', and another, 'Jumping Jehosophat—Papier Masche'. Some of the shikaras that passed us also had strange names such as 'Happy Perhaps', 'Me and My Girl', and 'My Blue Heaven'. It seemed that everything had to have a name and I felt sure that this strange idea and the peculiar names must have been introduced by the British in the first place.'

'As we came out of the waterways into an open part of the Dal Lake, we saw a pretty island with a meadow covered in wild flowers and a flock of sheep grazing there. When we came ashore, we discovered that the flowers were all of the same variety that one would find in an English meadow, and the scene reminded me of the English countryside, except for the magnificent backdrop of the range of snowy mountains. It was such a lovely spot that we decided this would be the ideal place to move our houseboat to, but at the time we had no idea what a major operation this would prove to be.

'This morning we moved the houseboat to the new location, and what an interesting feat it was. It took six men with long poles to do it. There were three men on each side of the boat, each with a long pole, which they used for punting. For two hours or more these men placed their poles down through the water, then walked the full length of the boat along the plank on the outside, pushing hard on the pole as they went. The awning on the sun deck had to be removed to enable the boat to pass under the arches of the seven bridges, which it had to negotiate. In some places the canals were so narrow that it seemed we would either damage the houseboat or knock down the walls of the little wooden houses on the edge of the water as we passed. Fortunately, these men were so skilful in the manipulation of their poles that no damage was caused. Seeing the houseboat was at least forty feet long and about twenty-five feet wide, and we were also towing

Fishing from Pintail

another houseboat that housed the kitchen and the servant's quarters, I think they accomplished an amazing task. I was astounded when we were still served a three-course lunch that had been prepared by our cook in the kitchen, whilst all this was in progress.

'We reached our desired haven about 3pm when we were tied up and the kitchen boat punted along to be moored in a little creek a short distance away. The houseboat staff had brought their chickens and ducks along with them, from our previous island where they had been kept by the kitchen boat. As they released them, they made a dreadful noise as they scattered across the field evidently approving of our new location. Thatch, too, was delighted as she raced about the meadow barking, but she was always so well behaved that we had no fears that she might worry them.

'We were so happy to be in this tranquil place that we just sat in our deck chairs until sunset, and drank in all the beauties around us. This is another world altogether and one in which I would like to remain always. The peace, stillness, and wonder of it all turns my thoughts to God the Creator and I am thankful to Him that I am privileged to see it.'

Now we had moved to this new location we had no electricity, so dined by candlelight. Afterwards, we went up onto the roof deck to relax in the deck chairs and enjoy the view of the snowy mountains as the sun set and reflected them in the still waters of the lake. It didn't get dark until around 9pm, and when the full moon rose it was so bright that father and a friend who had joined us (the same RAF padre who had named his Jeep after me,) played a game of chess by the light of the moon, whilst I played a selection of some lovely tunes from the Student Prince on the gramophone we had brought with us.

'Overhead the moon is beaming,
Bright as blossoms on the bough.
Nothing is heard but the song of a bird,
Filling all the air with dreaming…'

I thought these lyrics rather appropriate for the occasion, but as I listened to them my thoughts turned again to Bill, as I wondered where he was, wishing so much that he could have been with me to share these magical moments, and the beauties of this wonderful place. He was constantly in my thoughts and prayers as I longed for him to return. When we parted he had not been able to tell me where he would be going or what he would be doing, but I knew he was shortly being sent into action against the Japanese and, as I pondered this, I offered up a fervent prayer; 'Please God take care of him and bring him back to me soon.' I later learned that at the same time that I was sitting in the moonlight listening to this lovely music and thinking of him, he **was** fighting a fierce battle in most terrible conditions in the Burma jungle against the Japanese again, having been dropped behind enemy lines in a glider that crashed there.

He tells his own story about that terrible time in a book he has written called 'A Chindit's Chronicle'. On the back of the cover it reads:

Bill's Book

'On Sunday 5th March 1944 an airborne force set out from Lalaghat airstrip in Assam aboard gliders piloted by Americans of the 1st Air Commando USAAF. They were men of Special Force, otherwise known as 'The Chindits' led by their famous commander Major Genral Orde Wingate. In the brilliant moonlight they flew eastwards over the steep mountain range separating India from Burma, crossed the mighty Chindwin River, which lay like a silver glittering ribbon far below them, to land in a small clearing, codenamed 'Broadway' in the jungle 130 miles behind the Japanese front line. Despite the heavy casualties sustained in the glider landings, the survivors by dint of prodigious effort managed in a few hours to construct a rough airstrip, which on the following night received Dakota transport aircraft ferrying men, mules and equipment. They achieved complete surprise over the enemy and within a period of six days, in a total of 78 glider and 660 Dakota sorties, some of which alighted at a nearby airstrip codenamed 'Chowringhee', 9,052 men and 1,360 pack animals and 250 tons of supplies were landed in a brilliantly successful operation for the loss of a total of only 121 men killed or wounded. It was the biggest operation of its kind so far launched during the war, though only three months later it was to be followed by 'Overlord', the gigantic Allied invasion of Normandy.

'Serving with the 3rd Battalion 9th Gurkha Rifles, first as intelligence officer and later as adjutant, Bill was in one of the leading gliders and was one of the fortunate few who survived the whole of the five months long campaign. 'A Chindit's Chronicle' is his intensely personal, vivid, sometimes amusing and often very moving account of his experiences, telling amongst other things of how four Victoria Crosses were won, and the background to the struggle. What it was like to march, struggle and fight on in the jungle-clad hills. Also some of the striking characters who took part, as well as accounts of actions of remarkable courage and gallantry.'

We spent the next three weeks exploring the waterways, horse riding along the shores of the lake, fishing for trout, picnicking on the islands and visiting the beautiful Moghul gardens, or browsing amongst the shops full of exotic wares in the town of Srinagar. It is said that this place is one of the most beautiful garden cities of the world..

Whilst we were there, my parents had been planning and arranging a trek up into the mountains to the Zojila Pass on the borders of Ladakh. When I read the leaflet we were given about the trip, I realized that we would be going off the

Picnicking amongst the wild flowers

beaten track out into the wilds of the Sindh valley up to 3,529 metres, which would be higher than

I had ever been. The description of the road along which we would be travelling read; 'The rough road clings to the edge of sheer drops and there are times when you'll wonder if you were sane to make this trip.' Not a comforting thought as we planned to be trekking away from civilization for two weeks.

After such a blissful stay on the Pintail, we were reluctant to leave it and this peaceful corner of paradise, though full of anticipation at the prospect of the adventure ahead. We deposited most of our luggage with the agent in town and set off in a rickety old bus loaded with camping equipment and the servants for the trek. We bumped along a road full of potholes to the village of Gund, where we were to meet the ponies with their *syces*. Although the scenery was fabulous, we couldn't enjoy it as the road was a quagmire after two days of heavy rain. The bus was skidding all over the track, and as there were no proper seats in the bus, only narrow benches, we found ourselves hanging on for dear life to prevent ourselves being thrown to the floor. It was so bad in places that we decided to get out of the bus and walk behind, until it had negotiated a particularly dangerous part of the road, especially when there was a sheer drop over the edge of hundreds of feet to the floor of the valley below.

After four and a half hours of a hair raising drive, we were relieved to arrive at Gund, from where we were to start our trek on the following morning. We had booked the Dak bungalow for the night, which was in a lovely location by the rushing torrent of the Sindh River. Dak bungalows are to be found all over India and Kashmir, sited at strategic places, and although facilities were very basic, they were built especially to accommodate travellers and trekkers. After checking that everything was ready for an early morning start, we enjoyed a picnic in the garden, which was full of the most beautiful alpine flowers. Now we were up into the high mountain area, it was quite cool, so the servants lit a roaring log fire for us in the bungalow that evening and, as we sat around it, we discussed the plan for the following day.

We arose at sunrise and, when I looked out, I was stunned to count no fewer than twenty two pack ponies that had already been loaded with all our gear. They were standing there in line in front of the bungalow, each with its own *syce*, waiting patiently for the signal to move off. There were also six larger ponies that had been saddled up for us to ride. After what our cook described as a 'hearty full English breakfast', we set off about 9am. Mother recalls the sight.

'What a cavalcade we are, as we ride at the head of this long line of ponies and men. As we did not have enough ponies to carry all our kit, we had to hire five more coolies to carry the extra loads. Behind us, came the 'khansama (cook), his mate, the bearer, the 'bhisti', (water carrier) and the sweeper, all on foot. The scenery was grander than any we had seen before and the going was easy. We stopped for a delicious picnic lunch by a mountain stream near the village of Kulan and then remounted our ponies. As we were leaving the village, a woman came to us pleading with Arthur to come to her hut to help her husband who had hurt his foot. When he dismounted and went with her, he discovered that this man's leg was so badly infected that gangrene had set in and the poor man would soon die if we didn't do something to help him immediately. So it was decided that as he

A cavalcade of pack ponies

needed urgent hospital treatment, we must let him have one of our pack ponies to take him back to Gund with its *syce* where, hopefully, he might find transport to Srinagar and the hospital. Father paid the full cost for all this, and gave the *syce* some extra money so that he would not loose out by having to return. He seemed content with this arrangement and agreed to help the poor man. This incident made us all realize the hazards that we might also be faced with should any of us have an accident, as there would be no way of getting in touch with anyone who could help us. The only transport available in that region was by mountain pony.

'We were all rather upset by this incident, but had to continue on our way. From then onwards, the track became more precipitous and even more beautiful and although the snow was all around us up above, it was exciting when we had to cross a steep mound of it which had come down in an avalanche and had blocked our path. All the ponies were wonderfully sure-footed as they picked their way across the slippery snow with the loads on their backs. We then descended into a very beautiful valley and rode along a path by the raging river. All around us the hills were covered in tall snow-capped pine trees and ahead of us was a snow-capped mountain glaringly white in the bright sunlight, with the bluest sky above. At our feet, peeping out from the clefts in the rocks, were little violets, crocuses and other alpine flowers. These rocks were of different colours, some pink, some grey and others green marble. As we rode along the track past a waterfall, I heard the call of a cuckoo. It was all so overwhelmingly beautiful that one was spellbound.'

We had ridden for seven hours and covered fifteen miles on that first day, so were glad when the village of Sonamarg came in sight, where we were to stop for the night. Sonamarg was called the 'Meadow of Gold' because it was covered in yellow crocuses. All the meadows in the Kashmir Valley were carpeted with these flowers, and the Kashmiris had harvested them from ancient times for their rich dye and also for the saffron that they produce from their dried orange-yellow stigmas. Saffron was more valuable than gold—ounce for ounce.

Thatch had been happily running alongside my pony for most of the way, but whenever she was tired, she just sat down and barked at me, so I would stop, pat the front of my saddle and say—'Come on up', and she would leap up onto it and ride along, sitting in front of me perfectly balanced even when the pony trotted, until she felt rested and wanted to jump down again. She was always so full of life and her boundless energy, vitality and adaptability was quite amazing.

Drying off after a paddle in a cold stream

When we arrived at Sonamarg village we still had to climb a further 500 feet up an almost vertical track, much too steep to ride up, so we dismounted and climbed it on foot. When we reached the Forest Bungalow at the top, I looked down to see all the pack ponies coming up that same steep track with all their loads. These were true mountain ponies, because no other breed of pony would have been able to negotiate such a steep ascent, let alone with a load upon its back.

The bungalow was situated on a plateau, on the edge of the mountain with, as always in this region, awesome views all around us. It was such an ideal location that we decided to spend two nights there. We went for some lovely walks in the snow the following day, including one to a spectacular glacier not far away. Later we returned to a wonderful hot meal and a roaring log fire to warm ourselves afterwards at the end of the day.

The view from the verandah at the front of the bungalow was so breathtaking that no description does justice to it. We just sat there in awe as we watched the glow of the sun changing the whole range of the high, snow-capped mountains from pale gold to flaming orange, then to crimson, with the ever-changing colours in the sky which cast shadows down into the deep valleys. We saw this magnificent panorama both at sunrise and sunset and felt so fortunate to have been able to witness such a scene that has been denied to travellers for so long. Throughout the whole of that wonderful journey we were the only people making that trek up to the Zojla Pass, so it felt as though we had that whole part of the world to ourselves.

We were reluctant to leave this lovely place, but had to pack up and move on to our next stop which was to be at the tiny village of Baltal, at an altitude of 9,000 ft, about ten miles away. It is the last place at the foot of the Zojila Pass, which is the watershed between Kashmir and Ladakh. On one side you have the green, lush scenery of Kashmir and, on the other the dry, barren Ladakh.. We hadn't planned to go over the border into that area.

All the pack ponies had gone ahead of us, so that when we arrived at Baltal we found our tents had been pitched in a high meadow that was full of wild alpine flowers. That evening, the *khansama* had once again prepared a delicious hot meal for us, and we dined in grand style by candlelight under a starry sky. He had laid out the table with pretty bone china on a linen tablecloth with napkins and silver cutlery. Throughout the trek we never ceased to marvel at the gourmet meals that he was able to produce under the most primitive conditions, and that he was even able to bake fresh bread and cakes for us every day. One of the pack ponies had carried our gramophone and records, so we were able to enjoy music whilst we dined or sat around the fire in the evenings. I had been wondering, but now knew why we had needed so many pack ponies.

That night we had a heavy fall of snow, and when we emerged from our sleeping tents to make our way to the dining tent, we found that in spite of the difficulties created by the weather conditions, the khansama had **still** prepared the usual 'hearty English breakfast' for us.

All around us the snow was glistening in the morning sun and it looked like a scene from a Christmas card. But this scene was marred when one of the syces came to tell us that his pack pony had fallen off the edge of the mountain during the night and had broken its neck. Evidently the syces had driven them into a higher alpine pasture to graze as we were spending three days there, but as they had not anticipated the heavy snowfall, they had left the ponies there instead of bringing them back to a lower level. As it turned out to be a very cold, misty day with more snowfall, we decided to put off the ascent to the Zogila Pass until the following day. Mother describes the climb most vividly in her diary.

'We started out at 10am on foot and the climb was quite easy to begin with, but as we went higher the track around the mountainside became steeper and, as we looked back down the mountain, we

Thatch enjoys a ride with me

could see our little camp fading into the distance. Arthur and Patricia trudged on ahead because they wanted to reach the summit, but Justine and I were getting rather breathless due to the altitude, so we took our time. We walked for another two hours until we met a deep snowdrift across our path, and decided to turn back. On the climb up we passed two caravans of fifteen and twenty laden pack ponies that had come over the pass from Ladakh in Tibet, probably heading for Srinagar where they would sell their goods. We noticed that these men were very small, probably less than five feet tall, and that they had Mongolian features. Their ponies were also very small but amazingly sure-footed, because we saw them trotting down the steep and narrow snowy mountain track at great speed even though they were heavily laden.

On our return, we found another steep track, which led down to a stream near our campsite, but we didn't realize just how steep it was until we looked back at it from the bottom. We were surprised to see a large greenish-grey snake cross the path as we neared our tent and hoped he wasn't heading in that direction. This short cut brought us back much sooner, and we were glad that we had taken it because it avoided us having to step across our dead pony which we could see lying on the path nearby. As we passed, we disturbed a pair of mountain eagles that had found it, and we watched them in awe as these beautiful birds soared away above us.

'When we reached the spot where we had camped, we found that all our belongings had been packed up and that the ponies had taken everything back to Sonamarg to await our arrival. Our riding ponies were awaiting us, and a lovely picnic had been spread out under the pine trees. It was so peaceful sitting there without a sound, except for the occasional call of the cuckoo and the rush of the river close-by, but suddenly the stillness was broken by a loud crack, as of thunder, followed by a prolonged roar. We looked up to where the sound came from, and saw that it was an avalanche of snow thundering down the mountainside. This roar lasted for almost an hour and we were worried as to whether Arthur and Patricia were safe. We were relieved when the *syces* came running to tell us that they had caught sight of them. So we mounted our ponies and went to meet them. Arthur greeted me with the words, 'You spoilt my day. It was all so wonderful but it was spoilt for me, because you weren't there to share it with me'.

'They were in ecstasies over what they had seen and told us that the journey had not been a hard one and they felt sure that we could have done it easily, but I was not so sure about that, as they looked very burnt with the sun, glare and the wind.

'The ride back was most enjoyable, as the stretch between Baltal and Sonamarg is quite the

Resting by the roaring river

prettiest part of this trek as it runs alongside the rushing river. The steep mountains on each side of the track follow the river that winds in and out, so that one is always coming across a glorious view, which often holds one spellbound. Once as we rode around the mountain and looked up, we were all excited when we saw a large black Himalayan bear walking across one of the slopes. The air was full of bird song, and from time to time we caught a glimpse of the beautiful Golden Oriole.'

'By the time we approached Sonamarg it was about six thirty in the evening and it was becoming cooler. During the last part of the journey a snowstorm had been following us, but as we entered the plateau it caught up with us. The sky was heavily overcast and suddenly we were in the midst of a roaring gale. We had to dismount from our ponies and the syces had to lead them on with encouraging shouts. We still had to climb that steep track up to the bungalow and it took us nearly an hour. The syces tried to find a more sheltered route for our ponies, out of the gale. As we wrapped our coats tightly around us we had a real task to keep our feet as we struggled up the steep track. When we finally reached the top of the ridge, we were almost blown over and had to double up and hang on to each other. We were very relieved when at last we reached the shelter of the bungalow and found a roaring log fire burning in the hearth. The table was laid with a freshly baked loaf of bread, scotch pancakes and pots and pots of hot tea. Although it was almost suppertime we tucked in and still did justice to the meal that followed.

'The next morning we were relieved when we awoke to find that the gale had abated and there were blue skies and sunshine once more. After breakfast we set off on the ponies once again on the last lap of our trek for Gund. This took us about seven hours, but we had a very pleasant stop for a picnic lunch by a bubbling stream en route. The scenery was just as stunning on the return journey but the views were quite different this time, as we had been riding with our backs to it on the way out.

'When we reached Gund, we found that the whole Dak bungalow had been reserved for us, so we spread ourselves out and spent a very comfortable night. On our trek, we had passed a colourful group of Lama Tibetan Buddhist priests from Ladakh who were dressed in their bright orange robes with high pointed hats. These men had travelled those many miles all the way to Gund through the snow and the storm on foot, and were now camping on the meadow in front of us. One of them spoke perfect English and we found that he had been educated at the only English Mission School in Ladakh. We were surprised to learn that he was taking his younger brother, also a Buddhist priest, all those many miles to the military base at Rawalpindi to join the Air Force.'

In the morning we boarded our bus to take us back to Srinagar. Thankfully, as the weather had been dry and sunny in the area whilst we had been on our trek, the muddy road had dried out, which made the return journey much more pleasant than before. Even though, I was still not happy about the sheer drop over the edge of the road that I could see all along the way, so I tried to take my mind off it by looking at the banks of pretty flowers lining the road that had bloomed during the time we'd been away.

When we reached Srinagar, we handed back the camping gear and collected the remainder of our luggage in preparation for our stay in Gulmarg, a picturesque little town in the heart of the mountains. Sadly we had to say goodbye to father before we left, because he had to return to Calcutta to attend to business matters, so only the three of us would be making the journey. We hired a car and driver for the 57 kilometres to Tangmarg at the foot of the mountains where the paved road ended.

It was a beautiful drive from Srinagar through the vale of Kashmir, past picturesque villages and orchards laden with fruit. There were flowers everywhere as we drove along lanes lined with poplar trees and flanked by fields of verdant green.

As there was only a track up to Gulmarg from Tangmarg, our luggage was loaded on to pack ponies and porters, and we had to ride our horses up this steep track for the rest of the way. It was a lovely ride through the pine forests, and when we reached the top we came upon Gulmarg quite suddenly in a little dell, a bowl shaped meadow covered with a carpet of flowers. (Gulmarg literally means 'flower filled meadow'.)

The view of Gulmarg from Hut 57.

Mother describes our arrival in her diary:

'Dotted all around the slopes are picturesque wooden houses, rather like Swiss chalets, in a semicircle amongst the pine trees, and above them I can see snow-covered mountains. A silvery stream meanders across the hollow of the meadow, which is dotted with all kinds of alpine flowers such as blue gentians, edelweiss, crocuses and tiny blue and yellow irises. Our chalet is at 9,000 ft above sea level and commands a beautiful view, quite the best in Gulmarg. From the front of the house, we have the whole view of Gulmarg before us, dotted with sheep and horses grazing in the meadow below with the backcloth of the snow-capped mountain of Apharwat, and behind the house in the opposite direction, the whole Vale of Kashmir is spread far below us. In the distance, from east to west as far as the eye can see, is the Pir Pinjal range of snow-covered mountains with Nanga Parbat at 28,000 ft towering above them all. This is a truly beautiful place and I know we are going to enjoy our six weeks rest here.'

The 'rest' that mother had anticipated did not materialize, because there were so many things to do. There was no means of transport in Gulmarg other than by Doolies (a wicker basket chair carried by two porters with poles slung across their shoulders) or horses, so we walked or rode everywhere. There was a wide selection of wonderful horses, so we enjoyed riding every day. Wherever we went the scenery was magnificent, and even though we were at such a high altitude, the weather was sunny and pleasant, though it got quite chilly in the evenings. After supper we usually sat around a blazing log fire and listened to music on our gramophone, which accompanied us everywhere. I wrote to Bill every day even though I knew my letters would take many weeks to reach him, if at all. I felt I had to tell him about everything, because it was all so wonderful in this remote corner of paradise. With no radio or newspapers, we had no idea of what was happening in the rest of the world.

There was a pleasant interlude when an RAF pilot who had frequently visited our home in Calcutta, brought his bomber crew with him on leave, and rented a chalet close by. We enjoyed some happy times with them when we went riding around the mountain tracks or picnicking in the meadows, or when we joined Jack and his lads on the golf course, which is the highest in the world.

Our stay there passed all too quickly and it was soon time to make that long journey back to Calcutta. Even though I had enjoyed

We picnic with Jack and his RAF crew in Shalimar Gardens.

myself during this wonderful trip, I had missed Bill immensely and was anxious to return home to find the many letters that he was sure to have written to me, as none of them had been able to reach me whilst we'd been away. I realized that I had to face the fact that even when I got them, I still wouldn't know if he was still alive, and there was absolutely no way of finding out. All that I could do was to continue to pray fervently—and I did believe in the power of prayer—that God would protect him, and that we would soon be together again. Should he survive the terrible fighting, in which I knew he was involved, I resolved to return to Kashmir with him sometime in the future so that we could share all these wonderful experiences together.

CHAPTER 27

BACK IN CALCUTTA

At the end of this glorious holiday we returned to the hustle and bustle of Calcutta. Though it was a long and tedious journey, it was accomplished, thankfully, without any major hitches or disasters. I was delighted when I reached home and found the pile of letters from Bill awaiting me. Of course, because of strict censorship, he wasn't able to tell me anything about the five months he had endured in the jungles of Burma.

In the last of the letters he said that he had been flown out of there and was in hospital, so at least he was **still** alive, and it was only when we met some time later that he was able to tell me something of the terrible atrocities he had seen and the hellish conditions he'd endured for so long.

A month before we left for Kashmir, he had been flown by glider 130 miles behind the Japanese front line with the Chindit Force as I have mentioned earlier. I quote a short passage from the book he wrote many years later in which he graphically though briefly, describes what those Chindits suffered.

'We fought with grim determination against a fanatical and ruthless enemy with no quarter asked or given, and exerted a stranglehold over the enemy supply routes which impeded the Japanese divisions to the north, which were attempting to force their way into India via Imphal and Kohima. When the monsoon came, the fighting continued in a sea of mud. We were often starving and short of ammunition since the low-lying cloud prevented supply drops being made to us by the RAF and USAAF. Inflicting enormous casualties on the enemy, we also took heavy casualties from battle and sickness until at the last, broken in body but not in spirit, less than a twentieth of those who survived, were judged on medical examination to be physically fit enough to continue the fight'.

'We had entered the fifth month of the Chindit Operation, and as a result of the unremitting strain and hardship, and lack of proper rest and food we were physically and mentally at an extremely low ebb and didn't care any longer whether we lived or died. The small pack of American K rations were all we had and were not meant for extended use, and often even these didn't arrive and we were left to starve. The incessant rain meant that we were never dry and when our night stop happened to be by a stream, I used to take the opportunity to wash my clothes and put them back on again wet. I was supposedly fit, but a few weeks later when we did eventually get back to India, I spent five weeks in hospital recovering from general debility and a fever, which was never diagnosed and didn't respond to treatment. I cannot offer any clinical explanation, but my view is that whilst we were in Burma, the adrenalin was flowing and kept us going, but with the release from danger and stress, that flow stopped and our latent ills were able to manifest themselves.'

Not only had he suffered a great loss of weight due to the terrible conditions, but having trudged for hundreds of miles with a sixty pound pack on his back through the mud in the wet jungle, his feet were never dry and often covered with blood-sucking leeches which were difficult to remove. Their bites caused the leg to go septic, but he still had to march on.

Though Bill was often under fire, he had some miraculous escapes. One in particular was so remarkable that I want to relate it in his words. This happened in 1944 as he was leading a patrol and I wonder if Someone up there was listening to my fervent prayers for his safety.

'I was ordered to take out a patrol against the Japanese around a hilltop which we had just captured, and as I started out, I noticed that my men were rather edgy, so to give them confidence, I decided to go 'point' myself—that is to take the leading position and obviously the one of most danger. We passed over a small stream and ahead of me was a narrow path, climbing steadily up a gentle dead straight gradient for a hundred yards, until it turned right and was lost to view. On either side of the path, which was only a few feet wide, was thick jungle. As I could see no one ahead, I started to walk up the path, moving very cautiously with my M30 semi-automatic carbine in both hands across the front of my body with the safety catch off and my finger on the trigger guard. I had gone about eighty yards up the path, when suddenly, from my left front, a Jap sniper fired at me and missed. He reloaded in a flash and fired again and thankfully missed again, as I leapt left into the cover of the jungle. I shall never forget the sound of his rifle bolt flashing back and forth as he speedily ejected the spent cartridge case and rammed a new round into the breach for his second shot. It was so loud and clear and sounded just as if I were standing immediately behind him on the rifle range, so he must have been only a few feet away. I could tell he was a trained sniper by the great skill and speed with which he reloaded and fired again. I had seen nothing to worry me as I started along the path, so he must have been laid up in his hide all the time with an unobstructed view, with plenty of time to take careful aim, and to select the very best moment to press the trigger. To kill a British officer would have earned him a bonanza of brownie points! So why did he miss me when I was 6ft 2ins with a large frame, even though very slim at the time, standing upright and virtually unmissable, even to someone who had never used a rifle before? I hope that this does not sound pretentious, but the only reason I can think of is that God was watching over me! I have to add, that in times of great stress and danger, my simple faith has been a source of strength and encouragement.'

Every time we parted, I realised his life would be in constant danger and my heart ached for him. It was not until I was able to read what he wrote many years later about some of his experiences during that long campaign, that I realized just how lucky he was to have survived when he had been in the midst of such fierce fighting, and what terrible suffering and hardships that he and his men had been forced to endure for so long. Obviously these memories caused him pain and psychological torture even though he wasn't physically injured. How can one **ever** forget seeing their friends literally blown to pieces? There is one more incident that I feel constrained to mention because it shows yet again that God must have been watching over him.

During the course of the Chindit operation, they set up a block on the road and railway at a place, code-named "Blackpool" to prevent the Japs from supplying their forces in the Kohima battle. By this time the Japs had got the measure of the Chindits and brought in anti-aircraft armaments to shoot down the supply planes. Despite the valour of the RAF and USAAF pilots flying the Dakota supply aircraft, the Chindits were left without food and ammunition and, in close combat with the Japanese, who began to overran their position, they were forced to abandon Blackpool, leaving behind all their heavy equipment, guns mortars, the Vickers medium machine-guns and very sadly most of their precious mules. Those of their wounded who had any reasonable chance of survival, they took with them on hastily constructed bamboo stretchers, and the 'walking wounded' had to hobble along as best they could. Some of his men had been so severely wounded and near to death, they just couldn't be moved. Rather than leave them to be tortured or brutalised by the Japanese, as they were wont to do to men they captured, they were faced with no other choice than to put 19 of their grievously wounded comrades out of their suffering by shooting them.

Now with virtually no food or ammunition left and ahead of them the long hard haul over the mountains to Mokso Sakan, their position was critical as they retreated through what appeared to be a gap in the enemy lines out into a clearing in the jungle. As Bill's men were making for the cover of jungle on the other side, all hell broke loose when the Japs opened fire on them with mortars and machineguns from a ridge behind. Several of his men were hit and lay there screaming, with others lying still, probably dead. About thirty yards out in the open, Bill and his colonel Alec Harper, recognized their cipher sergeant who had also been hit and was sprawled on the ground writhing in pain. Without stopping to think of the danger, Bill and Alec rushed out to rescue him amidst all the firing. When they reached him they ignored his repeated pleas of 'Leave me sir—I'm done for!' as they dragged him back still under heavy fire, to the cover of the jungle, where Bill arranged for someone to dress the wound in his groin and organize a makeshift stretcher to be made so he could be carried along with them.

Back in India some months later, Bill unexpectedly came face-to-face with this same sergeant whom he saw hobbling about in the camp where they were both convalescing. He was certainly most grateful then that they hadn't left him on the battlefield to die, and Bill was pleased to know that the risks that they had taken in rescuing him had been worthwhile and that he was recovering from his horrendous injury.

The troops who fought in this bloody campaign called themselves 'The Forgotten Army'. They were given little credit and often the poorest supplies and equipment—and yet fought one of the fiercest and cruellest campaigns of the entire war, during which time 29 Victoria Crosses were won. After the horrendous attack on Pearl Harbour in 1941, the Japanese forces convinced that they would be victorious, swept across all the British territories in the region, capturing Malaya, Singapore, Hong Kong and then Burma. Their advance was finally halted along the border with India, during which time the Chindits operated behind the Japanese lines, as Bill describes in some of the actions in which he was involved. After the bloodiest battles at Kohimia and Imphal where the Japanese were defeated, British forces were finally able to advance against the Japanese and take back the lost territories. Three out of every five Japanese died in that campaign.

A few weeks after we had returned home from Kashmir, I was overjoyed to receive the wonderful news in a letter from Bill that he was now well enough to be discharged from hospital and hoped it would be possible for him to stay with us for a short while. In preparation for his arrival, I wanted a special gift for him and thought that he might appreciate something that had been denied him during those five months in the jungle, some pyjamas. So I visited the market and bought several yards of grey and crimson silk for our *derzi* to make up two pairs for him in grey with crimson facings. It hadn't been possible for him to let us know exactly when he would be arriving, so now I found the waiting intolerable, because of the months of uncertainty, wondering if he were dead or alive, or even if we would ever be together again. Now he was actually coming home.

One afternoon as we were sitting on the verandah enjoying afternoon tea, the bearer came to announce that the 'Major sahib' had arrived. Words cannot express my joy, relief and emotion as I rushed to see him. I wasn't the only one pleased at his return but also the rest of the family. During the short time we had all known him, he had endeared himself to us. Now we were determined to do everything possible to help him relax and forget the horrors of war. He was delighted with his luxurious pyjamas, which he said made him feel what it was like to be back in civilized society once more.

In the middle of the night we were suddenly awakened by a commotion on the verandah where Bill was sleeping. A bullock cart had rumbled past the house with its metal rimmed wheels making a loud grinding noise on the road, and Bill, thinking that he was under attack from the Japanese, had jumped out of bed to grab his rifle. After all that he had been through, he suffered from nightmares, and it took him some time to be rid of them.

We spent some happy days together. Sometimes relaxing by the swimming pool at the Calcutta Swimming Club, or visiting the famous Firpos restaurant on Chowringhee over-looking the Maidan, where we met and chatted to many other members of the forces. As our car was always available, we were often driven out to the Tolleygunge Golf Club for tea in the beautiful grounds.

One night I dressed up in an exotic evening gown because Bill wanted to take me out to the Great Eastern Hotel for a romantic candlelight dinner, and to listen to their live band. We sat there enjoying all the old melodious, nostalgic tunes of the 1930s and 40s, overwhelmed with joy and emotion, and hardly able to believe that we were actually together once again after all that Bill had been through. Being so much in love, I remember just sitting there in silence holding his hand

Calcutta Swimming Club

across the table and gazing at him through the candlelight which cast flickering shadows across his face, too thrilled to eat and wondering if it was all just a dream.

In the cool of the evening we often enjoyed a stroll on the Maidan with Thatch, and sometimes we returned to the Victoria Memorial to watch the sunset or the sunrise before breakfast. A place that brought back nostalgic memories of the day he proposed to me there early one morning before breakfast.

Those magical days passed all too soon, and Bill had hardly had time to recover from his recent ordeal when he was recalled for further active service, so sadly we had to say goodbye to each other once more. He was desperately hoping that he would be able to return to be present for my 18th birthday on September 26th, when we could officially become engaged, and had been trying to arrange for some of his friends from the regiment to be able to join us for that celebration. As the date for this special event drew near, I made plans for the party and designed and ordered a large cake from Firpos, the famous confectioners, which I wanted to be made in the shape of two large hearts entwined, pierced by a silver arrow, and a spray of red roses with Bill written on one heart, and another spray of yellow roses with Justine on the other.

Everything was ready for our special celebration, and I was thrilled and excited when Bill wrote to tell me that he had arranged to have leave and would be coming with his friends. But three days before my birthday, my heart sank as I received another letter from him to say that the military authorities had once again unexpectedly posted him to another zone of operations, so very sadly he could not attend, although his friends would still be

Our special engagement cake.

able to come to celebrate it with me. I had no idea who they were, but when they arrived I enjoyed their company, and they did their best to make it a happy occasion. Bill had asked Mike Bates (the actor who later starred in the TV comedy series 'It Ain't Half Hot Mum' as the saucy bearer '*Rangi Ram*') to act as proxy for him and put the engagement ring on my finger, which he kindly carried out in a spontaneous 'Engagement by Proxy' ceremony. Mike was the life and soul of the party with his exuberant good humour, which helped to make it a happy occasion, though Bill was sadly missed. We ate the half of the engagement cake with Bill's name on it, but I saved the other half of the heart with my name on it, with a request that they take it back to him as a love offering from me, as they expected to be joining him shortly. I thought it rather strange that Bill never mentioned receiving it in his letters to me, so asked him about this the next time we met. He seemed surprised because he knew nothing about it. When he asked them what had happened to it, they had to admit that they had eaten it all whilst on the long journey to join him.

It was sometime before we were able to meet again, because his regiment kept posting him to sort out trouble spots in different areas, but one day I was delighted to receive a letter from him telling me that he would be passing through Calcutta with the same officers that had been at my engagement party, and that he planned to visit us with them.

When they arrived, I was disappointed and puzzled to find that Bill wasn't with them again. Apparently just before their departure, he had met with a slight accident, but I was assured that it wasn't serious. They described what had happened. He had been demonstrating the use of a phosphorous grenade to his men, but it had accidentally hit something as it exploded, and he had been showered with phosphorous which had burnt off his hair and eyebrows, and pitted his face with burns. They added that he had a narrow escape and was lucky not to have been blinded by the explosion. Their assurance that the accident wasn't serious seemed like a gross understatement to me, so naturally I was most concerned. It transpired that, because he was so embarrassed by his appearance, he had asked his friends to act as an advanced 'warning party' so I would not be too shocked when he finally arrived. But I was horrified when I saw him a few days later and full of sympathy for him in his suffering.

It wasn't until years later that I discovered the real truth of what had **actually** caused that accident. In the camp where he had been stationed, flies, especially in the 'long drop' latrines, plagued everyone. Bill thought he had a good solution as to how to get rid of them. These outdoor latrines had separate cubicles with seat flaps over the holes. His plan to kill the flies was by flicking a phosphorous grenade into the void and quickly slamming the seat flap shut on top of it. This he did, but failed to appreciate that it was full of methane gas. There was an enormous explosion, and the whole of the toilet building leapt several inches in the air, as the seat flaps flew open then banged shut again. A great sheet of flame gushed out towards him, burning off his eyebrows and eyelashes and the front part of his hair. His face was spattered with specks of phosphorus, which burnt into his skin, but mercifully missed his eyes. He rushed up the hill to the Mess, where he was lucky to find the doctor who shouted for a bowl of water, and shoved Bill's face into it, then proceeded to dig the phosphorus out of his skin with a razorblade, which left his face pitted and sore. It was no wonder that he was hesitant about coming to visit me.

He certainly was very lucky not to have been blinded, and I dread to think of what could have happened to anyone had they had the misfortune to have been sitting on one of those seats in the latrine at the time. If I had realised that this disaster had been caused by such stupidity, I might not have shown him such sympathy when I saw his injuries. But it was probably punishment enough for him that he had to face all his friends in the battalion in such a shocking state. He told me that his hair took a long time to grow back again, but luckily he was not left scarred by the burns, so the next time we met I was glad to see that he was still as handsome as ever.

CHAPTER 28

RETURN TO KASHMIR

In February 1945, we planned another visit to Kashmir to escape the Hot Season. Father wasn't able to join us this time due to business commitments, so only mother, Patricia, our two dogs Thatch and Timmy and myself would be going. I wrote to Bill informing him of our plans, and hoped that he would be granted leave to join us for part of our time there. As mother had done previously, she rented the same houseboat on the Dal Lake in Srinagar for the first part of our stay, and the lovely wooden chalet in Gulmarg where we had stayed previously, for the latter part of our holiday.

Bill admiring the beautiful view.

Having been disappointed so often on previous occasions when Bill had planned to visit us only to be told that he had been ordered to go elsewhere, I dared not raise my hopes again. It had been my dearest wish that it would be possible for him to come to this corner of paradise with me, so I just lived in hope and waited. Imagine my joy when I received his letter telling me that he had been granted leave to join us.

On his arrival I was relieved to see that there was no evidence of his accident with the grenade, and that his dark wavy hair had grown back again. In spite of the fact that he had come straight from a war zone, he had made a quick recovery and looked remarkably fit and bronzed.

Bill travelled with us on that long journey from Calcutta, and I cannot remember experiencing any of the traumas or frustrations that we had suffered on the previous journey. Just being with him and in love, could probably have had something to do with it. I can only recall poor Bill suffering from carsickness on the journey from Rawalpindi to Srinagar as we wound around all those mountain hairpin bends, and that he was most apologetic and very embarrassed each time he had to ask us to stop. It was many years before any flights were available to this area, so there was no alternative to the long journey by road. All the discomforts were soon forgotten when we reached Srinagar once again and saw the beautiful houseboat as we were paddled over to it in our shikara appropriately named 'I For You-You For Me-We Shall Be Happy Together.'

In that magical setting, with the whole range of the snowy mountains reflected in the still, crystal waters of the lake, Bill was as enthralled as I was with the beauty of the place, as we sat together on the top deck of the houseboat in the sunshine, watching all the shikaras gliding by. It was so peaceful and I was pleased that he looked so relaxed and contented. I hoped this short respite with us in this wonderful place would help him to forget what he had been through and give him renewed strength to face whatever lay in store for him in the days ahead.

The weather was pleasantly warm, with sunshine every day, so we were able to enjoy magic

Thatch trying to catch fish

moments together as we were paddled around the lake and along the waterways in our shikara. Sometimes we took Thatch and Timmy with us, and it was amusing to watch our dear Thatch trying to catch the silver fish she could see as we drifted by. Once when she leant over too far she fell in, and then after we had fished her out, shook herself all over us. Some days we were paddled over to one of

the remote and beautiful islands where we picnicked in a meadow covered with many varieties of wild flowers. When the moon was full, Bill and I took the gramophone with us and listened to soothing music as we reclined on the richly embroidered drapes of the shikara, whilst the two boatmen silently dipped their heart-shaped paddles in the still waters as we glided along. There were other times when we were paddled across the lake to one of the many beautiful gardens built by the Moghul Emperors, where we spent the day wandering amidst the exotic flowers and fountains.

The Shalimar gardens in particular were one of the most beautiful. They were designed and created in 1616 by the Emperor Jahangir for his favourite wife Nur Jahan, meaning 'the light of the world.' The picturesque approach to this lovely place, with its

In a meadow full of flowers

ornate bridge at the entrance, was from the lake along a canal lined with chenar trees. These gardens had been laid out in terraces, with ornamental pools covered with lotus flowers and hundreds of fountains. They had the traditional pattern of a central channel running down through the terraces, with what appeared to be a fish-scale design, which caused the water to sparkle in the sunlight as it rippled over it. We climbed up through the terraces to the topmost terrace and wandered through a black marble pavilion where the Emperor used to entertain his ladies, known as '**The abode of Love**'. There were niches all around in the walls where flowers were placed in the daytime and flickering lights at night. As we sat there in that romantic setting, we recalled a Kashmiri love song that we had played on our gramophone.

'Pale hands I love beside the Shalimar,
Where are you now that lies beneath its spell?
Pale hands, pink tipped, like lotus buds that float
On those cool waters where we used to dwell.
I would have rather felt them round my throat
Crushing out life than waiving me farewell!'

There were many beautiful orchards in the grounds with the branches of the trees heavily laden with cherries, apples, apricots, peaches and all manner of luscious fruits. We were fascinated as we watched young boys whose duty it was to keep the birds out of their particular batch of trees, as they pulled on ropes attached to the top of them every time that a bird alighted.

We had always wanted to return to this beautiful garden once again, and one day this wish was fulfilled many years later when we were fortunate to have been present at a spectacular 'Son et Lumiere' in this magical place, which evoked so many poignant memories.

The last evening that Bill and I spent on the Pintail was memorable as we watched the sun go down behind the range of snowy mountains that lined the lake, lighting up the peaks in red and gold. There were lovely sunsets every evening but this one was even more spectacular than usual because of the cloud formations and the reflections in the waters of the lake. All along the banks of the island, the soft lights of the houseboats moored there shimmered on the still surface of the water and, every now and then, it was broken as we heard the soft swish of a paddle when a shikara glided past. A short distance away we watched as a fisherman stood poised on the tip of his bark canoe ready to spear the silvery fish as they darted past in the clear still waters. We sat on the roof deck gazing

Bill in reflective mood.

at this glorious scene until the sun disappeared behind the mountains and the full moon rose, and talked together about what we would like to do when the war was over.

I played records on our gramophone of Bing Crosby singing romantic songs, and an old recording of Nat King Cole's entitled 'Too Young', which reminded us of the day when Bill asked my parents' permission for us to become engaged, and they told us that they thought I was too young.

The following morning it was time to pack up and bid a reluctant farewell to our magnificent houseboat as we paddled back to the shore to the car that was waiting to take us on our onward journey to Gulmarg.

We drove along that picturesque route again as far as Tangmarg where the paved road ended. As there was still no navigable road for cars the rest of the way, our luggage was slung onto the backs of the pack ponies and hill coolies who climbed up the steep winding mountain track to Gulmarg, while we made that journey on horseback.

One particular memory I have of that ride which astounded me, was when I passed a coolie struggling up that very steep track carrying an upright piano slung across his back held by a broad band across his forehead. He would be taking it several miles to Gulmarg, which was still inaccessible to any traffic. I often saw the coolies carrying unbelievably heavy weights, and marvelled at their incredible strength. They were all quite small men, probably not much taller than about 5ft, neither did they appear to be powerfully built but must have had the stamina required to do this. I was concerned to see that several of them had such large goitres on their necks, some were even as large as tennis balls, and I wondered how they were able to work like that. For such heavy

Happy days together in Gulmarg

labour, they only earned a few rupees for each load, but that small amount of money made all the difference between eating and starving.

We were glad to have been able to rent Hut 57, which was the same beautiful chalet that we had stayed in on our previous visit. It was the one with the best position surrounded by meadows full of flowers and the breathtaking views of the great, snow-covered mountain range across the plains hundreds of feet below. Being Bill's first visit, he was astounded by the grandeur and beauty all around us.

In the evenings as it grew chilly, we sat around a log fire after enjoying a sumptuous meal prepared by our khansama, and listened to records while we planned what we would do the next

Ready for the horse race with Bill

day. Bill and I loved riding, so we often hired horses to ride through the pine forests and tracks that wound around the mountains. I remember one frightening experience I had when we hired two beautiful thoroughbred horses and decided to race each other across the meadow. We set off at a gallop, and as we approached a broad shallow stream, I had expected my horse to gallop through it as Bill's horse had done, but was taken by surprise when he jumped it in one mighty leap. Thankfully, I managed to stay on, but as Bill hadn't seen this, he wondered why I looked so worried when I caught up with him. Even though it was an unnerving experience, I had enjoyed the ride.

Apharawat at an altitude 14,500 feet, was the highest mountain that overlooked Gulmarg. One day the four of us decided to climb it. It was pleasantly warm with clear blue skies, so we hired horses to ride up the steep mountain track to the Khillanmarg meadow, which lay 2,000 ft above Gulmarg below the mountain, where we left the horses to await our return.

After enjoying a picnic spread in the meadow full of alpine flowers, we started the climb on foot along a steep winding track. When we reached the snow, the climb became tougher and we needed many rest stops to recover our breath. It took us over four hours to reach the top but, after the gruelling climb, we were rewarded with magnificent views in every direction. It was as if we were on 'the roof of the world'. As we wandered around the summit in the sunshine enjoying the amazing scenery, I noticed a long sloping ravine that ended in the meadow far below us.

There were two men at the top of it with toboggans available for hire. As the climb had been so steep and slippery, I suggested we might slide down on these instead of making the difficult descent on foot. Mother didn't like the idea at all and warned us it could be

Racing down the ravine

dangerous, but as Patricia and Bill were also willing to take the risk, we paid the men a few rupees and climbed onto the sleds. I sat behind Bill on one toboggan with my arms around his waist and, with Patricia on the other, we set off gathering momentum as we raced down the icy slope and kept going until we reached the meadow, twenty minutes later, where we had left our horses. As I look back, it was a crazy thing to do, but we were young and full of the 'joie de vivre', and it was an exciting experience. We had left mother on the summit where she had met some friends who agreed to escort her back to our cabin. We rode back the 6 km route through the pine forests to our cabin, and were pleased to find that a cheery log fire had been lit to warm us up again. When mother arrived later that evening, she was relieved to see we had returned safely, but when we told her what an amazing experience it had been, I think she wished that she had joined us.

Our time spent together in that beautiful place was filled with so many wonderful experiences, and I was happy that on this occasion Bill had been able to be with me there to share them.

As our holiday was soon coming to an end, Bill and I decided to take one last ride and climb to the top of a snowy range. As it would be a long day ride, we arose very early, and with a picnic packed in our saddlebags, we set off accompanied by our two *syces* to show us the way. Through the pine trees, we caught glimpses of the sunrise on the snowy mountains, as they turned from pale gold to flaming orange. The air was cool and crisp as we rode along the trail beside a sparkling mountain stream, and all around us was the sound of the dawn chorus as the birds awakened. Every now and then the vista opened to show the whole of the Vale of Kashmir, thousands of feet below stretching over to the Pinjal range with Nanga Parbat, the highest mountain, towering above the rest of them. It was so peaceful and, from what I remember, we seemed to be the only people on the trail that day. When we reached the top the view was even more wonderful. We stood there marvelling at the beauty that surrounded us—an unforgettable memory, which we still treasure.

CHAPTER 29

SEAC SECRET CYPHERS

All too soon the day arrived for us to leave this corner of paradise and return to the heat and noise of Calcutta. So once again we had to part, and each time it became harder, because neither of us had any idea of when or whether we would ever see each other again. Everywhere people were suffering the same heartache because of the war, which was a time for so many sad goodbyes. I quote a few lines from a poignant song sung by Robbie Williams, which expressed these sentiments, called 'Every Time We Say Goodbye'.

> Every time we say goodbye
> I die a little.
> Every time we say goodbye,
> I wonder why a little…?

Sadly for Bill, he had received orders to rejoin his battalion and sail to Rangoon, then proceed to Mingaladon to train for **Operation Zipper**, which was planned for the seaborne invasion of Malaya. If this operation had taken place, then certainly many more thousands of our servicemen, and possibly Bill, would have been killed, but because of the dropping of the atomic bombs in August 1945, and Japan's capitulation, it was mercifully cancelled. Bill was sent to Singapore instead.

When Britain was forced to surrender Singapore to the Japs in February 1942, they had captured thousands of our troops and thrown them into the infamous Changi Jail. Many of them had been forced to work on the 'Railway of Death' (depicted in the film 'The Bridge on the River Kwai') where terrible atrocities were committed against them, and where they were forced to work in inhumane conditions even when they were sick and starving. As a result many thousands of them suffered and died.

Bill sets off again

The day after the surrender of the Japanese, Bill had boarded the HMT 'Egret' and embarked on a twenty-day voyage to Singapore, where one of his tasks was to find an island where there was water, and where the Japanese prisoners of war could be taken as an interim staging post before being shipped back to Japan. While he was there, his men also had the joy of releasing from Changi Jail men of their 2nd battalion who had been taken prisoner in 1942. After he had completed this assignment, he was sent on to Surabaya in Java, setting sail on the HMT **Islamic** on October 30th 1945 to clear up a messy and very bloody situation, which had arisen there.

When he left me after that wonderful holiday in Kashmir, I had feared that he would be returning to more dangerous assignments, so once more I was left worrying if he would ever come through it all alive. The only way we could keep in touch was by letter, so all I could do was to pray that God would keep him safe and continue writing to him every day, but as he was being moved around continually from place to place, I wondered if he would ever receive any of them. It was a tense time for us when once again he was thrown into the thick of the fighting. I later discovered what a horrendous experience it was for him when he reached Surabaya.

It was after the Chindits had been disbanded and Bill had then joined 123 Brigade in the 5th Indian Division that he was sent to Surabaya. It was to take it over from the Japanese and also to arrange for the release and repatriation of the prisoners of war and the Dutch civilian internees. Another brigade had gone earlier, expecting a peaceful takeover, but were surprised when they arrived and found themselves confronted by many thousands of irregular troops who had been armed with modern weapons by the Japanese and who were intent on gaining independence from the Dutch. Brigade outposts and guards throughout the town were overwhelmed and massacred, and their commander, Brigadier Mallaby, was also murdered whilst endeavouring to negotiate with the insurgents. As Bill's boat arrived at the docks, he and his men were horrified and angered when they saw the dead bodies of their own men floating down the Kali Mas canal, which flowed through the town. Now they were given the most dangerous and difficult task of retaking the town, which was in a state of chaos.

Their first priority was to release the 2,000 Allied prisoners and Dutch civilians that had been held in the Kale Sosok Jail, which was being guarded by the insurgents. As Bill and his fellow officer, Lieut. Jim Vicary, approached the front gate of the prison, a rebel leant out of a window and shot at them. The bullet hit Jim, wounding him badly. (This injury left him with a paralysed left arm for the rest of his life). A fierce battle then ensued before they managed to take over the jail and release all those people who had suffered so much for so long. It took a further twenty days of bloody fighting to take possession of the whole town, and thankfully Bill once more miraculously survived all those battles, in an operation, which he said was the most unpleasant of his military service, because it involved the civilian population.

In contrast, one of his more pleasant tasks was in the Surabaya Zoo, where he let all the starving animals that he felt would pose no threat to the population, out of their cages to forage for themselves, and tried to arrange for the more dangerous ones still in captivity to be fed.

After this operation, he was posted back to Malaya to a place called Khota Bahru, in the far north-eastern part of the country. I found it impossible to keep track of his whereabouts because of his frequent movements, but we did our best to continue to keep in touch by letters, which usually arrived weeks after they were written. We were being forced to part so often, and each time it became harder to bear. We were never able to talk together over the phone, because there weren't any. All we had to comfort us were our letters, our hopes and our prayers, and anyone who hasn't been through this experience themselves can never know the worry, heartache and anguish that we both suffered at that time.

After returning to Calcutta from Kashmir, Patricia and I were offered 'top secret' jobs by the South East Asia Command (SEAC) with high salaries. I felt I should do more towards helping to win the war, so exchanged my pretty dresses for a khaki uniform. The job that I was given was in the department of Secret Intelligence, decoding secret ciphers. I found this very interesting and sometimes exciting, especially when I decoded a top-secret message on July 31st 1945, which read:

'A secret device is about to be used against the Japanese within one week, which it is believed will end the war in the Far East'.

Naturally I was curious as to what this meant, but at the same time elated, because I hoped it would mean that Bill wouldn't have to fight any more and be free to return to me. But this was not to be. That secret device turned out to be the **atom bomb** that was dropped on Hiroshima on August 6th 1945, exactly a week after I decoded that message. The second atom bomb was dropped on Nagasaki three days later on August 9th. This so surprised and terrified the Japanese as they realized what might happen to their other cities, that they surrendered on August 15th.

Even after this surrender there was a mammoth task ahead for SEAC to sort out, one of which was the operation in Surabaya, just mentioned, and also to repatriate troops, and deal with the areas where trouble still existed. Consequently, I remained at my job for a further period.

It was during this time that I violated the strict security code that was in operation for entering and leaving the building where I was working. This place was situated in a densely populated area of Calcutta, and overlooked a very busy road with heavy traffic. One day when I heard someone shouting loudly and looked through the window, I saw a man whipping his horse which had stopped, as it was unable to go any further. As I looked more closely, I saw the reason for this. It was harnessed to a loaded refuse cart, and one of its legs was swollen and so badly infected that it was impossible for it to bear any weight on it, let alone pull a cart. The poor animal's body was covered with white sweat and it was frothing at the mouth, so it must have been in great pain. I was aware that once I had entered the building, under strict security surveillance, we were not permitted to leave it without being checked again, but I was so incensed by what I had seen that I rushed past the guards out into the street without stopping to think of the consequences. Dodging the heavy traffic, I ran over to the cart and ordered him in Urdu to get off and un-harness the horse, but because he proceeded to give me excuses as to why he couldn't do this, I grabbed his whip and hit him with it and told him I would call the police and have him arrested. He was so scared by what I had done, that he jumped off his cart and ran away, leaving me to deal with his cart and the injured horse, all by myself. In the meantime all the traffic had stopped, and the drivers who had witnessed what happened were staring at me in amazement, but no one offered to help. There was no alternative but to un-harness the poor animal myself. Whilst I attempted to do this, the drivers in their vehicles further down the road who couldn't see the reason for a hold up, were tooting their horns. My hasty action had caused chaos. Because the cart was so heavily laden, I had great difficulty in releasing the horse from the shafts, but after struggling for some time, I eventually succeeded and led the poor, limping animal slowly through the traffic into the garden where I tied it up in the shade. After giving it some water to drink and hosing it down, I cleansed the gash on its leg that was covered with flies.

Fortunately at that time there was a very efficient RSPCA run by the British, so I was able to summon a horse ambulance to take it to the veterinary hospital where it would be treated and given the chance to recover. The cart remained there for the next few days, still causing a problem for the traffic, and every now and then when the wind was blowing in my direction, the stench of the garbage that was rotting in the great heat, wafted through the window to remind me of a very unpleasant incident. As expected, I was severely reprimanded for breaking the strict security regulations that were in force at the time, but I felt that my actions had been totally justified.

Throughout my life I have loved animals and cared passionately about all living creatures. Tragic sights in India like this, amongst the animals and especially amongst the poor people, surround you wherever you go, so whenever it was possible I felt I must help them. I once saw a pariah dog foaming at the mouth running round in circles that was obviously suffering from rabies, whilst a crowd of Indians stood around it helplessly looking on. Fortunately I could call the authorities at that time to deal with it. But I have returned to India on several occasions since then and been saddened when I have still seen the suffering there, but being a visitor, have been unable to do anything about it.

CHAPTER 30

COMMUNAL STRIFE

For generations there had always been strife and rivalry between India's Hindu and Muslim communities, but on August 16th 1946 it erupted into savage violence. It centred on Calcutta, the second city of the British India, which had a reputation for violence and cruelty, with the story of the Black Hole, which had been a painful memory to generations of Englishmen and a reminder of the savagery that the Indians had been capable of at that time. The slums of Calcutta contained the densest concentration of poor human beings in the world with interlaced Hindu and Moslem neighbourhoods, where there was ever rising tension.

At dawn on that day, howling Muslim mobs came bursting from their slums, waving iron bars, shovels, *lathis*, (heavy-weighted bamboo canes) or any other instrument that was capable of smashing a human skull, to beat to a pulp any Hindu in their path. The terrified police could do nothing to stop the carnage, so simply disappeared, and the murdered bodies of the victims were left lying in the gutters of the streets for days afterwards. Soon pillars of black smoke could be seen rising all over the city as the Muslims burnt the various Hindu bazaars. My father witnessed some of these tragic sights and told us about the chaos that followed these awful events.

It wasn't long before the Hindu mobs came out in revenge, looking for defenceless Muslims to slaughter. In one part of Chowringhee, a line of poor Muslim rickshaw coolies lay beaten to death where a Hindu mob had found them sleeping between the shafts of their rickshaws during the night. Never, in all its violent history, had Calcutta known twenty-four hours as savage and packed with such human viciousness. There were as many as six thousand savagely mutilated corpses lying all over the city, rotting in the great heat. It was not long before the vultures found them and moved in to feast. The terrible sight of hundreds more bloated bodies could be seen bobbing down the Hooghly River towards the sea. It had all erupted so fast that the City Corporation was faced with what appeared to be an insurmountable problem. My father was so incensed that he took his cine camera out into the streets to record some of this devastation. (I believe this film is now stored in the archive library of the BBC.)

This carnage became known as the Great Calcutta Killings and changed the course of India's history. The Moslem League had declared August 16th as Direct Action Day, to prove to Britain and the Congress Party that India's Muslims were prepared to get Pakistan for themselves by 'direct action' if necessary. It was Mohammed Ali Jinnah, their leader, who vowed that day: 'We shall have India divided or we shall have India destroyed.'

These terrible events sickened Mahatma Gandhi as it had also triggered bloodshed in Noakhali, where he was living at the time, and had spread as far as Bombay on the other side of India. He now had the awful vision of seeing the whole country embroiled in civil war, so made up his mind to embark on a Pilgrimage of Penance to the forty-seven separate Muslim and Hindu villages of Noakhali, where there had been so much violence and killing. In an effort to make peace between them he decided to walk the 116 miles barefoot, as a sign of his penitence. So on New Year's Day, four and a half months after the tragedy in Calcutta, he set off on the walk at the age of seventy seven, with his favourite nineteen-year-old grandniece Manu and four of his followers, determined 'to rekindle the lamp of neighbourliness' amongst them.

For seven weeks he endured hardship, rejection and even attempts on his life by sabotage, preaching non-violence amongst the enraged Hindu and Muslim villagers and setting the example of meekness by showing them basic hygiene methods, and even cleaning out their latrines. In every village he held an open prayer meeting inviting Muslims to join, when he was careful to recite verses from their Koran as well in part of the service. In this way he was helping them understand his message and the inflamed Muslims gradually began to let the terrified Hindus return to their homes.

So much has already been written about Gandhi that I may be in danger of repeating it but, because my father became a close friend of his during that tempestuous period that led up to the granting of Independence to India, I feel the need to include all that I know about him.

Mohandas Karamchand Gandhi was born to wealthy parents in 1869 in the South Indian city of Porbandar at Kirti Mandir. Although Gandhi, a Hindu, was destined to become India's greatest spiritual leader of modern times, he was not born into the high Brahman caste, but into the Vaisyas caste that were shopkeepers and tradesmen. When his father died, Gandhi was sent to England at the age of nineteen to study law in the hopes that he would be able to return to India to become prime minister of a princely state. As a result, he was pronounced an outcast from his own caste, because his Hindu elders believed that by crossing the seas it would leave him contaminated.

He was miserable in the sophisticated world of the Inns of Court and being barely five foot tall and painfully thin, he was sometimes mistaken for the errand boy. He decided that he had to change his image by buying a new wardrobe, and hiring an elocution teacher in an effort to set himself up as an English gentleman. That idea proved unsuccessful, so he completed his studies and, after he had been called to the bar, he returned to Bombay to practice law.

He tried desperately to find a case to plead, but failed to impress any of the magistrates in the courts of Bombay. This failure led to the first great turning point in Gandhi's life, when his family decided to send him to sort out a legal problem of a relative in South Africa.

In May 1893 Gandhi disembarked in South Africa, and a week later, dressed in the smart clothes of a London Inner Temple barrister and holding a first-class ticket on an overnight train to Pretoria, he was ordered out of the carriage by a white man who refused to share the same compartment because he was coloured. When he refused to leave, the guard threw him off the train at the next stop, and he was left there alone in the dark all night. This experience changed his way of thinking, and made him resolve to stand up for his rights in the future. He was so incensed by what had happened that he addressed a group of Pretoria's Indians urging them to unite to defend their interests and encouraged them all to learn English. He also managed to get the railway authorities to allow any well-dressed Indian to travel in a first or second-class compartment in the future. Throughout the years that he lived there he encouraged the many Indian settlers to oppose apartheid by passive resistance.

Mohandas (later known as Mahatma) Gandhi returned to India in 1915 after practising as a lawyer in South Africa for twenty years, to find India in a state of revolt against the British. He had arrived there at a time when the British parliament was giving the Indian courts powers to try political cases without a jury and also to imprison politicians without trial. This legislation so upset him that, to mark his protest, he called for *hartal*, (a day of mourning) when all activity had to cease for a day right across India. Unfortunately, all the protesters were not silent and started riots, the worst being in Amritsar where a vast crowd became trapped in an area with only one exit.

In an effort to restore order, General Dyer's troops were ordered to fire into the unarmed crowd, killing 379 people and wounding another 1,200. This notorious act set the anti-British feelings aflame and riots broke out across the whole of India. Gandhi then initiated a movement of non co-operation against the British and was thrown into jail.

From now onwards throughout his life he was a 'thorn in the flesh' of the British administration, because of his extremist views and the various protest movements of non co-operation, albeit non-violent, that he initiated. It was during his time in South Africa that he first began to experiment with his ideas of the simple life and helping the oppressed and the underdog. He had studied the life of John Ruskin, and read his book 'Unto This Last', and had been influenced by what he read. (We had stayed in the home of this great man, when our parents first brought us to England to leave us there in boarding school).

In March 1930, Gandhi organized a march in protest against the British Raj's monopoly of the production and sale of salt, and set off on foot with 80 of his followers who were made up of Muslims, Hindus and Harijans (Gandhi's Untouchables). This attracted large crowds along the 320km route to the sea, where they collected and boiled seawater to make salt. This act also provoked widespread demonstrations and, as a result Gandhi was imprisoned once again without a trial. Before he entered the prison, he managed to send a message to his followers;

'The honour of India has been symbolized by a fistful of salt in the hand of a man of non-violence. The fist which held the salt may be broken, but it will not yield up its salt.'

There was such widespread support for his movement that Lord Irwin, who was the Viceroy at this time, felt obliged to release him from prison in February 1931 and invite him to the Viceregal Lodge in New Delhi for a conference on the future of India. When Winston Churchill heard about it, he was so incensed that he made a speech in the House of Commons in which he referred to Gandhi as 'that half-naked fakir', as he visualized Gandhi walking up the steps of the Viceroy's palace in his loincloth to negotiate with the representative of the King Emperor.

Gandhi. A sketch created by Sian Rosumand.

This was the turning point in the independence movement, so that after he was released the following year, and as the acknowledged leader of the Indian masses, he renewed his efforts to strive for a united India, free from British colonialism.

Although he looked such a frail, emaciated and insignificant human being, he had a powerful charisma that attracted the masses that gave him the title of Mahatma ('Great Soul') and was much loved by them, and especially by the people who knew him and were his devoted followers. Although he was a Hindu, he had been educated in a convent, so knew all about Christianity, but embraced all religions. All the same, he held some strange beliefs and even stranger habits, one of which was that it was beneficial to one's health to give yourself a daily salt-water enema. Another was practicing yoga while standing on his head. In spite of his odd ideas, he had a clever way of getting what he wanted by threatening to embark on 'a fast to death' and, because he was such a powerful leader and had such wide influence amongst the politicians and other important people in high office, his threats were taken seriously, so had the desired effect.

In 1921 he gave up his western style of dress and donned the homespun dhoti, which was worn by poor Indian villagers whom he encouraged to take up spinning. He then committed himself to improving the status of the outcastes, whom he called Harijans ('Children of God'). These were the poorest of the poor, and there were millions of them right across India, who were born outside the caste system and therefore were without any status whatsoever, and would remain so throughout their lives as 'Untouchables.' In the 1930s they constituted a sixth of India's population believing that they were condemned by their sins in a previous incarnation to a casteless existence. They stood out from the masses with their dark skin and ragged clothing. If a Hindu came into the slightest contact with one, it would stain his caste, which could only be removed by a ritual purifying bath. It is hard to comprehend, but a caste Hindu believed that should even the shadow or the footprints of an Untouchable cross his path, he could be defiled. In some parts of India these poor people were only allowed to leave their hovels at night and were known as 'Invisibles'. In 1922 Gandhi made their cause his cause, and to thwart a political reform he feared would permanently institutionalise their separateness from Indian society, he embarked on a fast that nearly killed him.

Gandhi had set about this enormous task by example, when he went from village to village, teaching basic hygiene, cleaning their toilets or digging new ones. He chose to live in the slums with the villagers and a few of his devoted disciples, and always travelled in crowded and uncomfortable third-class train compartments, taking his message to the towns and villages across India. Wherever he went crowds rushed to see 'The Great Soul'. To them his humility, voluntary poverty, and his saintly air, made him like a holy man who could unite India and liberate it from the yoke of British rule.

Gandhi with a little beggar child.
Photo by the author.

Gandhi had always had a dream of creating a modern India that would be a living example to Asia and the rest of the world. He did not base his dream of his social ideals on an industrial and technological society, but on the thousands of villages across India that he wanted to become self-sufficient units. He also wanted to close down the textile mills and replace them with his spinning wheel, to give work to the unemployed and return to the old simplicity in a classless society. With the prospect of independence fast approaching, these ideals had become an embarrassment to his friend Nehru and other members in the Congress Party who wanted the very things that Gandhi was opposed to.

In March 1942, when the Japanese Army was threatening to invade India, Churchill sent an offer to the Congress party, over which Gandhi had a powerful influence, pledging to give India independence and dominion status after the War, but it contained recognition of the Muslim League's desire for an Islamic state, which was not acceptable to Gandhi's idea of a united India. So he decided that, as Britain would not give India its freedom at once, he would start a 'Quit India' campaign, which landed him and all his Congress leaders, including Pandit Nehru in jail, where some of them remained for the rest of the War. But Gandhi's followers continued to make life difficult for the British, especially in Calcutta.

During all the years I lived in India, I had been able to go anywhere on my own feeling totally safe, and wherever I went the local population had always shown me respect, but now the mood was sadly changing and noisy mobs were creating trouble and shouting 'British Quit India'. Our own servants remained totally loyal to us and were grieved by what was going on, especially after hearing what happened to me one day.

I often used to ride my bicycle when I went to shop in the New Market nearby, visit the hospital at the end of our road, or help at the WVS (Women's Voluntary Service) troops' canteen a short distance away, as I felt it was quite safe to do so. As I was cycling down the busy Chowringhee to return home one afternoon, a young Indian man came up to cycle parallel with me and, without any warning, he shot out his arm and shoved me violently off my bicycle, causing me to fall heavily onto the filthy road amidst the heavy traffic, as he shouted 'Quit India!' I was very lucky not to have been run over. It happened so quickly that he was gone before I knew it. In a state of shock, bruised, battered and grazed, I somehow managed to cycle back home to mother, who was horrified when she saw the state I was in, and indignant at what had happened. She found it hard to believe that anyone should have felt such animosity towards a young English girl. After this happened, Patricia and I were driven everywhere in our car which was always available for our use. But the changing attitude towards the British was evident everywhere. In the 'old days' when you walked down Chowringhee amongst a crowd of Indians, they would make way for you on the pavement out of respect, but as the 'Quit India' movement grew in momentum, it was **you** who would have to move out of **their** way, or you could be jostled. For the British, having lived happily and peacefully amongst the local population for generations, these were sad and worrying times, and it forced us to consider how much longer it would be safe for us to continue to live in India.

To add to all the tension, there was growing unrest again amongst the Hindu and Muslim communities. The slaughter that began in Calcutta 1946 was only an extension of what had been going on between these two communities for years. The most terrible atrocities were still being committed right across India, especially in Calcutta. During a riot one day, one of the religious groups took their captured victims to the Howrah Bridge and decapitated them. The group then threw their bodies into the Hooghly River, which became choked with the dead, and you could see the sickening sight of the vultures feeding off them as they floated down the river. But there were also other terrible sights all over the city of massacred Hindus and Muslims still lying in the streets for days after every riot, causing a grave risk of spreading disease. The problem seemed too great for either the police or the Calcutta Corporation to deal with.

My father was so distraught at what he saw that he joined the European Group in The House of Representatives in an effort to improve the situation. He was subsequently chosen to be their speaker. He had lived and worked in India for over forty years and, during that time, had grown to love the country and its people, so was well suited for this formidable task.

In Calcutta where the Muslim and Hindu communities lived in such poverty and close proximity to each other it would always be a place that was rife for communal strife. Almost anything, even a rumour, could spark off a riot and, before the police could take action, hundreds would be slaughtered in cold blood. Since the killings perpetrated on Direct Action Day in 1946, the tension between the two communities had not abated, so that riots and slaughter still continued. Gandhi was well aware of this and felt constrained to come to Calcutta to try and stop it. With a small group of his devoted disciples, and his faithful grand-nieces Manu and Abha, he arrived at a crumbling old mansion that had been lent to him at 151 Hydari House, Belgachia Road, in the heart of Calcutta. The news of his arrival soon spread, and before long leaders of both the communities were invited to his house to try and find a way to stop the violence. Through his leadership in the Central Peace Committee and his wise counsel, he managed to form a local group who agreed to become members of this committee, which consisted of ten Muslim and ten Hindu leaders who, with Gandhi, would seek to work out a way to get their message of peace across to the masses. Gandhi wanted to have a European on this special committee, so requested my father to visit him and join it. When he arrived, Gandhi greeted him warmly and called for a chair, which my father declined, choosing to sit on the floor with him as they discussed the problem. He was puzzled as to why he had been chosen by Gandhi to help in such a momentous task and, on one of his many visits to attend the committee meetings, father had a private interview with him and put forward this question. He was surprised at the answer that followed:

'In any discussions concerning the Peace Committee, all the members must have truth in their hearts. I have heard that you are a committed Christian, and as such I am sure that God will guide you to help us make the right decisions in the difficult task that lies before us. I have a Bible here and this book is my vade mecum, and I have learned all my teachings from that book, and seek to follow the teachings of Jesus Christ, especially from Christ's Sermon on the Mount where he said 'Blessed are the peacemakers, for they shall be called the children of God. Blessed are the merciful for they shall obtain mercy.'

As the committee met often to discuss ways to resolve their problems, a great spirit of friendship built up between Gandhi, my father, and the two groups who had initially been so opposed to each other. It was agreed that a rally be held on the Maidan and invitations were sent to all the important dignitaries and government officials in Calcutta to hear Gandhi making a speech calling for peace to be made between the Hindus and Muslims. Gandhi asked father if he could suggest a rallying slogan for them to chant at this meeting. Father thought about this for a few moments then suggested '*Hindu aur Musulman ek ho*' (Hindus and Muslims be one) which pleased Gandhi, who thought it appropriate, and the rest of the committee were happy to adopt.

On the chosen date, an enormous *shamyana* (marquee) was erected at a central and very busy site at the end of Chowringhee on the Maidan by the Ochterlony monument, with seating for the hundreds of people who had been invited. In front of this was a high platform from which the speeches would be made. Father recorded this special occasion on his 16mm cine camera and entered the following in his diary.

'Thousands of Muslims and Hindus were assembling to show their desire to end the strife in Calcutta. As Gandhi mounted the platform with Manu and Abha standing on each side of him, a cheer went up from the vast crowd. When it had subsided Manu read some verses from the Koran, (the Mohammedan's holy book, through loudspeakers, followed by verses from the Shastras, the Hindu's religious books, and recited by Abha. By this act of reading the Shastras and Koran, the idea was to show religious acceptance, an important asset to such a meeting. Then Gandhi made an impassioned speech to the masses, telling them that if they continued to kill each other and could not agree to live in peace together, he would embark on 'a fast to death.' Then the twenty members of the Peace Committee joined him on the platform and in unison started chanting the slogan '***Hindu aur Musulman ek ho***'. The crowd then took up the chant. After the rally ended, bands of right-thinking Hindus and Muslims went about chanting the slogan, and the city enjoyed a period of peace for a time.'

When my father was a Councillor of the Calcutta Corporation, he was asked if he would accept the Chairmanship of the Vigilance Committee, which had been established in an effort to control bribery and corruption, and improve the public services within the city. Whilst willing to serve, he was puzzled as to why they had chosen him, being a European, when all the other members were Indians. But as he had been elected by a unanimous vote he agreed to stand. In this capacity, he managed with the help of his fellow members to bring fresh water stand-pipes to the market places and crowded back-alleys, whereas before all they had was dirty polluted water. Another terrible eyesore and health risk, were the large open communal dustbins in all the streets of the city. These were gradually removed and replaced by house-to-house collections.

For years, the Calcutta Corporation had tried to ban the hundreds of rickshaws that were pulled by men who would run for miles in the heat and dust amongst the heavy traffic. The rickshaws weren't owned by these rickshaw *wallahs*, but by their bosses to whom they had to pay about 90% of their takings. Because they were responsible for the rickshaws, the poor men would never part from them, so at night when they weren't pulling someone along, you would see them sleeping by the side of the road between the shafts. They worked day and night for a mere pittance in order to survive. Even during the monsoon with the heavy rain lashing down on them, you would see them stripped to the waist, struggling to pull their heavily laden rickshaws through the flooded streets. For some reason I believe that Calcutta was the only city unable to remove them from the streets, whereas in other cities they were replaced by cycle rickshaws, and more recently by the noisy three-wheeled motorised '*tuk-tuks*'.

CHAPTER 31

HOME RULE

On the morning of March 24th 1947, Lord Louis Mountbatten mounted the viceregal throne in the Viceroy House, New Delhi, to become the twentieth and final Viceroy of India. He had been sent out from London to take over from Lord Wavell, and given the momentous task of handing over to India the Home Rule and Independence for which they had agitated for so long. But when he arrived he found a country that was in turmoil with violence everywhere and he knew that unless he could act quickly the country could be on the verge of civil war. He soon discovered that the Congress Party, with Jawaharlal Nehru as its leader and Ali Jinnah as the leader of the Moslem League, were so opposed to each other that they wouldn't come together in discussion and, if the proposed negotiations fell apart, he would have to assume the terrible responsibility of exercising rule over one fifth of humanity.

Mountbatten had a vision, together with Nehru and Gandhi, of a united India, but Jinnah had always wanted to create the state of Pakistan, and it was this wish, which caused the dilemma that now faced Mountbatten. He invited each one of them individually for discussions to Viceregal House, and after deliberating with them for several days, sadly came to the decision that **there was no other solution than to divide India.** The terrible tragedies that followed that momentous decision are now history and too awful to dwell upon. The irony of it all was that **if** Mountbatten, Gandhi and Nehru had known at that time about a closely guarded secret, that Jinnah had tuberculosis and was a very sick man and that he would soon die, it might have been possible to delay the hand-over of power for a little longer, which could possibly have saved the lives and displacement of millions of so many poor people, and changed the course of history.

To nearly all the British, including our family, the idea of partition was a horrifying thought that could only bring disaster to India and all of us who had made our home there. Strife, murder, displacement of millions and the grief that would be caused by this would be inevitable, and make the task that Mountbatten had been sent to India to accomplish, even more difficult.

In those last days before the handover of power, there was another thing that greatly troubled Mountbatten. It was what would happen in Calcutta at the stroke of midnight as the day of granting India its independence dawned on August 15th 1947. It had acquired the reputation of being the most violent city in India, and he feared that, even if he had sent a vast army of soldiers to keep the peace there, they would have been unable to do this. As he pondered on what should be done, he decided to send Gandhi there instead. He felt that perhaps he alone could achieve by his presence, the force of his personality and his non-violent ideals, what the army would be unable to do, so Mountbatten pleaded with him to remain there at this momentous time. But Gandhi had already resolved to return to his village of Noakhali to pray and fast, and try to protect his people there from the violence that was sure to erupt when independence was granted.

On the eve of Gandhi's departure from Calcutta for Noakhali, he had an unexpected visit from a man by the name of Surhawardy, who was the leader of the Muslims in the city. This was the same rogue who had organized the killings in Calcutta on Jinnah's Direct Action Day in August 1946, and the same man who in 1942 had diverted all that grain to the black market during the time thousands were suffering and dying as a result of the disastrous Bengal famine. Now he had rushed to Gandhi to beg him to stay in the city, as he believed that only he could save his fellow Muslims from the inevitable violence and slaughter he expected.

Gandhi sensed Surhawadys' genuine concern for his followers, and told him that he would only stay if he agreed to two conditions. Firstly, that he would have to give a solemn undertaking that all the Hindus would be kept safe from the Muslims in Noakhali, and that if a single Hindu was killed, he would fast to death, and the responsibility for this would be thrust on Surhawardy. The second condition was that he would have to give up his extravagant lifestyle in the city and come to live with him in a sordid slum of Calcutta, and that they would remain there together day and night unarmed and unprotected by any guards. Surhawardy realized that he had no other choice but to accept these terms.

News had spread of Gandhi's resolve to stay in Calcutta to keep the peace in the city and the reasons behind Surhawardy's sojourn with Gandhi. As the day approached, a great procession of Hindus and Muslims marched to Hydari House to see the little man who with his saintly presence might check the violence that was expected to erupt there on Independence Day.

When the day dawned thousands of Hindus and Moslems stood there awaiting his appearance on his prayer platform. When he appeared he spoke to them:

'Everybody is showering congratulations on me for the miracle that Calcutta is witnessing, but let us thank God for his abundant mercy, and not forget that there are still isolated spots in Calcutta where all is not well.' And he asked all the Hindus and Muslims to join him in prayer that 'the miracle of Calcutta would not prove to be a momentary outburst of passion.'

The crowds down Belgachia Road and around his house increased as the day wore on, clamouring for a view of Gandhi, so that every half hour he had to interrupt his meditation and his spinning to come out to speak to them from the platform that had been erected in front of his house. He congratulated them on what they had achieved in Calcutta, and hoped that their noble example might inspire their countrymen in the Punjab. It was there where the worst of the atrocities were being committed. After Gandhi had finished speaking, Suhrawardy, looking strained and fearful, addressed the vast crowd of Hindus and Muslims asking them to set their seal upon their reconciliation by joining him in crying out 'Jai Hind' (Victory to India.) There was a thundering roar from the crowd as they chanted these words. After this, the two of them got into

Gandhi's old car for a tour of the city, and as it made its way slowly through the crowds, they were greeted with cries of 'Gandhiji you have saved us' and they were showered with marigold petals.

Day after day Gandhi made his way to the Maidan where he held his regular evening prayer meetings, and each day the crowd that attended grew bigger. They came there in a spirit of friendship towards each other, with the eyes of the world upon them. One newspaper reported that 'The miracle of Calcutta had held and the city was the wonder of India.' Mountbatten wrote to him saying, 'In the Punjab, we have a military force of 55,000 unsuccessfully trying to keep the peace and there is still rioting, but in Bengal our force consists of **one man** and, as the last viceroy, I humbly ask to be allowed to pay tribute to my **One Man Boundary Force'**. But Gandhi still refused to accept the credit for what he had done.

Though there was mass rejoicing in New Delhi when Mountbatten presided at the special ceremony to declare home rule for India on the stroke of midnight, sadly elsewhere across that vast continent, instead of the rejoicing there were riots, brutal mass murders, looting, rape, terror, the burning of peoples homes, the list was endless. And the tragedy of it all was because of the partition of India that **Jinnah had insisted upon**. The scale of the carnage was so great, that neither the police nor the army were able to cope with it and restore peace or keep order.

In Calcutta on that same day when India was granted Home Rule, there was peaceful rejoicing between the Hindus and Muslims because of what Gandhi had been able to achieve there. So to mark this great occasion, my father in the capacity of Leader of the European Group in the House of Assembly, was asked to make a speech. The following is a transcript of it as recorded by his personal secretary at that time.

'This is perhaps the greatest occasion in the life of India. She has at last achieved the goal of her ambition. I was wondering what I should say in the House today in considering this great question, and a thought came to me, and that thought is the reflex of my mind. It is no idle thought but an expression from the very depths of my heart that God may be with you on this day and may you demonstrate to the world at large, that having largely achieved what you set out to get, you now bury the hatchet forever and join the two flags of Hindustan and Pakistan together. Without that being achieved, India will be missing a part of her life. I cherish the hope that there will be that conjoint feeling and sentiment in the hearts of all men of goodwill, despite the fact that you have not got entirely all that you wanted; but let this day be marked by love and affection for India and that can be best expressed through a change of heart in the people of our land. I, with my party, rejoice that India has achieved her ambition and I can assure you that in the heart of every Britisher there is still a place, a very warm place, for India. With these words, I support the proposal that has been put forward and trust that steps will be taken to mark this occasion in a manner that will show cordial relations between the two communities of India unsullied by any communal feeling.' The secretary adds a note. 'There was a long drawn out applause as Mr Wise resumed his seat, the House being touched by his sincerity.'

In hindsight, it transpired that the people of India were not yet ready for home rule. Not everyone wanted it, and it is doubtful if anyone would have, had they been aware of what would happen as the result of partition and the hand over of power.

The Indian Army certainly didn't want the abandonment and split up of their regiments. It had taken two hundred years for Britain to build up and unite these dozens of castes, creeds, colours, and beliefs together under one flag. They had remained loyal to their regiments and fought side by side with us throughout two bloody world wars, and countless numbers had laid down their lives for Britain. And now at the stroke of a pen they were to be divided.

The Commander-in-Chief of the Indian Army, who was Field Marshall Sir Claude Auchinleck, was given the awesome task of dividing the army in two with all its equipment. He recalled how his own regiment which consisted of half Muslim and half Hindus who had fought side by side, just wept on each other shoulders when it happened, and even after partition they remained 'staunch' through all the horrors that accompanied Independence. Many of the British officers felt that it would be wrong to stay on in the Indian army because they would have to choose to serve either the Mohammedan or Hindu Government and this would be impossible if you had to show a preference for one and not the other.

All over India people had to make difficult decisions as to whether they should stay in India or leave for England. Many felt that it would be impossible and even dangerous to remain. My father personally felt that he could not leave because of the important post that he held within his firm and as Leader of the House of Assembly and his work in the local Corporation. Fortunately he had already anticipated the problems that would arise when India gained her Independence, and felt it was imperative to start making plans for mother to take us back to England. I think he had seen 'the writing on the wall' warning of the trouble that would surely erupt in the days ahead, on the day I was so rudely pushed off my bicycle into the road by the Indian who shouted, 'Quit India'. So once more there would be another sad parting and the break-up of our home.

As soon as Independence was granted, there were riots in Simla, the place which held such happy memories for me, and which had been a favourite hill-station of the British for so long.. Mobs were racing down the Mall looting all those lovely shops, carrying off women to rape them, slaughtering all those poor innocent rickshaw *wallahs* who had for so long served the British there, and the bazaar area was going up in flames.

The situation deteriorated so rapidly that the British living there feared for their lives. Most of them were elderly English couples. Some were retired judges, former colonels of the best regiments in the Indian Army, and senior officers of the Indian Civil Service, all of them had given India the best years of their lives. They had come up to Simla to live out the rest of their lives peacefully in their little cottages in that beautiful tranquil setting. Now, for their own safety, they were given just an hour in which to pack one suitcase, lock up their bungalows and hurry down the valley to board the two buses that had been commandeered to rescue them and take them to Delhi to await flights back to England. The situation had been so dangerous, that a company of

Gurkhas had been deployed to guard them all the way. I don't think any of them were ever able to return again to reclaim their homes, which I'm sure, would have been broken into and looted and perhaps burnt to the ground.

The events of that dreadful day could possibly have accounted for what I discovered when I returned to Simla forty years later and went in search of my old school, Sherfield, and found it abandoned and in ruins with a tall pine tree growing out of the room that had once been our lounge.

While the tragedy in Simla and other parts of India and the Punjab was exploding, the truce created by Gandhi in Calcutta had been holding good, but in the early morning of August 31st 1947 after sixteen miraculous days, the peace of Calcutta was shattered by an outbreak of violence. The outbreak started in the bazaar with the rumour that Muslims had beaten a Hindu boy to death. That night a crowd of young Hindu fanatics burst into the courtyard of Hydari House, dragging out two blood-spattered Muslim youths whom they blamed for the killing. Yelling with rage, they demanded to see Gandhi who, disturbed from his sleep, came out to try and quell the commotion. When the Muslim youths saw Gandhi, they somehow managed to break free and hide behind him. The infuriated crowd then started hurling stones, narrowly missing Gandhi. One of his followers summoned the police who managed to disperse the angry crowd.

Worse was to happen the following day when a group of fanatics of the Hindu extremist movement, threw two hand grenades into a truck full of poor frightened Muslims, who were fleeing from their hovels to avoid the violence that they feared might follow the previous days' rioting. When Gandhi heard, he hurried to the scene and was sickened by the massacre. All that night he meditated about what he could do to stop this new wave of violence, and by the morning, found the answer, which he had been seeking. He would embark on a fast unto death.

Gandhi looked on fasting as a form of prayer and the perfect way in which to fulfil his constant need for penance. This time it was to be a public fast against his own countrymen who were causing such conflict, to save the lives of the thousands of poor innocent people who might die in Calcutta's violence. This great, but very frail little man was preparing to risk his life on their behalf to bring peace and harmony back to the city. He would shortly be seventy-eight years old.

Worried that this fast would probably kill him, his followers tried to reason with him that it would be pointless to embark on such a thing when he was dealing with *goondas* (lawless thugs) who wouldn't care if he lived or died and, if he did, it could make the situation even worse. But Gandhi pointed out that he wanted to touch the hearts of those who were behind the *goondas*, and no amount of persuasion would make him change his mind. So, on the evening of 1st September, he announced that his fast had begun saying,' Either there will be peace in Calcutta, or I will be dead'. News of his decision spread rapidly across the city, and the press and All India Radio issued frequent reports on his condition.

When my father heard of his fast, he was deeply concerned and hurried to see him. As a member of Gandhi's Peace Committee, they had spent many hours together discussing ways to create and maintain the peaceful atmosphere in the city, and now it seemed that all their efforts had proved to be in vain. During his visits with Gandhi, he had grown to love this wise and shrewd old man who had wrought such wonders by his life of penitence and example, and he couldn't bear the thought of him dying in this way.

On the second day of his fast, delegations of Hindu **and** Muslim leaders hurried to Gandhi's bedside to beg him to eat, but he was determined he wouldn't until peace had been restored. When Gandhi started to fast, his body was already in a desperately frail condition, so that on the third day his pulse had weakened so rapidly that it was feared he wouldn't survive much longer. A rumour that he was dying spread across the city, and the mood of both the Hindus and Muslims suddenly changed as neither of those groups wanted to be blamed for his death.

Another miracle occurred when a mixed procession from **both** groups converged on the slums where many of the atrocities had been committed, in an effort to restore calm. But what was even more amazing was when a group of twenty-seven *goondas* called at Gandhi's house to ask his forgiveness for what they had done. They brought all their weapons of murder and left them at Gandhi's bedside as a token of their pledge never to use them again. Later that same day they sent a truckload of weapons to be dumped in his courtyard. The leaders of both parties then issued a joint declaration promising him that 'they would never allow communal strife in the city again and would strive unto death to prevent it.' Gandhi accepted their promise and ended his fast. This time **The Miracle of Calcutta** was real, and **never again** in Gandhi's lifetime were there any further killings or communal rioting in the city. It is said that 'Gandhi achieved many things, but there has been nothing, not even independence, that is so truly wonderful as his victory over evil in Calcutta.'

CHAPTER 32

LEAVING INDIA FOR GOOD

For some time I had seen mother anxiously poring over the pages of The Lady magazine that arrived from England every month. She had been searching for a suitable house for us to rent there as she and my father felt that it was now time for us to say goodbye to India and set up home in England, and try and make a new life for ourselves there. It was a heartrending decision, as it meant a great upheaval and disruption for the whole family, as well as having to say goodbye to all the friends we had made there, and especially having to part from father yet again. He would have to remain behind at his job with his firm, as he was still too young to retire. What was worst of all for me was the fact that Bill's repatriation papers had not come up yet, so he would have to stay behind to continue to serve his regiment and be posted to places where there was still trouble, and where his life would continue to be in danger.

The other thing that grieved me was the thought that I would have to leave behind my precious little dog Thatch, as I couldn't take her back to England in a cage to suffer six months incarceration in a quarantine kennels, with all the suffering that would entail. She was a free spirit and had travelled everywhere across India with us as part of our family. She was my little shadow and I couldn't bear the thought of life without her, so with a heavy heart I had no alternative but to accept the fact that we would just have to leave her behind and try and find someone who would give her a home. This was not so easy, as when we came to contact our various friends, we found that most of them had also decided to leave India for good because of the political situation. Fortunately for little Timmy, an officer who visited us often and was stationed in Fort William in Calcutta had grown very fond of him and asked us if we would let him give him a home, so we were delighted and relieved that he had solved this problem for us, but I was still looking for a home for Thatch.

Mother was faced with the dilemma of not knowing where we should stay in England. We had no family ties, relatives or friends living anywhere in Britain, so it would have to be a matter of finding a suitable house or cottage somewhere to rent. Because The Lady magazine always had so many to choose from, I think she was bewildered and spoilt for choice. At any rate when she showed me the location on a map, I wondered if she had just closed her eyes and blindly stuck a pin into it and decided that wherever it landed, that was the place where we would go, because we discovered eventually that our new home was to be a small cottage in a remote farming village in a wild part of Wales where no one spoke any English.

As we would be leaving India never to return, packing became a major problem. What should we take with us, and what should we leave behind? We were only allowed to have one cabin trunk each and a suitcase for the journey. As there were five of us in the family including Claire, we would have ten pieces of luggage between us, more than enough to cope with.

Since my engagement to Bill I had been collecting various items for my 'bottom drawer'. I knew that it would be difficult to obtain anything without coupons or dockets in England, so planned to take all my household linen with me as well as the beautiful clothing that the *derzi* had made for my trousseau. As Bill and I had planned to get married once he had returned to England after he had found a job, mother wanted me to have her wedding dress that had been carefully stored in a lead lined trunk in one of our storage godowns in the grounds of our home. I was lucky to have been blessed with a slim shapely figure like hers, so knew that it would fit me. I had seen her wearing it in a wedding photograph and thought how lovely she looked in it, so was quite thrilled at the idea, especially when I realized that such gorgeous items were not available in England as a result of the war. She found the keys to the *godown* and the trunk, and took me to get it. But when she opened it and we looked inside, all we saw was a sea of sludge with some brass items sticking out of it. We were quite mortified when we saw what the white ants had done. This was meant to be an ant and vermin proof storage trunk, which was why it was lined with lead, but they had discovered an access through the keyhole.

When all the servants heard that we would be leaving for 'Blighty' and would never be coming back, they were most distressed. This had been their home together with their families, and we had housed, clothed and fed them for so many years, during which time they had all been cheerful, content and loyal in their service to our family. I know they considered mother to be a kind and caring *Burra Memsahib*, (a grand lady) that was why we had never experienced any problems with them. When they realized that they might be deprived of their job and their home, some of them wept. We couldn't find them new jobs with other British families, because most of them were also leaving India for good. Father decided that, for the time being, he would remain in the house and retain a few of the servants. His old bearer Hurree and another bearer, a sweeper, a cook and the *mali* to look after the garden, each of these would be essential to carry out those tasks that his caste would allow. The rest of them would each receive a generous pension to enable them to return with their families to live in their own villages. That is if those villages had not already gone up in flames.

All our servants had come from various parts of Bengal, and were gentle-natured people. In fact the local people and all the Indians we had ever come into contact with, had always been kind, willing and respectful towards the British, so it was hard to fathom how such people could now be capable of so much hatred towards us and amongst themselves as to cause the eruption of such terrible and violent acts. It has to be remembered that throughout the time that the British had ruled India, all these people who were now locked in strife, had lived amicably together, which made one wonder what benefits were achieved for them by the carve up of India.

The turmoil and disruption affected everyone, from the lowliest beggar to even the Maharajas, some of whom were now shortly to become prisoners in their own palaces. The vast scale of the problem was almost impossible to imagine. As far as the British were concerned, it also meant the split up of many families as they hastened to leave India and, because of this general exodus, it was difficult to obtain passages on the liners leaving for England. Since the end of hostilities, there were thousands of troops that also had to be repatriated.

The various members of the forces who had made our home their 'home from home' and were still in Calcutta, were sorry to hear that we were planning to leave India and that they might never see our family again. To cheer them up we decided to hold a farewell party for them in the garden. We were deeply touched when many of them made moving and heartfelt farewell speeches. Later in the evening we went indoors and they treated us to an impromptu concert when some played the piano and we all sang along together. Father cheered them when he told them they would still be welcome to come to our home whenever they wished.

We managed to book our passages to England on the P&O liner the Stratheden, leaving from Bombay. I can't remember the date or the month but I believe it was in the autumn of 1946. This time the voyage would take three weeks through the Suez Canal that had been reopened, and I was not looking forward to making the journey. The reason for this was the heartbreak that I was suffering at the thought of leaving my home and way of life that I had enjoyed for the past six years, and father whom I had quickly grown to love and respect. Now I wondered how long it would be before we would all be together again. Finding a home for Thatch proved to be a problem, but eventually we found an old lady who said that she was too old to face the upheaval of moving to Britain, so offered to have her, but it was far from ideal as she lived in a block of flats. When I left her there I was devastated, because she had been so much a part of my life, and never left my side. I know that she was only a little dog, but she had such character and was always so full of life. As I look back to that sad time I can still see her now with her little paw raised, quivering with excitement as I threw a ball for her, and the way she used to romp around the garden with little Timmy. I know I am in danger of repeating myself but she was quite special, and of the many dogs I have owned since then, there has never been another quite like Thatch.

I was also devastated and heartbroken at the thought of leaving my precious Bill behind and wondering if I he would be killed or wounded, and whether I would ever see him again. The uncertainty of starting a new life in a country that was strange to me after being away from it for so long, added to my state of turmoil and despondency.

When the day arrived for us to leave, there was no joy in any of our hearts, especially when I saw mother bidding father a tearful farewell as we boarded the express boat train at Howrah Station. Some of our servants followed us to the station to take care of our luggage, and as they lined up on the platform to see us off, they too looked sad as they put their hands together in a farewell gesture.

When we arrived at the Bombay docks, we made our way to the boat followed by a long line of ten coolies carrying our trunks and cases. Crowds of noisy excited troops who had also been travelling on the same train, surrounded us. As usual there were the wolf whistles when they saw us, but by now we had grown accustomed to hearing them, so we just greeted them with a wave and a smile as we walked up the gangplank to meet the ship's officers waiting to welcome us aboard.

The troops were in jubilant mood. They had survived the war and all the hardships of their term of service in India, and were on their way back to Blighty. Up on deck I watched as they filed up the gangplank in pairs with their topees on and kitbags slung over their shoulders. They were the lucky ones, but how many of their comrades would be remaining behind 'in a corner of a foreign field that is forever England', having made the ultimate sacrifice for their King and Country?

As the ship drew away from the quay side, a Military band struck up the tune of Auld Lang Syne and everyone joined in the singing as we threw the coloured paper streamers we had been given, back on to the quay to those who had come to wave farewell. As the ship passed the great arch of the Gateway of India, I saw the troops that were lining the rails cheering and waving, pleased no doubt that it was their last sight of India. But for me it was quite the opposite. I was leaving behind a way of life that I had grown accustomed to, my dear father, my beloved Bill, and my dog. I wept as I watched it fade away beyond the horizon. What had I got to look forward to in

My last view of the great arch of the Gateway to India
Photo by the author

England? Only the day when he would return to me.

I can't remember much about that voyage, probably because I felt so despondent all the time. But there were two things however that I do recall because I found them rather amusing. The first happened as the ship sailed away from Port Said into open waters, which it was believed is where the East ended and the West began. It was the point where as a final farewell ritual, the troops returning to England from India, were paraded on deck, and at the given signal they all cheered as they flung their topees into the sea. The second amusing incident I remember took place as we were passing close by to the Rock of Gibralter. We were standing on the deck looking at this wonderful sight when I noticed Patricia in animated conversation with a young army officer in uniform, who appeared to be 'chatting her up'. She was usually painfully shy and not in the habit of speaking to strange men let alone walking off with one. So I was surprised when I saw her allowing him to lead her away. She returned shortly after, looking flushed and extremely angry, her eyes flashing with indignation. When I asked her where she had been and why she had gone off with a complete stranger, she told me that he had suggested taking her to a place where she would have a better view of the Rock, but it transpired that he had other intentions, because he had led her to a quiet spot on deck and wouldn't release her until he had taken her in his arms and kissed her passionately. I know for a fact that she had never had a boyfriend before, and had never allowed any man to kiss her like that, let alone a complete stranger, so could understand her distress. But I have to admit that the rest of the family had found the incident rather amusing, and it made matters worse when we jokingly suggested that it might have been a prelude to a beautiful romance, but she was **not** amused. Now whenever 'that Rock' is mentioned even to this day, we tease her about what we refer to as 'your Rock of Gibralter experience'.

When we reached the Bay of Biscay, the seas were mountainous, whipped up as always by gale force-winds. The dining room emptied and only the hardiest of passengers who had found their 'sea legs' were seen trying to walk around the decks as the ship pitched and tossed, and rocked and rolled. Feeling miserable in more ways than one, I went to my cabin to lie on my bunk, and it was a couple of days before I felt able to surface again. I'm sure everyone was relieved when we reached the calmer waters of Southampton and tied up at the quay.

As the ship approached the dock, I was surprised at the sight of so many women, but very a few men, who had come to meet the boat. They were all anxiously looking up at the soldiers lining the rails of the troop deck hoping to catch a glimpse of their loved ones. When we were allowed to disembark, there were tumultuous and emotional scenes all around us as these happy men were reunited after years of separation. As there was no one to meet us, we felt quite excluded, so went in search of our luggage and porters who led us to the office of our agents Cox and Kings. There we collected the keys to our rented cottage and the rail tickets for the train journey to London, then onwards to Wales.

When we arrived at Waterloo station, there were more jubilant scenes as people were reunited with family and friends, and the Salvation Army was there handing out mugs of tea to the men. Their kind gesture brings to mind a poignant remark I once heard from one of these soldiers about this.

After having been away from England for years serving in the Far East with his regiment, which had seen some of the bloodiest fighting of the war, he had arrived at Waterloo station with no one to welcome him and nowhere to go having lost all his family in an air raid when their home was bombed. A young girl dressed in the uniform of The Salvation Army, came up to him and offered him a mug of tea with the comment, 'Well done, and welcome home.' After giving the best years of his life to serve Britain, this was a sad homecoming for him. But at that time there were thousands more like him arriving back in England who would have to start their lives all over again. I hoped that they too had the same welcome and were also handed a cup of tea.

We transferred to Euston station for our onward journey to Newtown, Montgomeryshire. When we arrived, once again there was nobody there to welcome us, so we had to find our own transport to the cottage that was on the outskirts of the village. When I saw it my heart sank. The rooms were very small and sparsely furnished and as I looked out of the window I saw the fields surrounding us were full of sheep. I sensed that mother was also disappointed with the place because she never made any remarks about it. When she booked it in India, she couldn't have known much about the place when all she had to go on was a small advertisement in The Lady magazine. The last time that mother came to England and rented a house was in1940 when, on that occasion, she had been able to find a maid and a housekeeper to help her, but now we would have to manage on our own. This would not be easy because of our lifestyle in India that was so different. It was useless to rent a car because none of us could drive and as there wasn't a phone or wireless in the house either, we felt totally isolated, and apart from going for walks, there was nothing else to do, so we felt bored.

Each day I hoped for news of Bill but there wasn't any. So to cheer me up mother suggested that we should buy a dog. We saw an advertisement for a young Welsh sheepdog that had been trained to round up sheep, in the local farmer's journal, so went in search of it. We found him in a farm nearby, tied up in a disused pigsty. He was a very pretty, friendly dog, though nervous of strangers. What we didn't know at the time was that he was 'gun shy' and was absolutely petrified of fireworks. We felt sorry for him living in the pigsty, so decided to buy him, and paid the farmer the asking price of £5. We walked him back home, but when we tried to get him to come into the house he was so scared he refused, probably because he had never been indoors before. We named him Laddie, and with patience, love and attention, he soon relaxed and became part of our family, and we grew very fond of him.

Our new Welsh sheepdog Laddie.

In these days of advanced telecommunication technology when it is possible to speak to anyone in any part of the globe for a minimal cost, it may be hard to appreciate the fact that at that time we couldn't just pick up a phone and speak to my father or Bill out in India, but had to rely on sending or receiving cables, or letters by sea mail, which could take weeks because there was no airmail service. During the war, the censor office carefully scrutinized every letter in case it contained some information that might be of use to the enemy, so you could receive a letter with whole sentences blackened out making it difficult to read. After the end of the war it was possible to purchase an aerogramme, which was a stamped single sheet of airmail paper only available for purchase from a post office. I sent these to Bill regularly, but had no idea if they would ever reach him. I was worried as I hadn't heard from him for some time but, discovered later, the reason for this was because he was involved in operations in many different and often remote regions, so it was impossible for him to send any letters to me. During our time in Wales it was even difficult to keep in touch with what was going on in the world around us because we hadn't a wireless. This was long before the advent of television. As the days passed we were beginning to feel very isolated there so mother decided to relocate the family and move near the seaside.

This time she found us a lovely furnished house called Sea Cottage at Felpham, near Bognor Regis in Sussex. It was so near to the beach that whenever there was a gale blowing off the sea, you couldn't see through the windowpanes because they were plastered with sea foam. But we were delighted with the house and its' location, and especially the garden which led directly on to the beach. I felt so much happier there as I was able to take Laddie for long walks along the shore, and enjoy a dip in the sea during the summer months, while he frolicked amongst the waves.

During our first winter there which was the coldest on record, a strange phenomena occurred when the sea froze all along the edge of the beach. One morning I saw an unusual sight of a flock of white swans by the water's edge not far from the house. Thinking that they were probably starving because of the frozen conditions everywhere, I broke up a loaf of bread and went to feed them. They rushed towards me and devoured it hungrily, looking for more. Feeling sorry for them, I was about to return to the house to get some more when they charged at me, hissing and flapping their wings. I was terrified and had to run for my life as they chased me. I was lucky to reach the garden and slam the gate shut just as they were about to grab me. The following day I saw an article in the local newspaper about this flock of swans, which said that they had come from the lake in the grounds of Arundel Castle that had been frozen for so long, that they had flown to the sea in search of food.

Not long after we had settled into Sea Cottage, I saw an advertisement for someone to help in a riding stable in Pagham, so applied for the job and was delighted when I was offered it. This meant that I had to leave the house at 6am and cycle seven miles to The Eagle Rock Stables to help out and escort the rides. Even though I worked a six-day week, and it involved hard physical work, I enjoyed working there until the winter when it got dark early and the road conditions proved to be too dangerous for me to cycle there and return in the dark at night.

I found another job as matron in a Holiday Hotel for Children in Bognor Regis. I was in charge of about twenty children who had been left there whilst their parents went on holiday. It was my task to keep them occupied and amused, so I took them to the beach for picnics and other places of interest. Even though the job involved working a seven-day week, for long hours and was hard work, I found it an enjoyable experience. Unfortunately it closed for the winter so I sought another job.

This time I was offered the post as a care assistant in an old people's nursing home. On my first day there I was concerned when I took a patient her medicine but was unable to wake her up. When I called a member of staff, she discovered that she was dead. This shocked me and, even more so, when I was asked to assist her in 'laying her out'. Having had no previous nursing experience I felt that this was not the right job for me so tendered my resignation.

Not having a car or a driving licence, I purchased a new Raleigh bicycle for £5 and cycled everywhere with Laddie following close behind. He could run for miles and never seemed to tire. He loved to travel on

Playful Laddie

the bus with us when we went to Bognor, where everyone made such a fuss of him. One day I decided to cycle to Felpham with him and left him sitting outside a shop guarding my bicycle.

When I returned he had disappeared. I asked some people who were sitting on a bench by the bus stop, if they had seen my collie dog, and was shocked when they told me that they had seen him board the bus heading for Arundel. I raced down the road on my bike and caught sight of it a long way ahead. Just as I was despairing that I wouldn't be able to catch up with it, it stopped and I saw Laddie get off. When I reached him he was overjoyed to see me again, but I dread to think where he could have ended up had the bus conductor not turned him off the bus before it had gone too far.

While we were at Sea Cottage, we continued to receive mail redirected from India. One day I was surprised to find a letter from Jock, the sailor that I had met on the Orion in 1940 on our voyage to India. Some years before, I had written to tell him that I had become engaged, so expected his letters to cease, but I was wrong. They didn't. Seven years had passed since that meeting, and in this heartrending letter, he **still** wanted to me to marry him and asked if I was **sure** that the man I was going to marry was the **right one** for me. He told me that he was still a sailor but would be willing to give this up and take a land job if that was the reason for my having rejected him. I felt so sorry for him, and still can't understand why he never gave up hoping I would change my mind after the passing of so many years.

CHAPTER 33

BILL IS DEMOBBED

Imagine my joy when the long awaited letter from Bill arrived with the wonderful news that his demobilisation number had finally come up. He was preparing to return home from Singapore and, all being well, we would be together again in about three or four weeks. I thanked God that in spite of all his terrible experiences, my prayers had been answered and that he was returning fit and well. Some time later I received another letter giving me the expected date of his arrival, so travelled to London to stay with Auntie Andre, who had been our guardian when we were at school, to await his phone call when he arrived at Waterloo station. When it finally came, I can't describe the relief I experienced and the thrill of hearing his voice again after so long, but my joy soon turned to dismay when he told me what had just happened. Unknown to him, he had been followed all the way from the boat by a man with the sole purpose of stealing his suitcase which contained all he possessed in the world. Evidently, it had been too large to fit into the phone box with him, so he had propped it against the door whilst he turned to dial the number, but in a flash it had disappeared. So after having given seven years of his life to serve his King and Country, this was the hero's welcome that awaited him. He was left with nothing at all, just the army uniform that he was wearing. One thing that upset him most was the loss of twelve pairs of silk stockings that he had brought for me from Singapore and the other was the loss of all the photos that he had taken of his Gurkha soldiers that had fought with him in Burma.

At this time everything in Britain was strictly rationed and nothing could be obtained without the allotted dockets or coupons. Everything was in short supply because of the shortages caused by the war. So many thousands of our forces were arriving back in Britain each day that neither the military nor the government could offer any help to Bill, or to the others who had suffered the same fate. When he finally found a policeman to report the theft, it was of no comfort to him when he was informed that they were already well aware of the fact that there was a large network of thieves operating across Britain, especially at all the ports. They were specifically targeting all officers in the three forces who were returning from abroad, as they thought they might be bringing back gifts and other items of value that would fetch high prices on the Black Market. The problem was too vast for the depleted police force to cope with so, what should have been a joyous homecoming was marred by the theft. It was some days before Bill was able to collect his demob suit that was being given to all the members of the forces, to help them start their lives afresh on 'Civvy Street'. Bill's was an ill fitting, dark brown striped, 'off the peg' suit. After being dressed in his smart army officer's uniform for so long, he felt embarrassed to go out in it until he was able to find a tailor to alter it to fit him. Even after it was altered at a cost of £3, he said he felt uncomfortable to go out in it. He was also supplied with a brown tweed overcoat, which he treasured for many years.

On his return home, Bill bought a silver cigarette case to give to his old battalion commander, Lt Col Noel George, as a joint present from him and his fellow officers. Bill was fighting under his command when this poor officer had become seriously ill in the jungle and had to be evacuated during the early stages of the Chindit operation. It was discovered later that he was suffering from poliomyelitis. He was lucky to have survived this and be given a desk job at the War Office, where Bill sent him the gift. He had heard that Bill was engaged to me, and I was aware that he thought a great deal of him, because in his 'thank you' letter Noel said—"I hear Bill that you are 'walking out' and I reckon she's a very lucky girl". Bill was well pleased to receive this accolade from his old CO, but he freely admits that there was a great deal of luck on his side too. (The term 'walking out' usually meant that the couple were engaged)

These were incredibly difficult days for all these poor men in the forces who were returning to their homeland. Nearly all of them were without jobs, and many had no homes to go to. Others had lost their girlfriends, wives or families, and this was before the days of the welfare state, though this was visualized. Thousands were searching for jobs and there weren't many available. For the few that there were, hundreds applied. Now Bill faced the same predicament. Before the war he was contemplating studying law and qualifying as a solicitor, which would have required serving five years Articles. The war changed all this and the prospect of a long period of training, though now reduced to two years, was daunting. We had already been engaged for a long time, and didn't want to have to wait before we could get married. Moreover, how were we to finance our living expenses?

We were facing this predicament when we heard of a Government scheme—the Further Education and Training Grant—so Bill applied for this and was granted £5 per week. This sum would have to suffice for the two of us once we were married. For the time being I remained at home in Sea Cottage and Bill returned to his family in Devon to study and seek acceptance as an articled clerk with a law firm there.

We wrote and told father of our plans to marry in October the following year and he was delighted to hear the news, and we were pleased when he replied to say he would be coming home on furlough in September, so would be there to give me away.

CHAPTER 34

GANDHI'S ASSINATION

We heard the dreadful news that Gandhiji—known as 'Bapu' to those who were close to him—had been assassinated in the afternoon of January 30th 1948 as he walked through the crowds on his way to his prayer meeting in the grounds of Birla House, New Delhi.

A congregation of about 500 devotees had gathered there to attend, and as Gandhi, supported by Abha and Manu, the two young women he called 'My walking sticks', approached the steps of the prayer platform to climb up to address the crowds, a Hindu extremist by the name of Godse, lunged at him firing the three shots into his chest that killed him. As the last shot rang out Gandhi was heard to cry out '*Hey Rama*! (Oh God!) Godse committed this crime because he believed the Mahatma was defiling the highest ethics of the Hindu religion by his beliefs. Father wrote to tell us of his grief and gave us a vivid account of the funeral, which he travelled to Delhi to attend. He was also able to take cine photos of it, which he showed us when he came to England. Many of the scenes were deeply moving.

As the three shots rang out and Gandhi sank to the ground, the people nearest to him heard a frenzied man in the crowd shrieking, 'It was a Moslem who did it'. If this had in fact been the case, then there would have been the most ghastly massacres the world had ever seen. As the news of his assassination quickly spread, and the director of All India Radio was informed that a Hindu by the name of Godse had committed the crime, he took an extraordinary and responsible decision: instead of sending the news flash and interrupting the nationwide circuits, he ordered the programmes to continue as normal until the 6 o'clock news 35 minutes later, so it would give the headquarters of the police and army time to employ their emergency telephone circuits to put every major army and police command in India on an emergency footing to enable them to be prepared for the chaos that was sure to erupt. At 6 o'clock the radio announced to a shocked world:

'**Mahatma Gandhi was assassinated in New Delhi at twenty minutes past five this afternoon. His assassin was a Hindu.**'

Because of this announcement wholesale slaughter across India was averted.

When Louis Mountbatten received the news, he hurried to Birla House where he found Nehru in tears and Patel transfixed as he gazed at the body of Gandhi. Manu sat cradling his head and weeping. Someone in the group around the palette on which he lay handed him some rose petals that he scattered over the frail little body. As he stood there looking at the man he used to affectionately refer to as 'his dejected sparrow', he realized that as Governor General he would have the mammoth task of arranging a funeral that thousands would want to attend.

India reacted to the news with a *hartal,* a national day of mourning. Bombay was a ghost city. From the mansions to the slums, everywhere people wept. There was no one on the Maidan in Calcutta. In Pakistan millions of women smashed their trinkets and baubles in a traditional gesture of grief. From villages everywhere, people started to march towards Delhi.

Jawaharlal Nehru was heartbroken by the death of Gandhi. At Louis Mountbatten's request he was asked to speak to the nation. All India Radio broadcast his words across that vast country and beyond as he faced the microphone and spoke from the heart.

'The light has gone out of our lives and there is darkness everywhere. Our beloved leader Bapu, as we called him, the father of our nation, is no more. The light has gone out, I said, and yet I am wrong. For the light that shone in this country was no ordinary light. In a thousand years that light will still be seen…the world will see it and it will give solace to innumerable hearts. For that light represented something more than the immediate present; it represented the living, the eternal truths, reminding us of the right path, drawing us from error, and taking this ancient country to freedom.

Messages of condolence poured into Delhi from all over the globe. Gandhi's death moved London as no event had done since the end of the war. George VI and his ministers sent their condolences. Bernard Shaws' comment was; 'shows how dangerous it is to be good' and from South Africa where he had spent so many years, Field Marshall Smuts' simple tribute was; 'A prince among us has passed'. Mohammed Ali Jinnah, Gandhi's principal political rival wrote in his condolence, 'He was one of the greatest men produced by the Hindu community'.

On the day of the funeral, just after eleven in the morning, Gandhi's body draped in the saffron-white-and-green flag of Independent India, was brought from the house and carried through the crowds to be placed on a weapons carrier to be transported across the city to the banks of the river Jumna where the funeral pyre was prepared for his cremation.

A force of 250 of his countrymen, sailors of the Royal Indian Navy, were waiting to tow it by the four ropes attached to its bumper along the five mile route littered with marigolds and rose petals to the River Jumna. The way was lined with thousands of spectators occupying every vantage point. A mixture of grieving humanity followed the cortege. Maharajahs mingled with Untouchable sweepers, veiled Moslem women and representatives of every caste, colour and creed, all united by their grief.

My father was present with Louis Mountbatten, his wife Edwina and their daughter Pamela, to witness the final ritual on the funeral pyre. He recorded that it was a very emotional experience.

There was no doubt that Gandhi's life had left a great impression on the masses, and in fact the whole world, and in particular on those who had the privilege of knowing him. Throughout his life he had always preached non-violence, forgiveness and love. To quote his own words;

'Non-violence is the greatest force at the disposal of mankind. It is mightier than the mightiest weapon of destruction devised by the ingenuity of man!' And of forgiveness;
'Forgiveness is the quality of the brave, not the coward.' And of love; Love is not love which asks for a return.'
He also said this during one of his times of fasting;
'For me the only way love punishes is by suffering, and the only way for knowing God is non-violence and ahisma (love).'

That anyone should have been filled with so much hate as to want to kill a man of such greatness and influence for good in the world is beyond comprehension.

After father's return to Calcutta from Gandhi's funeral, he was asked to pay a tribute to him in his capacity as leader of the European Group in the House of Assembly, and a member of Gandhi's Central Peace Committee. He sent us a copy of his speech:

'In associating myself with the deep grief and sorrow that has over-shadowed India and the world, I trust that after his death, there may come about a realisation of the need for that unity for which he sought and ultimately died at the hands of his own people. Mahatma Gandhi's life and devotion to the cause of freedom, in the setting of true democracy, has emblazoned in letters of gold, the way he ultimately found to direct his people in achieving that end. He toiled along life's pathway and laboured out of love for his people and this country, in a manner that will go down to posterity and live in the hearts of the people as a monumental achievement fought without weapons of war, strife and bitterness. He endeavoured to radiate with his presence that peace and calm which comes about in the life of a man when his heart has been changed towards his fellow man, regardless of caste, colour or creed.'

Father adds in his letter, that all his fellow members were moved by these words and deeply upset at the death of such a remarkable man.

Hundreds of Pilgrims still come daily to the home and shrine of this 'Great Soul' Gandhi.   Photo by the author.

I have recently returned from a visit to India where I went to several sights associated with Gandhi. Adjacent to the house at Kirti Mandir where he was born, an elaborate shrine has been built commemorating his life, and thousands of people, including children, from that vast country, as well as people from all over the globe, make a pilgrimage to visit it. As I travelled to various parts of India, I saw many statues of him, and there were always garlands of fresh marigolds that had been placed around his neck by devotees. So even after all these years since he was killed, he is still honoured and remains a much loved and revered charismatic leader and Father of the Indian Nation.

CHAPTER 35

THE ATTIC

Later in the year we were delighted to welcome father home and be a complete family once again. It was twelve years since he was last in England, and strict rationing was still in force. By now mother had found a housekeeper-cook, a Norwegian lady by the name of Edith, so was free to spend more time with him. At first, father enjoyed the novelty of going shopping for her, but was not used to the queues in England. There was not even a word for this in India where nobody ever queued. Because of the shortage of everything, mother had told him that whenever he saw a queue he should join it, because he could be sure that it would be for something worth having. So the first time that he saw one, he joined it, even though he appeared to be the only man. As he waited in line, he noticed that his presence was causing some amusement, so asked what they were queuing for, only to be told that the queue was for the ladies toilet!

Another time when father went shopping for some vegetables, he forgot the name of them, so asked the greengrocer for the cabbage's babies, when he should have requested Brussels sprouts. He did his best and tried to be helpful even though he found it difficult to get used to this new lifestyle. On another occasion out shopping, he came home very pleased with something he had bought from the butcher, which was whale steak. He had been told that it was a good substitute for beefsteak. Meat was still rationed and we were only allowed a few ounces each week, so finding interesting food was a problem. Edith looked through the cookbook in vain, to see if there was a recipe for this unusual delicacy, so she tried frying it. The smell that it produced was awful and it was as tough as leather. She gave it to Laddie, and even he refused to eat it. As it was impossible to obtain tins of dog food for him, I used to buy a complete sheep's head and boil it, then remove all the parts that were edible for him, —a very unpleasant job that I detested. After such wonderful food in India, it was very difficult to enjoy meals, which consisted of tripe, brain cutlets, heart, pig's trotters and offal, all of which was available without coupons.

In the late spring of 1948, I travelled with Laddie to Bill's home in Devon to stay with him, meet his family and make plans for our wedding in the autumn. Fortunately, he had been given a few days off work to spend some time with me. We enjoyed blissfully happy days together walking on Dartmoor and visiting his childhood haunts of Marldon, and Compton Castle and picnicking amongst the bluebells in the woods around Berry Pomeroy Castle near the old farm where Bill was born. There were so many beautiful little villages in the area and along the river Dart that we visited, and one sunny day we took the steamer for an interesting trip down the scenic river from Totnes to Dartmouth.

Bill was working in the office as an articled clerk in a law firm in Torquay and studying hard to complete the required training for the period now reduced to two years. He didn't receive any salary because law students in those days were required to **pay** the firm a premium for the privilege of being able to train with them. So he had to give them eighty pounds the total sum of the meagre army gratuity pay that he had received on his demobilization. Not only that, but he also had to pay eighty pounds stamp duty on the Articles of Clerkship, the written contract between himself and his principal. Later on a further sum lent to him by a kind relative to enable him to complete the course. This left him with nothing except the weekly allowance of £5 from the Further Education and Training Grant, which was only available to ex-servicemen and women.

While in Devon with Bill, we discussed our proposed marriage and how this could be arranged when were both so short of funds. I know he was unhappy about us having to live on such a small weekly allowance, but because we both loved each other and longed to be together, I assured him that somehow we would be able to manage. We discussed this with my parents who, seeing our determination to go ahead in spite of the government's meagre allowance, kindly offered to pay for the wedding, and as their wedding gift to us they said they would arrange and pay for us to spend our honeymoon in Lucerne, Switzerland. As we had no furniture, they would also give us a bedroom suite, though at the time we still had nowhere to live and not enough money to pay any rent, but 'where there's a will, there's a way'. So we started to make plans as to when and where the wedding should take place.

Mother approached Auntie Andre, the rich lady in Twickenham, who had been our guardian when we were in boarding school, and she was delighted to offer us the use of her home for the occasion. She also said she would introduce us to her friend who was the minister of the Richmond Baptist Church, so that we could arrange to be married by him there. Bill was so delighted when I told him about this, and came up from Devon at Auntie's invitation to spend the weekend making all the arrangements.

The date fixed for the wedding was 5th October 1948. Coupons were still needed to buy clothing and as we didn't have any to spare, we contacted Moss Bros in London and arranged to hire everything required for a white wedding. I remember the hire cost of my white satin wedding dress and veil was £5 and Bill's complete outfit, including the grey top hat, cost the same. Auntie Andre's generous wedding present to us would be the reception she would arrange in her house, so we were thrilled that at last everything was falling into place.

The urgent problem now was where we could live afterwards. As we didn't own a car, it would have to be within easy reach of Bill's office. A kind young couple by the name of John and Ruth, who attended the same church as Bill, heard of our predicament and offered to help. When we told them of our marriage plans and the shortage of funds making it difficult to find accommodation, they offered us a disused attic at the top of their Village Store. When Bill went to view it with them, he discovered that the two small rooms were in the apex of the roof with one window at each end with a narrow spiral staircase leading to the entrance at the top which was only three feet high under a beam. As he was 6ft 2ins tall he had to bend double to get in, and careful not stand up too quickly or else he would bang his head on the sloping roof. Besides this problem, it had never been decorated and was festooned with spider's webs, neither was there any electric light or power in it. But as they offered it to us for £1 per week to rent, Bill gratefully accepted.

He wrote to tell me all about it and said that if I was willing to live there with him, he would lime wash the walls and wire it up himself, even though he admitted he had never done anything like that before. So I travelled to Devon to stay with his family, and we went to view it. He had described it so vividly in his letter that I was not surprised by the state of it. The only thing that worried me was sharing a kitchen on the ground floor, which meant carrying meals up three flights of stairs. But as I thought about it, seeing that I didn't know how to cook, maybe I could learn from our friends. Poor Bill was apprehensive about the whole idea. After we had discussed the matter and I offered to stay and help him, he decided to look on this project as a challenge. If in the end it meant that after all the years of waiting because of the war, we could at last get married and begin living together, then it would all be worthwhile.

Bill managed to get some time off from the office to enable us to do the renovation. As the weather was very hot that summer, and the two rooms were right up in the attic, working there in the heat was exhausting, but it was rewarding to see them being transformed into our own little home. At the end of a couple of weeks, the work was almost finished and ready for the furniture to be installed. We hadn't realised the problem we now faced as to how to get it into the rooms because of the spiral staircase and the low beam at the entrance. Fortunately a friend solved our dilemma by arranging for the window to be removed and the furniture winched up through it.

Once it was furnished, albeit it very sparsely, it looked quite cosy and we were thrilled that at last Bill and I could look on it as our own little home after all those years of waiting.

CHAPTER 36

THE WEDDING

October 5th 1948. As our wedding day dawned, I looked outside and my heart sank when I saw the thick fog. Bill had travelled up from Devon the previous day with his parents and brother to join me and my family, to spend the night at Auntie's house, which was so large that it could accommodate us all. Just before midday, when it was time for everyone to leave for the church, the sun broke through and the fog cleared miraculously. When I walked down the drive on father's arm to the car to go to the church, the sun shone brightly upon us.

As I entered the church to the sound of the organ playing the tune 'Here Comes The Bride' and saw Bill standing there at the alter as he turned around to smile at me, my heart skipped a beat. He looked so radiant and handsome.

The wedding service was a most wonderful, though emotional experience for us both as we exchanged our vows. Words fail me as I try to express the thrill I felt as I walked down the isle on Bill's arm afterwards, amidst smiles from our families and friends, while the organ played Mendelson's Bridal March. Outside, we were showered with rose petals and confetti as we entered the decorated wedding car to be driven to the reception.

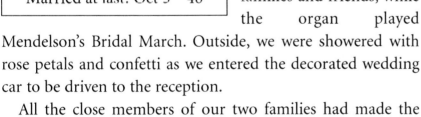

Married at last! Oct 5th 48

What a wonderful memory!

All the close members of our two families had made the effort to be present and this was a great opportunity for them to meet us, and each other. In spite of the rationing restrictions the caterers laid on a lavish reception in the luxurious lounge. Telegram greetings were read out, including some from friends we had known in India. A rather clever telegram from Bill's old wartime friend, Tony Grist read: 'Though one has ceased to be wise, no one will ever know which. May you enjoy your marital ties, and be happy, healthy, and rich'. (The pun on the word 'Wise', being my maiden surname). As we cut the magnificently decorated two-tier wedding cake, everyone applauded. After all the speeches were made and everyone had dined, we changed into our going away outfits, said goodbye amidst a chorus of good wishes and showers of more rose petals and confetti, and were then driven up to London to catch the overnight train to Lucerne in Switzerland where we were to spend our honeymoon.

The Hotel des Balances where we stayed, was right on the edge of the lake by the old covered wooden bridge. From the balcony of our room there was a beautiful view across it to the snowy mountains beyond. The weather was perfect for the whole of the two weeks that we were there, which made our trips on the lake and to mountain villages all the more enjoyable. What a wonderful honeymoon it was, filled with happiness and precious memories.

We returned to Devon with Laddie, to live in our little attic, which we had done our best to make feel like home. The time we spent there in our very cramped little abode, with so little cash, were some of our happiest days together—life seemed so simple and carefree. While Bill was working in the office, I sometimes took Laddie for long walks in the woods or on Kingskerswell Downs, and at weekends we often walked through the quiet country lanes, the eight miles to the home of Bill's parents to have a meal with them, then back again afterwards, with Laddie enjoying every minute of it.

As I recall those early days of long ago, I am grateful for the experience and hardships that we endured together then, and the valuable lessons learnt on how to budget and manage one's finances on 'a shoe string'. Because of the lifestyle I had enjoyed in India, it had never occurred to me to learn to cook, so my early attempts proved disastrous and there were often 'burnt offerings' for supper for which I apologized. In spite of this, dear Bill realized that I was struggling to do my best, so never complained about the food, but was patient, understanding, longsuffering and always loving.

Every morning Bill had to rise very early and put in some hours of study before he left to catch the bus for the office. When he returned at the end of a hard day's work there, he would resume his studies after supper, often working late into the night. We hadn't a car, a wireless or even a gramophone to distract us, so I spent my time reading, sewing or embroidering, whilst Bill studied. I often helped Ruth and her husband in their shop while Bill was at the office or watched her preparing a meal in the hopes of acquiring basic cooking skills.

In March 1950 the time came for Bill to go to London to attend Law School and take the Final Exams of the Law Society. My parents had bought a house in Sutton, Surrey and invited us to go and live with them there during this time. When Auntie Andre heard that we were leaving Devon, she kindly offered to come and help us pack up and transport our belongings to Sutton.

On the day she arrived, Bill had to return to his work in the office, so I greeted her and helped her up the winding stairs to our rooms. As she was a lady of large proportions, she found this difficult, especially when she reached the top and decided that the easiest way to enter the room was on all fours. I left her packing up, while I went down to the kitchen to prepare a snack for us.

I hadn't been there long when John and Ruth's little girl came running in shouting that there were two legs sticking out through the ceiling over her mummy and daddy's bed. I rushed up to find out what had happened, and discovered that Auntie had gone through the small door into the eaves to put a carton in there, and not realizing that the floor wasn't boarded, had stepped on the thin lathing which had given way. The poor dear was trapped because the broken slats were sticking into her thighs. A further complication was that, because it was so hot up there, she had removed all her underwear. I tried to pull her back through the hole but couldn't, because she was too heavy. I called to John who tried to help me but, we didn't manage it either, so I hurried to the shop below to phone Bill for some advice. When I told him what had happened, I thought that the line had gone dead because he didn't reply. It was no laughing matter, but he had seen the funny side of what had happened and had put his hand over the mouthpiece because he was helpless with laughter. Eventually he came back on the line and suggested we call the farmer next door who could help John, which we did. Eventually they managed to extricate her with great difficulty. She was most apologetic and embarrassed about what had happened, especially as we were all looking up at her. When she saw the large hole that she had made in John and Ruth's bedroom ceiling, and the pile of lathing and plaster on their satin bedspread, she offered to pay for it. So much for her kind offer of help, but she was a dear kind-hearted and well-meaning old lady, and we all felt sorry for her mishap.

Our time spent in that little attic was full of happy memories in spite of our lack of creature comforts and the shortage of cash. Sometimes we would reminisce about those early days in India when we first met, and that romantic holiday we spent together in Kashmir, or talk about the dinner parties we had every night with our friends in the forces, when dressed in a lovely evening gown, I sat down with them to enjoy a sumptuous gourmet meal, waited on by servants. Then, with a mischievous twinkle in his eye, Bill would tease me and say, 'How the mighty have fallen!' But in spite of everything, we were blissfully happy together; in fact as I look back across the years I think they were some of the happiest years of our lives, and we were thankful to God that we still had each other after all the trials and tribulations of the War years. Even though our lifestyle was so different now, we were glad that we could look back and say that we were lucky to have lived **'In Those Days!'**

What happened next is another story!

EPILOGUE

India Then and Now

When I left India in 1946 the population was very roughly 300 million and is now over one billion. Despite the huge pressures on the economy, which this enormous population explosion must impose, people in general appeared to me on recent visits to be more prosperous. While pestilence, poverty, illiteracy and helpless backwardness still exist today; it seemed not as prevalent as it was in the last century.

During the British rule the Hindus and Muslims lived together without much conflict. After partition the differences and conflicts between them was exacerbated by what today we call ethnic cleansing, when communities were forced out of homes and land they'd occupied for generations and compelled very much against their will to go to another country where they had no place to live.

I have returned to India seven times since I left it amidst turmoil and strife and it continues to draw me back. As I have travelled all over that vast country, each time I am made aware of the changes that are still taking place. On a visit in November 2004 when I went on a 'Rajasthan Railway Adventure, I was able to get close to the people and found that I could remember the Urdu that I learnt all those years ago when I lived in India, so was able to speak to them in their own language, which appeared to cause them some amusement. I returned to South India again in February 2005, and wherever I went I was welcomed by friendly people and felt safe to walk about freely without feeling I must look over my shoulder. I noticed too how clean everybody looked in their brightly coloured clothes and the children especially looked healthy and well dressed. But on the other hand, there were always the poor beggars, and the thin pariah dogs everywhere and hoards of wild pigs scavenging amongst the rubbish that I saw as I drove through the villages, and the holy cows all over the streets, but even they looked well covered and healthy. Some things will probably never change.

ARTHUR WISE. In 1950 my father left India after spending twenty five years in business out there to retire in England, where he and my mother bought a house in Sutton, Surrey to set up home there. But after the very active life they had led in India, the sedentary pace of life and cold winter weather didn't suit them. So two years later they returned to Karachi where father went into a business again. Four years later they returned to finally settle on the south coast in Sussex, where they bought a lovely house with a view of the sea and where the family came to spend happy holidays with them.

Throughout his life he was a committed Christian who played an active part in church life. When he was 85years old he took up oil painting and created many 'masterpieces' that hung in the rooms around their house. At the age of 93 years he continued to enjoy good health and was still driving his car. He wrote and published a book entitled 'Ninety Two Years of Miracles', the story of his life. He was a kind, genial old gentleman who easily made friends with everyone he met, and was sadly missed when he died just short of his 97th birthday.

IVY WISE. My mother remained in England after our wedding in 1948 for a short while before returning to join father in Calcutta, but returned again in 1950 to set up home in England with him on his retirement. She was also very active in the church both in India and England. With her happy disposition, she spent her life helping those who were less fortunate than herself, and was much loved by all who knew her. She was a vivacious, fun loving person who enjoyed entertaining her friends and eventually, she mastered the art of cooking. Her five grandchildren adored her and she was a wonderful mother to Patricia, Claire and me. They had the joy of celebrating their Diamond Wedding in 1985 when they met many old friends once again that they hadn't seen for years. We were devastated when she was diagnosed with terminal cancer in 1984 and had the very sorrowful task of helping father nurse her at their home in Banstead Surrey, until she died on May 18th 1985 at the age of 80 years.

My parents Arthur and Ivy celebrate their Diamond Wedding

PATRICIA. My sister trained as a welfare worker for the blind, and went to North Carolina, USA, to a family there to care for their deaf and blind daughter who she found nobody had been able to 'reach' before, but through her skilled help was able to introduce to a better quality of life. She then returned to England for a short while, but decided to join our parents who were living in Karachi at that time. It was while she was there that she met Edwy, the son of missionaries in India. He was training to be a Chartered Accountant. They married in Karachi in 1956 where they remained for sometime before returning to England to set up home in Banstead. He then joined a firm of Accountants. We have always remained in close contact and have never lived far from them. In 1965 they became parents to Caroline, who has been a great help to me in producing my memoirs by proof reading and correcting any errors, for which I am most grateful.

CLAIRE. My youngest sister trained as a nurse in Guys' hospital London after completing her education at the same boarding school that I attended in Malvern, which had relocated to Wales. Whilst nursing a member of the police force who had come in as a patient after being coshed by a thug, they fell in love and later married, and have lived in a pretty little thatched cottage in Wiltshire ever since. They have two daughters; the elder is also a nurse.

BILL and I lived in our attic until 1950 when we moved to stay with my parents in Sutton, while Bill travelled to London to take his final Law Society Examinations, which he passed at the first attempt. His first job was as an assistant to a solicitor in Acton, west London, where we bought our first home, a little semi-detached house with a heavy mortgage and a loan from Bill's father. He remained with this solicitor, working long hours on a pitifully small salary for three years before moving on to another firm in Ewell, with an increased salary of £1,000 per year. This meant that we would have to sell our house in Acton and buy another one nearer to his work. We found a nice house in Cheam, which we purchased with a greatly increased mortgage. After working in that firm for three years Bill decided to branch out on his own, and set up a practice, which he built up successfully and ran for 28 years before retiring 18 years ago.

JUSTINE. In April 1951 I gave birth to our first baby, a little girl whom we named Diana, and four years later to our second daughter Anthea, who like me, grew up with a passion for horses. This has resulted in my still being involved with them to this day, because she runs a successful Riding Centre from our home in Surrey, an attractive house set in a wood with 18 acres of pasture where the horses graze. We have always kept many different breeds of dogs and also bred German Shepherds. During our time here, twenty-eight foals have been born, reared and trained, from the different breeds of my brood mares. We have also rescued and reared various other animals, some of which were wild rabbits, 3 orphaned lambs, two goats, dogs including abandoned greyhounds, a piglet, cats, orphan foals, abused horses and ponies, some of them rescued and brought to us by the RSPCA, and numerous distressed racing pigeons which had arrived here battered by gales and bad weather. After restoring them we returned them to their owners.

DIANA trained and qualified as a nurse when she was 18 years old and has nursed ever since, but is now specializing as a palliative care nurse in a hospice for terminally ill cancer patients, as well as nursing for Marie Curie Cancer care. Like her Mum and Dad, she has a passion for classical music, opera and travel, and has accompanied us on various holidays to all parts of the world. Now, in our old age, we are grateful for the care and attention that she so lovingly bestows upon us.

ANTHEA. Throughout her life she has been involved with horses, which she bought and trained for show jumping, and successfully competed with them at various shows, as well as others carefully chosen and schooled for the riding school. She is an 'out-door-girl' and loves to camp amongst the wildlife of Botswana, which she visits to help with the horses in a riding safari camp out there. She also loves scuba diving and has been lucky to be able to do this in various exotic sites in different parts of the world. She has been taking flying lessons and hopes shortly to obtain her pilot's license, and is hoping she will then be able to fly the little plane into the Okavango Delta, in Botswana when she returns there again this year!

We celebrate our 57th Wedding Anniversary on October 5th 2005 and are thankful for the measure of good health we still enjoy. They have been eventful and interesting years as we have travelled to many parts of the world. Throughout the years that Bill and I have been together, he has been a wonderful husband and father, always kind, caring, gentle natured and supportive, and at

We visit the Taj Mahal on a Wedding Anniversary

heart, **still** a romantic. We have experienced many joys but also sadness at the passing away of loved ones, and lately of so many of our old friends. So as we look back on our long lives, we praise God for the happy years that we have been able to spend together and would like to believe that ours was '**A marriage made in Heaven**'

In the early 1950s there was a popular song sung by the beautiful Irish singer Ruby Murray, though wildly sentimental, expresses the way that I still feel about us.

You are my first love
My first and last love
We'll make this love last
for evermore…
★★★★★★★★★★★★★★★

Till the sun grows cold,
Till time stands still,
We'll feel the magic thrill
Of our first love.
★★★★★★★★★★★★★★★★

978-0-595-36350-6
0-595-36350-4

Printed in the United Kingdom by
Lightning Source UK Ltd., Milton Keynes
140321UK00001B/20/A

9 780595 363506